U.S.A. FIFTIES

Volume 3

Formosa/Taiwan — Law and Order

www.scholastic.com/librarypublishing

First published 2005 by Grolier,
an imprint of Scholastic Library Publishing,
Old Sherman Turnpike,
Danbury, Connecticut 06816

Set ISBN 0-7172-6082-8
Volume ISBN 0-7172-6085-2

Library of Congress Cataloging-in-Publication Data
USA 1950s.
p. cm.
Includes indexes.
Contents: v. 1. Abstract Expressionism–China—v. 2. Chosin Reservoir–Foreign policy—v. 3. Formosa/Taiwan–Law and order—v. 4. Lebanon–Pauling, Linus—v. 5. Phillips, Sam–South America—v. 6. Southeast Asia—Zhou Enlai.
ISBN 0-7172-6082-8 (set : alk. paper)—ISBN 0-7172-6083-6 (v. 1 : alk. paper)—ISBN 0-7172-6084-4 (v. 2 : alk. paper)—ISBN 0-7172-6085-2 (v. 3 : alk. paper)—ISBN 0-7172-6086-0 (v. 4 : alk. paper)—ISBN 0-7172-6087-9 (v. 5 : alk. paper)—ISBN 0-7172-6088-7 (v. 6 : alk. paper)
1. United States—Civilization—1945—Encyclopedias, Juvenile. 2. Nineteen fifties—Encyclopedias, Juvenile. I. Grolier (Firm)

E169.12.U78 2005
973.921—dc22 2004061903

For information address the publisher:
Grolier, Scholastic Library Publishing,
Old Sherman Turnpike,
Danbury, Connecticut 06816

Printed and bound in Singapore

For The Brown Reference Group plc

Project Editor:	Claire Chandler
Deputy Editor:	Chris King
Editors:	Felicity Crowe, Jonathan Dore, Jane Edmonds, Mark Fletcher, Lee Stacy, David Tombesi-Walton, Sylvia Tombesi-Walton, Elizabeth Wyse
Designers:	Ron Callow, Q2A
Picture Researchers:	Becky Cox, Laila Torsun
Cartography:	Darren Awuah, Mark Walker
Index:	Kay Ollerenshaw
Production Director:	Alastair Gourlay
Senior Managing Editor:	Tim Cooke
Editorial Director:	Lindsey Lowe
Consultants:	Professor Mina Carson, Oregon State University; Professor Richard C. Crepeau, University of Central Florida; Professor Sharon Ullman, Bryn Mawr College

ABOUT THIS SET

This book is part of a six-volume reference set that explores all aspects of life in the United States in the 1950s. The set covers not only the major political events of the decade but also developments in the arts, sciences, and popular culture.

Politically the 1950s were dominated by the Cold War, the hostile relationship that developed after World War II between the United States and the Soviet Union and their respective allies. At the beginning of the decade the United States' commitment to fighting communism drew it into the Korean War, a conflict that lasted from 1950 to 1953 and cost thousands of American lives. Anticommunist suspicion at home, meanwhile, was stoked by the investigations of Senator Joseph McCarthy and the House Un-American Activities Committee.

The rivalry between the superpowers also manifested itself in efforts to develop ever more devastating nuclear weapons. By 1953 both the Americans and the Soviets had tested hydrogen bombs. Four years later the Soviet Union became the first country to send an artificial satellite into orbit, marking the beginning of the space race that would continue throughout the 1960s.

The 1950s were a decade of great cultural change. Popular music was transformed with the birth of rock 'n' roll, musical theater flourished on Broadway, and there was continued experimentation in the world of jazz. Television came to dominate all other media and had a huge influence on the daily life of the average American family.

Growing prosperity after the deprivations of the Great Depression and the war meant that families had more money to spend on consumer goods and more time to spend on leisure activities. By the end of the decade most families owned a car, and many white Americans had moved to the suburbs. The good times were not shared by all, however. Black Americans faced discrimination in many areas of public life, and racial segregation was still a reality in the southern states. During the decade key Supreme Court decisions regarding desegregation paved the way for further successes for the growing civil rights movement in the 1960s.

This set contains more than 270 illustrated articles, arranged alphabetically for ease of reference. Many contain boxes that provide more detailed examination of key topics. Each entry contains cross-references to related articles, while every volume features a comprehensive set index, together with a timeline, a reading list, and useful websites for further research.

CONTENTS

FORMOSA/TAIWAN

Formosa, now usually known as Taiwan, is an island located 100 miles (160km) off the coast of southern China. It was the center of one of the great international crises of the 1950s, when Mao Zedong's Communist forces threatened to invade the Nationalist-held island.

The names "Formosa" and "Taiwan" refer to the same land mass: "Ilha Formosa" is Portuguese for "beautiful island," while "Tai Wan" is Chinese for "big bay." Both descriptions are apt for the island now usually called Taiwan. Today it is a major trading center and the home for 23 million people, yet ownership of the island remains a deeply unsettled question. Historically, the connection between the island and the Chinese mainland has never been very strong. The indigenous people of the island are most closely related to the original settlers of the Philippines. Ethnic Chinese settlement began in the 14th century, although the rulers of the Ming dynasty then made such emigration illegal, and Taiwan was considered not to be part of China. The island was briefly ruled by the Dutch from 1624 to 1662, and in 1684 Taiwan was brought under formal Chinese control for the first time.

Japanese control

In 1887 Taiwan was made a separate province of China. That status was short-lived, however: China ceded the island to Japan at the end of the Sino-Japanese War of 1895. Taiwanese rebels (including both ethnic Chinese and indigenous Taiwanese) rebelled against the Japanese takeover, declaring an independent "Republic of Formosa." The rebellion was suppressed, and the Japanese retained control over the island until the end of World War II (1939–1945).

The peace treaty between the Allies and the Japanese did not make provisions for final legal control over Taiwan. On Japan's defeat the U.S. government declared that sovereignty over the island was "an unsettled question subject to future international resolution." However, General Douglas MacArthur (1880–1964) had to arrange for the surrender of the Japanese forces on the island. He left this task to the wartime ally of the United States, the Nationalist government of the Republic of China, led by Chiang Kai-shek (1887–1975). Chiang sent his own forces to Taiwan.

Taiwan quickly became embroiled in the civil war that had been raging in China since the 1920s. Chiang's Nationalist party, the Kuomintang (KMT), battled the Chinese Communist Party of Mao Zedong (1893–1976) all across the country. In

Buildings are covered with banners written in Chinese characters in Taipei, Taiwan, in 1955. They were built by the Japanese during their occupation of the island, 1895–1945.

1947 a rebellion broke out on the island against the corrupt and oppressive KMT government. The rebellion was not connected to Mao's movement, but it was savagely repressed anyway. Nationalist forces killed 20,000 Taiwanese.

Civil war

Elsewhere in China the civil war did not go well for Chiang. By late 1948 some KMT members had begun migrating to Taiwan. As Chiang's forces were defeated elsewhere in China, he gradually shifted as much of his army as he could to the island. By May 1949 some two million mainlanders had relocated to Taiwan, including around 500,000 KMT soldiers. Chiang himself abandoned the mainland. He relocated his administration to the island and declared the city of Taipei to be the "temporary capital" of the Republic of China.

Following the Communist victory in the civil war, Mao declared the People's Republic of China (PRC), which had effective control of all of mainland China. He claimed that Taiwan was also rightfully the property of the People's Republic. Chiang argued just the opposite: Mao's PRC forces were merely "Communist bandits," and Chiang's own Republic of China government was still the legal ruler of all of China, although at the time it controlled only the island of Taiwan. To Mao in Beijing, therefore, Taiwan was a rebel province, while to Chiang in Taipei, it was the rest of China that was in illegal rebellion.

The stalemate might have been quickly settled by a Communist invasion from mainland China. However, the onset of the Korean War in 1950 brought the United States into the controversy over Taiwan. In June 1950 President Harry S. Truman (1945–1953) sent the U.S. Seventh Fleet to patrol the Strait of Taiwan, the stretch of water separating the island from China. The U.S. Navy was ordered to protect Chiang's KMT regime on Taiwan from invasion from the mainland, but it was also put in place to prevent Nationalist troops on Taiwan from raiding the mainland. Truman's blockade had the effect of establishing Chiang's wobbling regime in its last stronghold.

Korean War

Mao brought China into the Korean War in October 1950, and the open conflict between the People's Republic of China and the United Nations (UN) coalition led by the United States isolated mainland China still further. In 1953 newly elected President Dwight D. Eisenhower (1953–1961) lifted the blockade on Taiwan: The U.S. Navy would no longer try to prevent Nationalist forces from leaving the island. Chiang dispatched forces to raid the mainland. He also sent some 75,000 troops to seize the islands of Quemoy and Matsu, which were located less than 10 miles (16km) off the coast of mainland China.

The KMT garrisons on Quemoy and Matsu, which were far closer to mainland China than they were to Taiwan, were an irresistible provocation to Mao. In September 1954 PRC artillery began to shell the KMT forces on Quemoy in preparation for an invasion. The United States quickly sided with Chiang and the KMT. In November 1954 the Communists retaliated by sentencing 14 U.S. airmen captured in Korea to long prison terms. The next month the U.S. government signed a mutual defense treaty with the Republic of China. In so doing, the United States promised to defend the KMT regime in Taiwan.

From late 1954 to early 1955 the situation deteriorated. While Mao continued to shell Quemoy, members of Congress openly advocated using nuclear weapons to prevent any invasion of Nationalist-held Taiwan, Quemoy, and Matsu. In April 1955 Mao backed off from the brink of war by agreeing that the situation could be resolved by peaceful negotiation. The shelling of Quemoy ceased on May 1, and the tensions gradually diminished.

There was no permanent settlement, however, and the Quemoy crisis flared up again in August 1958. The Communists resumed shelling of Quemoy and Matsu. In response, the Eisenhower administration dispatched U.S. Air Force fighter-bombers, capable of nuclear strikes, to be based on Taiwan. PRC troops stood by to invade Quemoy and Matsu, and the only option America believed it had to stop such an invasion was nuclear attacks on the Communist troop concentrations on the mainland. The United States and China were on the brink of nuclear war in the Strait of Taiwan.

In October 1958 Soviet Premier Nikita Khrushchev (1894–1971) raised the stakes. In a letter to Eisenhower Khrushchev declared that he would

Chiang Kai-shek, the leader of the Chinese Nationalists, addresses a gathering in Taipei, Taiwan, in October 1952 to commemorate the foundation of the Republic of China in 1911.

CHANGING RELATIONS

Since 1958 much has changed on the issue of Taiwan, but the stalemate of the 1950s remains in place in many ways. All American combat forces were removed from the island in 1974 following President Richard M. Nixon's (1969–1974) visit to mainland China. Nixon and Mao agreed that Taiwan was a part of China. And on full American recognition of the PRC as the legitimate government of China the U.S. government endorsed the proposition that Taiwan was a rebel province of China. The mutual defense treaty with Taiwan was canceled in 1979.

However, the United States continues to sell advanced weaponry to Taiwan and has repeatedly sent forces to the area to deter any possible PRC invasion of the island. The PRC continues to consider Taiwan to be a rebel province, but the Beijing regime has also declared that it will not invade the island unless Taiwan declares independence.

Taiwan, meanwhile, has become independent from China in all but name. Thanks in part to massive American economic aid in the 1950s and 1960s, the island has become very wealthy. It has the world's 21st largest economy and the 14th largest volume of foreign trade, with a particular strength in computer chips and consumer electronics. Taiwan has become so economically well developed that its investors now look outside the country to invest money, increasingly to the PRC itself.

Also in contrast to the PRC, Taiwan has become a meaningful democracy. Chiang Kai-shek died in 1975, and his KMT party has gradually allowed greater political competition. The Democratic Progressive Party (DPP) now competes on an even basis with the KMT, and the DPP's platform endorses independence for Taiwan, ending the fiction that the Taipei government is the legal authority for all China. However, for all that has changed, the essential relationship among the People's Republic of China, the Republic of China (Taiwan), and the United States remains where it was in the days of "brinkmanship" in 1958.

consider any nuclear strike by the United States on his ally China to be the same as a nuclear strike on the Soviet Union. The Soviet Union would then retaliate against the United States with nuclear weapons, and a new world conflict would be underway. Eisenhower's Secretary of State John Foster Dulles (1888–1959) responded to the threat by saying that while the United States had no desire to start a worldwide war, it would take "timely and effective action to defend Taiwan."

Members of the Chinese People's Liberation Army shout slogans on the streets of Beijing in 1958 in support of the Chinese government's handling of the Quemoy crisis.

Brinkmanship

Once again Mao defused the tension by essentially conceding defeat. The shelling of Quemoy and Matsu ceased in late October, and all sides gradually scaled back their troop buildups and their apocalyptic rhetoric. Dulles considered the truce on the issue to be a victory for the United States. In order to attain a favorable resolution to Cold War crises, he believed it would be necessary to pursue the American position even to the brink of war. Negotiating for peace through an open willingness to go to war became known as "brinkmanship," and the 1954 and 1958 Quemoy crises became the best examples of "brinkmanship" in action.

Although the immediate threat of Communist invasion subsided, no amount of "brinkmanship" could win a permanent solution to the issue of Taiwan because neither Mao nor Chiang would relent in their claims that each represented the one true government of China. American air and naval forces stationed on Taiwan until the 1970s (*see box*) prevented a Communist invasion of the island, but this did not make Taiwan independent. Neither Mao nor Chiang was interested in recognizing a separate, sovereign Taiwan.

See Also:

China • Cold War • Dulles, John Foster • Foreign Policy • Korean War • Mao Zedong • Soviet Union • Zhou Enlai

FRANCE

After World War II France had to rebuild both its economy and system of government. While the French economy thrived during the 1950s, the Fourth Republic collapsed in 1958 and was replaced by the Fifth Republic, with Charles de Gaulle as president.

At the end of World War II (1939–1945) most French people wanted a new system of government to be established, but they were divided over what form it should take. General Charles de Gaulle (1890–1970), who was treated as France's greatest hero when Paris was liberated from German occupation in 1944, was head of a provisional government. However, his belief that any future government should be led by a strong president was rejected by the assembly that was elected in October 1945 to draft a new constitution. It insisted that the president should continue to be little more than a titular head of state, and that all effective power should lie with the legislative National Assembly. De Gaulle resigned in January 1946, and in October the new constitution of France's Fourth Republic was accepted in a referendum by a narrow majority.

The Fourth Republic

Following de Gaulle's resignation, France was governed by its three largest parties: the Communists, Socialists, and the Popular Republican Movement (MRP). Their leaders had all played a significant role in the resistance movement during the war; but this was not enough to preserve the unity of their government, and in 1947 it fell apart. A pattern was now set until 1958, with France being governed by a series of short-lived coalition governments made up of Socialists, Radicals, and the MRP, while the Communists and Gaullists were kept out of power.

Despite its political problems, the Fourth Republic did much to restore the French economy through a series of four-year development plans. What was to become known as the *trente glorieuses* ("30 glorious years") got under way, during which time people generally became more prosperous. As French industry thrived, the nation's economy grew between 5 and 10 percent each year, and more and more people moved into the towns and cities.

One of the factors that helped make this expansion possible was the financial support—more than $2.7

Men work in a steel mill in Hayange, France, in 1952. The steel industry thrived after France became a founding member of the European Coal and Steel Community in 1951.

FRANCE AND ALGERIA

The French protectorates of Morocco and Tunisia in North Africa were granted independence in 1956. However, the French were determined to hold on to Algeria, thus provoking a particularly bitter eight-year guerrilla war. The conflict began with a declaration of independence by the Algerian National Liberation Front (FLN) in 1954. Acts of terrorism by the FLN met a violent French response. In 1956 the French army was given a free hand to conduct the campaign as it chose, and a regime of brutality and torture ensued. By 1958 there was still no political party in France demanding that Algeria be granted independence. However, President Charles de Gaulle knew that the situation had to be resolved, and the following year he began negotiations with the FLN. Fearing that they were being sold out, the French settlers in Algeria founded the Secret Army Organization (OAS), which launched another terror campaign. When the violence spread to France in 1961, public opinion began to turn in favor of independence, and this was finally proclaimed after a referendum in Algeria in 1962.

billion in grants and loans—that France received from the United States as part of the Marshall Plan to rebuild Europe. Another was the formation of the European Coal and Steel Community (ECSC) in 1951. Made up of France and five other Western European nations, its aim was to create a common market for coal and steel from which all members would benefit. The success of the ECSC led to the establishment of the European Economic Community (EEC), or Common Market, in 1957. A third factor was the creation of the Commissariat général du plan, an agency established by economist Jean Monnet (1888–1979) that set out to make the economy more efficient through the coordination of the state and private sectors.

General Charles de Gaulle speaks at a press conference in Paris in May 1958, declaring that he is ready to take control of the French government as president.

Changes in society

It was not only the nature of the economy that changed in postwar France; there were great social changes, too. The birthrate increased dramatically, doubling the number of young people under the age of 25 in just 20 years. This baby boom helped trigger the creation of a social welfare system that provided a range of benefits, including financial support for large families, a minimum wage, pensions for older people, and subsidized medical care.

The chief role of women in the 1950s continued to be that of wife and mother. French women had finally received the vote in 1945, a generation after it had been won by American and other European women—but they subsequently made little progress toward achieving equality in other areas of life. The number of women elected to the National Assembly actually declined in the 1950s.

Indochina and North Africa

The Fourth Republic presided over the collapse of France's overseas empire in Southeast Asia and North Africa. In Indochina (present-day Laos, Cambodia, and Vietnam) French troops suffered heavy losses in battle against Communist Vietminh guerrillas in northern Vietnam. At a peace conference in Geneva, Switerland, in 1954 France agreed to withdraw completely from Indochina. It also recognized the independence of Morocco and Tunisia in 1956.

In May 1958 France faced a domestic crisis arising from events in Algeria, where the French army was attempting to suppress the nationalist movement (*see box*). The government proved unable to control the situation; and on May 13, when French settlers in Algeria declared that they were seizing power, there were fears that there might be a military coup in Paris. Leaders of the French army in Algeria appealed to de Gaulle to form a government, and after complex negotiations the National Assembly reluctantly voted him supreme power for six months. In September de Gaulle presented a new constitution that gave the president new powers. In a referendum 80 percent of the French people voted in favor of the new constitution, thus establishing the French Fifth Republic, which survives to the present day. De Gaulle was elected its president in December 1958.

See Also:

European Common Market • Foreign Policy • Germany • North Atlantic Treaty Organization • Southeast Asia • Suez Crisis • Vietnam

ALAN FREED 1921–1965

Alan Freed was one of the first white disc jockeys to champion African American performers and their music. He is often credited with coining the phrase "rock 'n' roll." His career, however, was blighted by controversy over the payola scandal.

Freed was born Albert James Freed on December 15, 1921, in Johnstown, Pennsylvania. He grew up in Salem, Ohio, where he led a jazz band called the Sultans of Swing during high school. An ear infection cut short his music career, and he began broadcasting in 1942, working at various radio stations, including WKBN in Youngstown and WAKR in Akron, Ohio.

In 1951 Freed began working for WJW in Cleveland. He took the name "Moondog" and began hosting a late-night show eventually called *Moondog Rock 'n' Roll Party*. Freed played rhythm and blues (R&B) records by black artists—what was then known as "race music"—and attracted a white teenage audience. He began to refer to R&B as "rock 'n' roll" as a way of making it more acceptable to whites. Ironically, it was actually a slang term used by black youths to describe sex.

On March 21, 1952, Freed and dance promoter Lew Platt organized the Moondog Coronation Ball, a concert at the Cleveland Arena to which many people now date the birth of rock 'n' roll. The show had to be stopped after only one song due to overcrowding. Freed's radio program survived, but he returned to using his own name after being sued over the right to use the name Moondog.

Alan Freed began broadcasting for WABC in New York City in 1958. The following year he was accused of taking bribes from record companies during the payola scandal.

WINS career

In 1954 Freed joined WINS in New York City. He refused to play covers by white artists of songs originally recorded by African American performers, as was the practice in the segregation era, and continued promoting concerts that brought together black and white fans of the new music. Freed also bought the publishing rights to several songs and starred in various movies, including *Rock around the Clock* and *Don't Knock the Rock* (both 1956). In 1957 he hosted a rock-'n'-roll show on ABC, but it was canceled after the African American singer Frankie Lymon enraged the network's southern sponsors by dancing with a white girl.

In 1958 Freed was indicted for incitement to riot after violence erupted at a concert in Boston. Although the charges were dropped, WINS refused to renew his contract, and he faced serious financial problems. He was hired by WABC but was then subpoenaed to appear before the U.S. House Oversight Committee investigating payola (the practice of record companies paying for their records to be broadcast on radio). Freed refused to sign a statement from WABC confirming that he had never accepted payola. In 1962 he pleaded guilty to charges of commercial bribery. He served no prison sentence, but his career was destroyed. In 1964 he was indicted for tax evasion. Freed began drinking heavily. He died penniless on January 20, 1965, in California.

See Also:

Black Americans • Popular Music • Radio • Recording Industry • Rock 'n' Roll • Segregation and Desegregation

BUCKMINSTER FULLER 1895–1983

Buckminster Fuller was a man of many talents. During his long career he worked as an architect, engineer, lecturer, and philosopher. His most famous invention was the geodesic dome. He was also a prolific author, publishing almost 30 books.

Richard Buckminster Fuller—always known as "Bucky"—was born on July 12, 1895, into an affluent Massachusetts family. Born with poor eyesight and one leg shorter than the other, Fuller learned to overcome his physical defects through an inquiring and sharp mind. Despite his intelligence, he failed to graduate from Harvard University and at 19 became an apprentice at a Canadian cotton mill.

Fuller's early life was marked by business failure and personal tragedy. In 1917 he married Anne Hewlett, the daughter of a well-known architect. The couple's eldest daughter, Alexandra, died at age four in 1922, a victim of an influenza epidemic. Her death prompted Fuller's interest in housing and the role of drafty houses in spreading disease. He began reading and thinking about changes that might help people. As a result he designed a mass-produced house, but it was turned down by the American Institute of Architects.

Buckminster Fuller found fame in the 1950s with the widespread use of his geodesic domes. By the 1960s he was considered one of the world's experts on modern technology.

Undaunted by this failure, Fuller continued to design new types of houses. He anticipated that there would be a housing shortage when World War II (1939–1945) ended and the servicemen returned home. His solution was one of his most famous creations: the Dymaxion house (DYnamic MAXimum tensION). The house was designed to be energy-efficient and low-cost, produced on an assembly line and made from the same light-weight material used in plane manufacture. In 1946 he produced a prototype at the Beech Aircraft Company's plant in Wichita, Kansas. It was the first successful application of Fuller's ideas, but his obsessive tinkering with the design lost him his financial backers.

Geodesic domes

After the Wichita house failed to go into mass production, Fuller turned to academia. He lectured on his ideas, sometimes for five hours at a time, and was able to refine his thoughts further. Fuller still wanted to prove that cheap, mass-produced housing was possible. While teaching at the experimental Black Mountain College in North Carolina in 1947, Fuller built his first geodesic dome. The spherical structure comprised a complex network of different-sized triangles. It was the lightest, strongest, and most cost-effective structure ever designed. Geodesic domes were widely used during the 1950s for military and industrial purposes, including one built for the Ford Motor Company in Detroit in 1953. Fuller was awarded the patent for the geodesic dome in 1954 and earned royalties from each one built, which allowed him to concentrate on lecturing.

With his new fame and fortune Fuller's international career as a writer, academic, and designer took off. Throughout the 1950s he traveled the world continually, lecturing or, as he called it, "thinking out loud." By the 1960s lecture halls were packed with students who regarded him as the guru of modern technology. Despite the fact he never completed his formal education, Fuller was awarded almost 50 honorary doctorates and countless awards. He died on July 1, 1983, in Los Angeles. Today there are more than 300,000 geodesic domes still in existence.

See Also:

Architecture • Civil Engineering • Design • Housing and Household Appliances • Suburbs

GAMES AND PASTIMES

In the prosperous postwar era Americans were able to embrace many new pastimes. Spectator sports, especially football and baseball, became increasingly popular, while for children there was a wealth of new games and toys available.

The postwar era was a time of booming prosperity, when at last the country emerged from wartime privations and was free to focus again on the good life. Secure in their green and spacious suburbs, complete with a gas-guzzling car in every drive, a new generation of middle-class Americans had both the money and time to pursue fun in a dazzling variety of ways.

On the road

In the 1950s the automobile reigned supreme. As an increasing number of Americans (an estimated 60 percent) achieved a "middle-class" standard of living—the average income for a white family was more than $4,000 by the middle of the decade—car ownership boomed. By 1954 General Motors was the leading American company, with annual sales of $10.2 billion. Car ownership made far-flung communities accessible and allowed for the development of new suburbs. The Federal-Aid Highway Act of 1956 initiated an ambitious program of road-building. The new multilane freeways ensured that motor transportation was king and hastened the decline of the railroad industry.

Automobiles were much more than simply the cheapest and most convenient way to travel: They were also a symbol of success and a national pastime. From the increasingly bizarre tail-finned sedans at the smart end of the market to the wood-trimmed family station wagons, cars were seen as status symbols and playthings. The American love affair with the automobile spawned a whole range of car-related leisure activities. The spacious cars of the 1950s were used as places to relax and have fun as much as to get around. By 1958, for example, there were close to 5,000 drive-in movie theaters in the country, an increase of more than fourfold over the previous decade. The drive-ins ranged from small venues that could hold only 50 cars to gigantic complexes such as the All-Weather Drive-In at Copiague in New York, which held 2,500 cars. Families, groups of friends, or dating couples could watch a vast screen from the comfort and privacy of their own car, enjoying a snack while they viewed.

Eating quickly became an aspect of car culture. The notion of "fast" food reflected a culture that valued speed and efficiency. Roadside restaurants, which began to appear in the late twenties and thirties, initially catered to car-owners in suburbia. In affluent postwar America restaurant chains started to exploit the drive-in concept: Car-owners simply drove up to a booth to place their order and pay for their food before driving on to another booth, where the food was dispensed. In an ever-more competitive drive-in market novelty was key. Meals were delivered by "carhops" in striking uniforms, who frequently arrived at the driver's window on roller skates. Among the most important drive-in chains were A&W Restaurants, Sonic Drive-in, and Steak 'n' Shake.

By the mid-1950s, however, drive-ins were increasingly seen as the hangouts of teenage hooligans and

Children buy popcorn at a fair in 1954. When television became popular in the 1950s, popcorn sales made a sudden and substantial rise—as much as 500 percent.

McDONALD'S

In the late 1940s Richard "Dick" and Maurice "Mac" McDonald owned a small drive-in restaurant in San Bernardino, California. To improve business, they experimented with a new concept based on speedy service, low prices, and high volume. They dispensed with carhops in favor of self-service at the counter, and they reduced the choices available on their menu to hamburgers, cheeseburgers, soft drinks, milk, coffee, potato chips, and pie, adding french fries and milkshakes later. They slashed the price of their hamburgers to just 15 cents. Within a few years they had almost doubled their annual revenue, and in the catering industry the brothers were big news. They were soon receiving enquiries from all over the country about franchising their operations. Their first franchisee was Neil Fox from Phoenix, Arizona. The brothers decided to make his operation a prototype for the nationwide chain they were envisaging. The red-and-white tiled building, with "golden arches" on the side soon became a model for McDonald's operations, as did the efficient assembly-line kitchen. For as little as $1,000 franchisees would receive the McDonald's name, a basic description of their Speedy Service System, and the services of Art Bender, the McDonald brothers' original counterman, who helped get the new restaurant started. In 1954 a milkshake machine salesman named Ray Kroc saw the McDonald's operation firsthand and was impressed by the spectacle of a rapidly moving line of customers buying bags of burgers and fries. He realized that this was a concept that would thrive anywhere in the country. In 1955 he formed a new franchising company under the name of McDonald's System, Inc., having purchased the rights to the name McDonald's in 1954.

On April 15, 1955, Kroc's prototype McDonald's restaurant began business in Des Plaines, Illinois. Rather than tinker with a successful format, Kroc retained the McDonald's formula of a limited menu, consistent food, an assembly-line system, and fast, friendly service, adding to that his own demanding standards for cleanliness. The franchise fee was limited to $950 for each restaurant, with a service fee of 1.9 percent of restaurant sales. Kroc was a persuasive salesman: By the end of 1956 there were 14 McDonald's franchises; in another four years there were 228 restaurants reporting $37.6 million in sales, and the company had sold its 400-millionth hamburger. McDonald's was only at the beginning of an amazing trajectory that was to export its restaurants and fast food worldwide over the next four decades. However, it had already transformed the eating habits of a nation and attracted many imitators.

motorcycle gangs, and families began to look for other family- and car-friendly dining venues. The hamburger restaurant quickly met this need. The double-patty "sandwich" hamburger was invented in the late 1930s by Bob Wian and sold by his Bob's Big Boy restaurants, the first national hamburger chain. Bob's supremacy was not to last for long, however. When a milkshake machine salesman named Ray Kroc (1902–1984) met two brothers named McDonald, a new American brand was born. The McDonald brothers opened their first self-service restaurant in 1948 in San Bernardino, California (*see box*). They were soon followed by other chains—Burger King, Wendy's, and Hardee's. All four chains were intent on selling cheap, standardized, fast food (burgers, shakes, and fries) to ever-growing numbers of Americans. Located at convenient points on the new interstates and furnished with vast parking lots, they were truly accessible restaurants. "Eating out" fast became a national pastime.

Automobiles were also to have a major influence on the American shopping experience, turning it into an immensely popular pastime. As cars became the dominant form of transportation, downtown city centers began to decline since they were unable to provide the necessary parking facilities. In many cases new highways bypassed historic town centers. Against this background out-of-town shopping malls began to dominate the retail scene. Seattle's Northgate shopping mall, the largest in the country, opened for business in 1950. Such specially built complexes concentrated a great array of retail outlets in one accessible space. They were supplied with large parking lots and fast-food restaurants, and were air-conditioned in summer and heated in winter. Shoppers could walk through these spaces in comparative comfort, and shopping was transformed from a chore to a pastime that could be enjoyed by all the family.

Popular entertainment

By the mid-1950s two-thirds of American homes owned at least one television, and as a result more traditional entertainment venues, such as movie theaters, nightclubs, and dance halls, saw attendances plummet. Hollywood struck back with a new emphasis on spectacular entertainment. The 1950s were the golden age of the musical, with a string of hits, many of which originated as Broadway productions: *Annie Get Your Gun* (1950), *Show Boat* (1951), *Singin' in the Rain* (1952), *Oklahoma!* (1955), *Guys and Dolls* (1955), *The King and I* (1956), and *South Pacific* (1958). Even

Marilyn Monroe (1926–1962), the ultimate screen goddess of the 1950s, sang in movies such as *Gentlemen Prefer Blondes* (1953). Lavish biblical epics, including *The Ten Commandments* (1956), exploited the potential of the big screen, as did experiments with widescreen Cinerama and three-dimensional viewing (*see box*).

Popular music really took off in the 1950s with the arrival of rock 'n' roll. Essentially a form of rhythm and blues (R&B), with its roots firmly planted in the black musical culture that originated in the South, it was distinguished by a steady, pulsing beat, prominent guitar, and suggestive lyrics. The term "rock 'n' roll" was coined or at least popularized by the disc jockey Alan Freed (1921–1965), who featured black R&B artists on his radio show. This form of music proved extremely popular with white musicians, and soon they were beginning to make their own rock 'n' roll. Bill Haley and His Comets had a huge hit with "Rock around the Clock" in 1955. Hits from both black and white artists such as Chuck Berry (1926–), Little Richard (1932–), Jerry Lee Lewis (1935–), and Buddy Holly (1936–1959) soon followed. Elvis Presley (1935–1977), the ultimate rock-'n'-roll star of the 1950s, had his first success with "That's All Right" in 1954.

Rock 'n' roll appealed to teenagers. It was very different from the kind of music enjoyed by their parents and was, above all, music to dance to. The swing dances of the 1940s (the jitterbug and lindy hop) were adapted to the fast, insistent beat of the new sound. Teenagers danced at high school proms (*see box on p. 17*), at dance halls, in bars, and even coffee shops,

3-D MOVIES

At the start of the 1950s Hollywood executives were worried that television would steal their audiences. They decided that they needed a gimmick to bring people back to the movie houses and came up with the idea of three-dimensional, or 3-D, films. Arch Oboler's *Bwana Devil* premiered in November 1952 and starred Robert Stack, Barbara Britton, and Nigel Bruce. Promoted with the strap-line "A Lion in Your Lap, a Lady in Your Arms!" the movie was about man-eating lions. The audience was issued with glasses that facilitated the 3-D effect, which aimed to create the illusion that the lions were actually jumping out of the screen.

Three-dimensional movies depended on delivering two separate images to the viewer taken from a camera with twin side-by-side lenses. Two projectors showed the two camera views, which were run through a polarizing filter. The audience's special glasses had polarized lenses that enabled the viewers to process the two different images as three-dimensional. Projection of 3-D movies was a fine art; any mistakes, and the image just looked blurry. In addition, many people found that watching 3-D movies gave them headaches. Nevertheless, several reputable films were shot in 3-D as well as 2-D, including *Kiss Me Kate* (1953) and *Dial M for Murder* (1954), although the 2-D versions usually proved more popular. Inevitably, 3-D movies became low-budget productions, notable for their novelty value if nothing else.

An audience wearing 3-D glasses watches the movie *Bwana Devil* at a screening in Hollywood in February 1953.

A young woman looks through records at a record shop in the 1950s. Record sales to teenagers rapidly increased as rock 'n' roll took the country by storm.

anywhere that could boast a jukebox and a selection of the latest hits. In 1949 RCA Victor introduced the 7-inch, 45-rpm vinyl record, and by 1950 the first jukebox designed to play these records had been launched. The leading jukebox manufacturers—Wurlitzer, Seeburg, and Rock-Ola—shipped thousands of models to venues throughout the country. Popular music had never been so accessible.

Western craze

While teenagers passed their time listening to the new music and congregating at a variety of venues from soda fountains and malt shops to pizza parlors and drive-in movies, younger children were enjoying playing with an unprecedented array of toys and games. Throughout the 1950s a range of fads and crazes swept the nation, promoted by advertisements, television programs, and comic books.

The most enduring fad of the 1950s was for Wild West gear and cowboy games. The fad was a direct result of Disney's *Davy Crockett* (1954–1955; part of its *Disneyland* TV series), which broadcast the mythology of the American West to an entire generation. *Davy Crockett* was introduced with the line "Tall tales and true from the legendary past" and starred Fess Parker as the eponymous hero (very loosely based on the real-life frontiersman who died at the Alamo). Crockett was initially portrayed as a carefree fighter who punctuated each piece of daring with a wink and a grin. Over the course of the series, however, he was transformed from a wisecracking character into a wholesome role model for children, distinguished by his trademark coonskin cap. Millions of children idolized Davy Crockett, and to prove it they all wanted a coonskin hat of their own. An astonishing $100 million-worth of raccoon caps were sold in a single year. Other merchandise included capguns, moccasins, and lunch boxes. The western craze was fueled by other television heroes: Roy Rogers, Hopalong Cassidy, the Lone Ranger, and for the girls, the "cowgirl" Dale Evans. There was even a Hopalong Cassidy board game by Milton Bradley that cashed in on the western craze, and others soon followed.

Dolls

Despite the introduction of TV characters such as cowgirl Dale Evans, the 1950s were marked by clearly differentiated gender roles. Nowhere was this more apparent than in the creation of the Barbie doll, the ultimate symbol of all things feminine and a favorite toy for successions of small girls. The first Barbie was launched at the end of the decade, but she had several predecessors. In the early 1950s the Alexander Doll Company in New York City began to utilize plastics and the new artificial fibers such as Dacron to create fashion dolls that showcased the revolutionary fashions of French designer Christian Dior's "New Look." In 1955 Alexander launched Cissy, the first "fashion doll," who was described in the company catalog: "Her long slim body, her molded bosom, her beautifully shaped feet that wear only high heeled shoes made just for her, and her elegant costumes, designed for her alone, make Cissy the shining wonder of the doll world." With her fine-quality hair, jointed arms and legs, and "sleep" eyes that opened and shut, Cissy

Six-year-old Jackie Smith draws a toy gun during a fast-draw competition in Topeka, Kansas, in October 1959. The fad for cowboy gear was fueled by television heroes.

was a young girl's dream. She was expensive, however, ranging in price from $16.99 to more than $60 for dolls dressed in ball gowns.

In 1956 the Ideal Toy Corporation launched the Revlon doll, its riposte to Cissy. The Revlon doll's hair was rooted into a vinyl head, rather than glued on, enabling little girls to "dress" the hair. She was also much cheaper and soon became a runaway success, especially when she was sold with an accompanying boxed wardrobe. In keeping with the new recognition of the teenage years as a separate step between childhood and adulthood, the American Character Doll Company took a familiar childhood doll, the Toni doll, and revamped her into a fashionable, high-heeled teenager.

In 1959 the toy company Mattel bought advertising on the television show *The Mickey Mouse Club* to launch "Barbie, the Teen Age Fashion Model Doll." Barbie was depicted as an independent, glamorous, globetrotting model; she seemed to represent everything a 1950s girl should aspire to.

Crazes and collections

One of the biggest crazes to sweep the nation during the decade was Silly Putty. First created by General Electric's laboratory in New Haven, Connecticut, in an attempt to develop a synthetic rubber, this silicone-based polymer stretches without breaking but can be "snapped off" cleanly. It bounces higher than a rubber ball and even keeps its shape when hit with a hammer. It was first marketed by Peter Hodgson, an advertising consultant, in 1950 and has since been bought by an estimated 70 percent of American households. The putty was packaged in one-ounce lumps in plastic eggs that sold for $1. In August 1950 *The New Yorker* magazine, intrigued by the product, published a story in its "Talk of the Town" section, and the craze began, with more than 250,000 orders placed in three days. Initially launched as an adult novelty item, Silly Putty was soon being sold primarily as a children's toy and in 1957 was marketed in one of the first TV advertising campaigns that specifically targeted children.

Another toy fad of the decade was the Hula Hoop, which owed its existence to Richard Knerr and Arthur "Spud" Melin, founders of the Wham-O Company. In 1957, when an Australian visitor told them that at home children twirled bamboo hoops around their waists in gym class, Knerr and Melin immediately saw the possibilities and created a hollow plastic prototype using Marlex, a lightweight but durable plastic. They chose the name "Hula Hoop," which came from the Hawaiian dance the hoop's users seemed to imitate. The hoop was marketed nationwide in 1958, and children and adults alike were immediately hooked; Wham-O sold 25 million hoops in just four months. At the peak of their popularity Wham-O was manufacturing 20,000 hoops a day. More than 100 million international orders ensured that Hula Hoops soon spread beyond the borders of America. However, not every nation was enthusiastic: In the Soviet Union Hula Hoops were denounced as an example of the "emptiness of American culture." By the end of 1958, after Wham-O had made $45 million in profits, the craze was dying down. However, Wham-O already had a new toy to promote: That year it had relaunched its Pluto Platter, a plastic flying disk, as the Frisbee, and another craze was soon to follow.

Children were able to watch the triumphs of their sports heroes on television for the first time, and the extensive media coverage devoted to baseball spawned yet another craze: collecting baseball cards. Cards featuring photographs of baseball teams date back to the 19th century and were initially handed out as "trade cards" as a means of promoting a business such as a sporting goods store. By the 1880s baseball cards were often included in packets of cigarettes, and in the early 20th century they were also introduced in packages of candy. In the 1950s the cards began to appear in packages of chewing gum and bubble gum. The bubble-gum manufacturer Topps introduced the practice of signing baseball players to exclusive contracts to appear on its cards. After several years of competing over player contracts, Topps enjoyed a largely unchallenged monopoly for more than two decades.

Most collectors of baseball cards in the 1950s were children. They traded their "extras" (duplicate cards) with other children to get cards they did not have. The craze for collecting cards closely mirrored the baseball season and in particular the World Series, when the whole country became obsessed with the sport. Many of the 1950s stars who were featured on baseball cards—for example, Sandy Koufax, Mickey Mantle, Willie Mays, Stan Musial, and Jackie Robinson—are still icons of the sport today, while the baseball cards themselves have become highly sought-after and valuable items.

Spectator sports

Americans still followed their two most popular sports—baseball and football—with a passion in the 1950s. However, attendance figures at live games steadily declined as more and more people turned to television coverage of their favorite teams.

During this period baseball began to expand its geographical range, becoming a truly national sport. Western cities acquired teams, either by luring them to move from the East Coast or by forming so-called expansion teams with players made available by established teams. With

DATING

Young men and women sit together in a pizzeria. Teenagers were given more freedom to go out on dates than ever before.

Teenagers in America were granted more freedom than ever before in the 1950s. Going out on dates was a sign of their new-found liberty. The sexes were allowed to mix freely away from adult supervision and enjoy the wide range of activities that were available to them. They could go to the movies, visit a restaurant, ice-cream parlor, or coffee bar, go dancing, bowling, or simply take a drive. On a more formal level they could accompany each other to high school dances and proms. Yet many unwritten rules governed the way the teenagers behaved.

It was unheard of for a girl to ask a boy out on a date. It was a girl's job to attract a boy, and there were many handbooks published in the postwar years that offered advice. Once out on a date, it was universally accepted that the boy should pay. According to an article in June 1959 in *Seventeen* magazine entitled "How Much Money Do Boys Spend on Girls?" a typical boy could be expected to spend $7 a month. This amount would pay, for example, for two high school football games, six sodas, three movies, two bags of popcorn, and gasoline for the car. The latter item was vital because cars offered an ideal location for sexual experimentation in the 1950s, affording privacy and comfort (the automobiles of the decade were large and well-upholstered). Any form of sexual contact in a car became known as "parking." Adults became concerned about "parking" and tried, where possible, to contain the practice. A police chief in New Jersey, for example, only allowed cars to park in country parks at night with their lights on. They were then watched over by police patrol cars.

THE HIGH SCHOOL DANCE

High school dances were popular events in the 1950s. They were a way for teenagers to meet and mix, and had the official sanction of both school and parents. Most dances took place in the school gym, and in order not to ruin the floor, teenagers were asked to remove their shoes, hence the term "sock hop." High school dances were relatively staid affairs, closely supervised and monitored. The main craze of the day was a foot-scuffling, partner-twirling couple dance that dated back to the 1940s called the jitterbug. Students spun and swung to songs such as "Wheel of Fortune" by Kay Starr or the "Bye Bye Blues" by Les Paul and Mary Ford. Songs like Johnny Ray's "Cry" provided slow beats for equally popular slow dances.

Another variant on the dance formula was the "sweater dance" in which dancers wore cardigans; "steady" partners donned matching sweaters. Some schools even turned dating conventions upside-down with "vice versa" dances at which girls asked boys to dance or paid for their date's ticket.

The big event of the high school year was the formal prom, or "Farewell" dance, normally held in June, at which graduating seniors bade farewell to the school. The gym was especially decorated with paper streamers and flowers. Corsages—small bouquets worn on the bodice of an evening dress—were an important tradition in formal high school dances. Boys were expected to buy their dates a corsage, and there was much competition about who had the most unusual or expensive corsage.

Couples dance at the senior prom at Anacosta High School, Maryland, in June 1953. This was the main social event of the high school year.

increased media exposure individual players were lionized. Their careers were followed on the television, in newspapers, and in sports magazines. Fans collected baseball cards or acquired products endorsed by their heroes. One of the most noteworthy of the 1950s sporting legends was the Brooklyn Dodgers' Jackie Robinson, a gifted athlete who became the first African American player in the major leagues in 1947. (Prior to Robinson black players had been restricted to the Negro leagues.)

Pro football

Professional football came of age during the new television era. The National Football League (NFL) was reorganized in 1950 into 13 clubs: the New York Yanks, Baltimore Colts, Chicago Bears, Chicago Cardinals, Cleveland Browns, Detroit Lions, Green Bay Packers, Los Angeles Rams, New York Giants, Philadelphia Eagles, Pittsburgh Steelers, San Francisco 49ers, and Washington Redskins. In the same year a new rule was introduced allowing the unlimited substitution of players. This move led to increasing specialization among both players and coaches, and helped make the game more appealing as a spectator sport. Pro football attracted a huge and growing TV audience. In 1958 the NFL Championship Game between the Baltimore Colts and New York Giants was televised nationally. It was the first such game to be decided by a sudden death play-off in overtime, and the nail-biting finish, which saw Alan Ameche give the Colts the game, captured the nation's imagination. That 1958 broadcast is today considered by many to be the turning point in the popularity of the professional game.

Meanwhile, at the local level football continued to arouse fierce loyalty among the fans of a particular school, town, or region. When spectators went to a football game, complete with its complement of smiling cheerleaders and perky drum majorettes, they were participating in the life of small-town America, where the entire community rallied around the local team and turned out in all weather to watch games.

In the 1920s and 1930s inter-collegiate football had become a national passion, uniting fiercely partisan supporters who enjoyed watching games at a local level.

A vendor sells cokes to a group of young football fans watching a game from the stands in 1954. Homecoming football games were especially popular in the 1950s.

However, with the country's entry into World War II in 1941 many colleges put their football programs on hold. In the postwar years big-time college football dominated as schools competed with each other for talented players and successful coaches. At the same time, however, attendance figures at college games began to fall. While the NFL was embracing the new medium of television, the organizers of college football did not recognize the enormous revenues that television could deliver until the 1960s. Nevertheless, on special occasions college football managed to pull the crowds.

The homecoming football game is one of the great traditions of collegiate sports and dates back to before World War I (1914–1918). Alumni of a university returned to campus for a weekend that revolved around a high-profile football game. The weekend was a festive occasion, with bonfires, fireworks, parades, and rallies, and most importantly, the election by the student body of a homecoming king and queen. Parades of floats, including the queen's, would make their way through the town and were displayed at halftime during the football game. Such events were enjoyed with renewed enthusiasm in the 1950s, especially after homecoming festivities were suspended during World War II.

The sporting life

Many Americans chose to play sports as well as watch them. The growth of the suburbs encouraged the development of country clubs and golf courses, and both tennis and golf were popular sports that combined a good game with an opportunity for socializing. Belonging to a country club had a certain social cachet, and participation in such sports was seen as a way of sealing business and social partnerships.

Miniature golf and bowling

At the other end of the social scale miniature golf and ten-pin bowling were two immensely popular games that were freely and cheaply available. Miniature golf dates back to the 1920s, when "Tom Thumb" golf courses, complete with carefully designed hazards such as ponds, sand traps, and whimsical sculptures became immensely popular. Such courses sprang up all over the country; it is estimated that between 25,000 and 50,000 courses were built across the United States. However, the passion for miniature golf eventually dwindled and was not revived until the 1950s, when minigolf was marketed as a wholesome pastime for families living in the suburbs. At this time miniature golf courses were paired with fast-food concessions, motels, and drive-in movie houses, becoming an important part of the nation's roadside architecture. Courses also sprouted up on beachfronts, near campgrounds, and around other tourist attractions.

Al and Ralph Lomma are recognized as the creators of modern-day miniature golf. They began to develop ingenious stunt courses that featured moving hazards. They built their first course at Scranton, Pennsylvania, in the early 1950s, and they soon established a successful business manufacturing and selling prefabricated courses. While large franchises such as Don Clayton's Putt-Putt Golf and Games were popular during the decade, many roadside courses were less sophisticated affairs constructed from concrete, timber, and chicken wire. As automobiles took more and more people onto the roads, these ramshackle courses proliferated.

Primitive forms of bowling date back to the ancient Egyptians, but the ten-pin bowling game did not evolve in America until the 19th century. With the development of rubber balls at the beginning of the 20th century the game gained a new following. Properly organized, with standardized rules, the game grew in popularity. In 1951 another technological breakthrough set the stage for massive growth. The American Machine and Foundry Company purchased the patents to Gottfried Schmidt's automatic pinspotter, and by late 1952 pinspotters were gradually being introduced in bowling alleys. Proprietors of alleys were no longer obliged to rely on the services of "pinboys" to set the pins. Fully automated bowling alleys began to spring up all over the country, and the sport soon proved popular among all age groups. Bowling promoters even tried to tap the elusive upper-class market: The sporting-goods manufacturer Capezio, for example, introduced a line of bowling shoes with advertisements showing society ladies bowling.

As with so many other sports, television embraced bowling in the 1950s, and the game's popularity grew accordingly. NBC's show *Championship Bowling*, which premiered in 1954 and featured tense one-on-one matches, was the first network coverage of bowling. TV coverage increased with shows such as *Make That Spare*, *Celebrity Bowling*, and *Bowling for Dollars*.

Television

If the huge range of family entertainment on offer failed to impress, there was always the option of staying at home and watching the new mass media sensation, television. Millions of families chose to stay indoors and watch favorites such as *Kukla, Fran and Ollie*, *I Love Lucy*, *The Honeymooners*, *Your Show of Shows*, and *Gunsmoke*. They could follow the World Series in baseball, tune in to network news, and be entertained by a varied diet of quiz shows, situation comedies, and soap operas.

Swanson Foods introduced the first frozen TV dinners—prepared meals presented in a three-compartment aluminum tray for reheating in the oven—in 1954. Some 10 million TV dinners were sold at 98 cents each during the first year, ensuring that

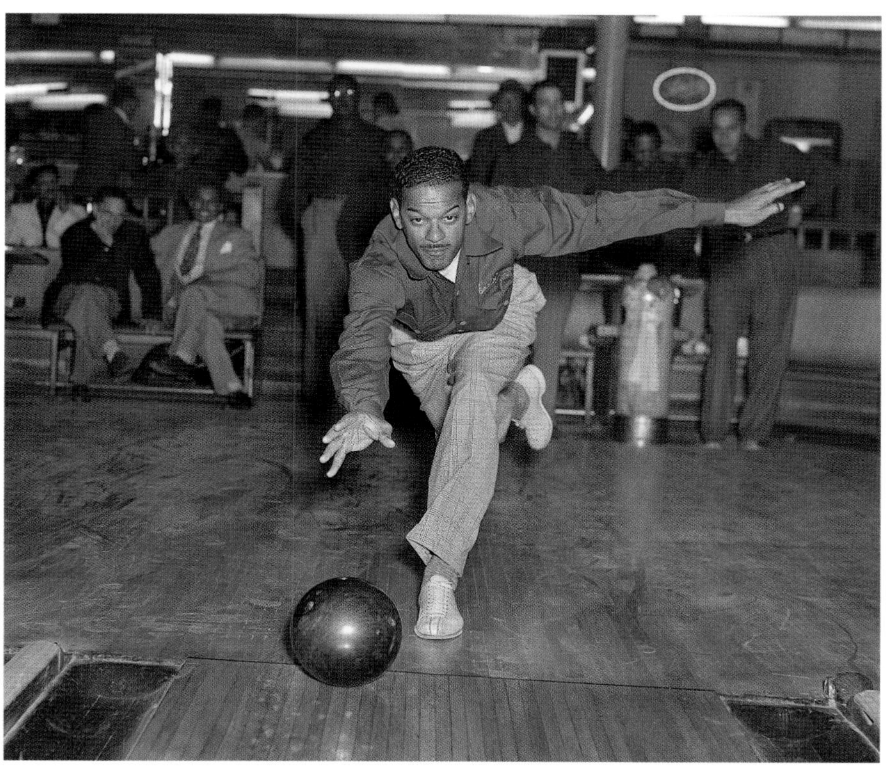

A young man bowls in Harlem, New York City, in 1953. The introduction of fully automated bowling alleys helped make it one of the most popular participation sports.

SCRABBLE: A 1950s CLASSIC

In the 1950s the Scrabble Crossword Game took America by storm, and it has continued to grow in popularity. In fact, the game dates back to 1930s, when Alfred Butts, a passionate enthusiast of crossword puzzles, created a crossword board game called "Criss Cross Words" that combined both chance and skill. He developed the game primarily as a home entertainment for family and friends, supplying them with his own hand-made sets of 100 letter tiles and 225-square boards. Butts's approaches to established game manufacturers were firmly rebuffed. In 1948 Mr. and Mrs. James Brunot, owners of one of the original Criss Cross Words sets, thought the game should be marketed and sought permission from Butts to manufacture the game. It was James Brunot who came up with the new name, Scrabble. The Brunots formed a production and marketing company, and rented an abandoned schoolhouse in Connecticut. With the help of friends they turned out 12 games an hour, stamping letters on wooden tiles one at a time.

In 1949 the Brunots made 2,400 sets and lost $450. In the three years from 1949 to 1951 sales of Scrabble remained at the disappointingly low level of fewer than 10,000 sets each year. However, the orders gradually increased as news about the game spread, mainly by word of mouth. In 1952, when Jack Strauss, president of Macy's, played and enjoyed Scrabble on vacation, there was a sales breakthrough. On returning to work, Strauss was surprised to learn that Scrabble was not on sale at New York City's famous department store. When the Brunots returned from a trip, they found their little factory deluged with orders. Once Scrabble was stocked by Macy's, the game caught on and became a national craze.

Residents at the Retired Officers' Residence in Asbury Park, New Jersey, enjoy a game of Scrabble in 1955.

The Brunots licensed the Selchow and Righter Company the rights to market and distribute the game in North America. Within two years the company had sold more than four million sets. Today Scrabble is one of the leading board games in the world and the most popular word game in the United States. It ranks just below Monopoly as the best-selling game in American history.

A idealized scene from the 1950s: A young boy and girl sit on the living-room floor playing cards while their parents sit on the sofa watching a baseball game on television.

nothing—not even mealtimes—was going to interfere with the nation's viewing habits. Watching television had become America's favorite pastime.

See Also:

Automobile Culture • Barbie Doll • Baseball • Basketball • *Crockett, Davy* • Dance • Football • Freed, Alan • Leisure Industry • Rock 'n' Roll • Sports • Teenage Culture • Television

JUDY GARLAND 1922–1969

The actress and singer Judy Garland found fame in the late 1930s when she was still a teenager. Although her subsequent career was plagued by drug addiction, she continued to give memorable performances on both stage and screen.

The singer who became known as Judy Garland was born Frances Ethel Gumm in Grand Rapids, Minnesota, on June 10, 1922. She gave her first performance at age two, invading the stage during her family's vaudeville act to sing "Jingle Bells." Frances joined her siblings in the Gumm Sisters Kiddie Act, which toured the United States between 1927 and 1935. She was billed as "the little girl with the great big voice." The sisters changed their name to Garland in 1934, but success still eluded them. However, when the trio split, Judy, as she now called herself, was personally signed to the MGM film studio by company head Louis B. Mayer. She made her MGM debut in the two-reel short *Every Sunday* in 1936 and became a star when she appeared in *Broadway Melody of 1938*, stealing the show by singing "You Made Me Love You" to a picture of actor Clark Gable. In 1937 Garland made *Thoroughbreds Don't Cry*, the first of nine movies in which she starred with Mickey Rooney (1920–).

Judy Garland, pictured here in 1956, was one of the most popular and enduring performers of the 20th century.

Garland became famous throughout the world for her portrayal of Dorothy in *The Wizard of Oz* in 1939. The role earned her an honorary Oscar for most outstanding juvenile performance. During this period Garland was being prescribed pills to control her weight, help her sleep, and give her energy. Her movie successes continued with *Meet Me in St. Louis* (1944), *The Harvey Girls* (1946), and *Easter Parade* (1948), but behind the scenes she was suffering from the side-effects of drug addiction. Her behavior became increasingly unreliable, and in 1950 her MGM contract was terminated.

Comeback in the 1950s

Temporarily turning her back on Hollywood, Garland resurrected her career by concentrating on live performances. In April 1951 she began a four-week run of concerts at the London Palladium, England. Later that year she embarked on a similar series of concerts at New York City's Palace Theater. The show was scheduled to run for four weeks but was so successful that it stretched to almost five months.

In 1954 Garland made a return to acting in *A Star Is Born*, delivering what is considered her greatest screen performance. The movie, in which she played a young actress whose ascending fortunes contrast with those of her alcoholic husband, earned Garland an Oscar nomination.

For the remainder of the 1950s Garland continued to perform to enthusiastic audiences in the United States and Europe. She also released a string of hit albums. On April 23, 1961, she gave the most famous stage performance of her career at Carnegie Hall, New York City. The concert was recorded and released as a double album. It sold more than two million copies and won five Grammy Awards.

Garland fought against drug addiction throughout her career, and she became notorious for her erratic behavior. She was prone to fits of depression and made several suicide attempts. Garland eventually died of an accidental overdose of barbiturates in her London apartment on June 22, 1969.

See Also:

Broadway • Movie Industry • Oscars • Popular Music

GERMANY

At the end of World War II Germany was divided between the Allies. Eventually two separate countries emerged: the pro-Western Federal Republic of Germany and the Communist German Democratic Republic. The Federal Republic's economy gradually began an amazing recovery.

Germany lay in ruins at the end of World War II (1939–1945). Most of the country's major cities and industry had been badly damaged or destroyed by Allied bombing. With no central government the country came under the control of the United States, the Soviet Union, Britain, and France, who divided it into four zones of occupation. Throughout 1946 and 1947 there were discussions about amalgamating the zones, but the Soviets were determined that communism should be fostered in their eastern zone. In May 1949 the three western zones were unified to become the Federal Republic of Germany (also known as West Germany), while the Soviet zone became the German Democratic Republic (East Germany) in October 1949.

Federal Republic of Germany

The constitution of the West German republic was initially based on a federation of 11 states (*Länder*). The federal government in Bonn consisted of two houses: the Bundestag, whose members were elected by the people, and the Bundesrat, whose members were designated by the governments of the states. A federal chancellor was to be elected by the Bundestag.

After elections in August 1949 the Christian Democratic Union (CDU) emerged as the largest party, and the first federal chancellor was its leader, Konrad Adenauer (*see box*). Throughout the 1950s Adenauer was to dominate German politics and—with the aid of Ludwig Erhard (1897–1977), the economics minister—built the foundations for West Germany's economic recovery. Evidence of this recovery lay in the fact that while unemployment was a major problem in 1949, by the late 1950s there was a shortage of labor. People were intent on putting the past behind them and rebuilding their country, and labor relations became less confrontational as 16 union groups amalgamated to form one strong federation that rarely resorted to strikes.

KONRAD ADENAUER

Konrad Adenauer (1876–1967) had long been active in politics when he became federal chancellor of West Germany in 1949. He had become mayor of Cologne in 1917 and in the 1930s he had twice been briefly imprisoned by the Nazis. He was reappointed mayor of Cologne by the Americans in 1945 but was subsequently dismissed by the British for his failure to organize the clearing of rubble created by the Allied bombardment during the war. He then became involved in the affairs of the newly formed Christian Democratic Union (CDU) and in 1949 became its chairman. In the Bundestag elections of that year the CDU was the largest party, but it required the support of other parties to form a government. In September Adenauer was appointed federal chancellor by a majority of just one. In 1957 he led the CDU to an outright victory in the polls and then stayed firmly in power until his retirement in 1963. Throughout his career Adenauer maintained a strong grip on government, ensuring that West Germany adopted an anticommunist stance and became allied with the rest of Western Europe, particularly France, while overseeing its transition from an economically crippled to a prosperous nation.

Konrad Adenauer became the first federal chancellor of West Germany in 1949 and remained in power until his retirement in 1963.

WALTER ULBRICHT

Walter Ulbricht (1893–1973) was a founder member of the German Communist Party (KPD) in 1919. Elected to the Reichstag (parliament) in 1928, he fled Germany following the rise of Adolf Hitler to power in 1933. He spent time in Paris and Moscow as well as in Spain during the Spanish Civil War (1936–1939) before being based in the Soviet Union between 1941 and 1945. On returning to Germany in April 1945 after the defeat of Hitler, Ulbricht became head of the KPD in the Soviet-occupied zone. He subsequently played a major role in the formation of the Socialist Unity Party (SED) through the merging of the Communist and Social Democratic parties. In 1949 he became deputy premier of the German Democratic Republic and in the following year general secretary of the SED and thereby effective ruler of the country. He established a repressive regime with close links to the Soviet Union and continued to pursue Stalinist policies even after the Soviet dictator's death in 1953. In 1960 Ulbricht became the official head of state, and he remained in that position until his death in 1973.

Additional factors that contributed to economic recovery were grants and loans to the value of almost $1.4 billion from the U.S. government as part of the Marshall Plan and, from 1951, West Germany's membership in the European Coal and Steel Community (ECSC). The success of the ECSC led to the formation in 1957 of the European Economic Community (EEC), of which West Germany was a founder member.

German Democratic Republic

From its establishment in October 1949 the German Democratic Republic was governed by the Communist-controlled Socialist Unity Party (SED). The party's general secretary, Walter Ulbricht (*see box*), soon became the country's effective ruler. A totalitarian regime was established under which economic policies were introduced that caused much dissatisfaction. In June 1953 workers in East Berlin started a strike and political demonstrations that were finally quashed by Soviet tanks. Ulbricht's position as ruler was confirmed, and the SED was purged of many members who opposed his hard-line policies. Some were sent to prison.

The East German government had begun to collectivize agriculture (merge individual farms) in 1952 and 1953. The process continued in 1959 and 1960. Meanwhile, resources were poured into expanding heavy industry; the production of consumer goods was largely ignored. While West Germany began to prosper, East Germany very obviously did not, and many inhabitants began to escape westward. The border between West and East Germany was closed after 1952, but it was still possible to get from the eastern to the western side of Berlin, the divided former capital city that now lay within East Germany. From West Berlin people could then travel to West Germany, and throughout the 1950s they did so in large numbers. The exodus came to an abrupt end in 1961, when the East German authorities erected a wall across the city. The Berlin Wall divided friends and families, and sealed the division between East and West Germany for three more decades.

An enraged rioter tears down the radio antenna of a Soviet tank during a rebellion and general strike by workers in East Berlin in June 1953.

See Also:

Berlin • Cold War • European Common Market • Foreign Policy • France • North Atlantic Treaty Organization • Soviet Union

ALTHEA GIBSON 1927–2003

Althea Gibson was the first great African American tennis champion. She broke the color bar in her sport two years after Jackie Robinson had done so in baseball. Tall and rangy, she often dominated her opponents with a powerful serve and forehand and wide reach at the net.

Althea Gibson was born on August 25, 1927, in South Carolina but grew up in a poor neighborhood of Harlem, New York City. In a public recreation center she was spotted playing paddle tennis. She had such quick reflexes and power that others encouraged her to try out playing tennis instead. Her first lessons were at the Harlem River Tennis Courts, where she excelled. From there she joined the Harlem Cosmopolitan Tennis Club, a group made up of African American players. In 1942, at age 15, she won the girls' singles title at the American Tennis Association (ATA). The ATA was an all-black circuit and provided the only opportunity for African Americans to play competitive tennis since the major tournaments were closed to them.

From Harlem Gibson moved back to the South, where she improved her game and went to college. In 1953 she graduated from college and got a job as athletic instructor at Lincoln University, Missouri. By this time she had already broken the race barrier at the all-white major championships.

In 1949, at age 22, Gibson became the first African American woman to compete in a white tournament when she was invited to play in the National Indoor Championships, where she reached the quarterfinals. "I had the notion," she wrote in her autobiography, "that, having done so well in the Indoors, I would almost as a matter of course be invited to play in the summer grass-court tournaments, the big ones. But nothing happened. The U.S.L.T.A. [United States Lawn Tennis Association] acted as though I wasn't there." Officials who refused to invite Gibson to play in white tournaments justified their decision by saying that she had no previous record to prove that she should or deserved to be invited.

In 1950 the *American Lawn Tennis* magazine published an article by Alice Marble, a white tennis champion, accusing the major tournaments of bigotry for not allowing Gibson to play.

International recognition

Soon after, Gibson was invited to play that summer in the important Eastern Grass Court Championships at the Orange Lawn Tennis Club in New Jersey. Later that same year she played in the National Clay Courts Championships, where she lost in the quarterfinals to Doris Hart, and finally in the U.S. National Championships at Forest Hills, New York.

Gibson won her first grand slam title in France in 1956. A few weeks later she arrived at Wimbledon as the favorite for the women's singles title but lost in the quarterfinals to Shirley Fry. The next two years were different. She won both the Wimbledon singles and doubles in 1957 and 1958 and the U.S. singles titles in the same years. She retired from amateur tennis in 1958 and was inducted into the International Tennis Hall of Fame in 1971.

Althea Gibson, seen here on her way to winning the U.S. National Championship title at Forest Hills, New York, in 1957, was the first black woman to play in a grand slam.

See Also:

Black Americans • Connolly, Maureen • Gonzales, Pancho • Sports • Tennis

ALLEN GINSBERG 1926–1997

The poet Allen Ginsberg was one of the leading figures of the Beat movement. His best-known work was the poem "Howl," a lengthy attack on contemporary American values that led to the poet's publisher being charged with producing obscene material.

With his friends the novelists Jack Kerouac (1922–1969) and William Burroughs (1914–1997) the poet Allen Ginsberg formed the core of the Beats, the bohemian, antiestablishment literary movement that protested against what it perceived as the soulless and materialistic culture of 1950s America. Ginsberg's most important work of the decade was also his first to be published: the fierce and anarchic "Howl" (1956). It sought to define the experience of a generation of disaffected, rebellious youths. The poem would take on an iconic status within the counterculture of the following decade.

Early life

Ginsberg was born on June 3, 1926, in Newark, New Jersey. His father was a moderately successful poet, while his mother was a communist who suffered severe bouts of mental illness and spent much of her life hospitalized. Ginsberg's youth was marked by poetry writing, half-hearted study, drug use, drunkenness, and intense homosexual love affairs. He met Kerouac and Burroughs in the early 1940s while studying law at New York City's Columbia University, from which he was suspended for a time. In 1949 he was arrested on suspicion of burglary but was released on condition that he spend a period in a mental institution.

In 1954 Ginsberg moved to California, where he met his lifelong partner, the painter Peter Orlovsky, and began his literary career in earnest. On October 13, 1955, he gave a drunken reading of "Howl" at San Francisco's Six Gallery. The end of each of the poem's long sentences was met with an encouraging shout of "Go!" from Kerouac. The poem was published in a collection entitled *Howl and Other Poems* by the San Francisco bookstore City Lights in October 1956.

Allen Ginsberg, picture here in 1958, was one of the most acclaimed poets of his generation.

In "Howl" Ginsberg evokes his bohemian life in New York in fragmented, incantatory, and largely punctuation-free verse. The poem is both a lament for and celebration of a "lost" generation of "angelheaded hipsters" scarred and broken by drug addiction and mental instability. It is also an attack on the materialism that Ginsberg felt dominated U.S. culture. The poem was dedicated and addressed to a friend he first met during his time in a psychiatric institution.

Inspired by writers such as Walt Whitman, William Blake, and William Carlos Williams, Ginsberg wanted to bring poetry "back to the streets," free from the intellectualism that characterized much of the American poetry of the 1920s and 1930s. He saw poetry as largely an oral art form, one that should have an immediate emotional effect.

In May 1957 City Lights was served with a warrant for printing, publishing, and selling "obscene and indecent writings, papers, and books, to wit: *Howl and Other Poems*." Although a judge soon acquitted the bookshop of the charge, the controversy generated by the warrant meant that sales of the poems rocketed. Ginsberg gained a national readership as well as widespread notoriety.

Ginsberg returned to the United States in July 1958 after a ten-month stay in Paris. In February 1959 he read his new, long poem "Kaddish" to a packed McMillan Theater at Columbia University. Eventually published in 1961, the poem was a lament for his mother, who had died in 1956.

In the 1960s Ginsberg became immersed in the U.S. counterculture. He became a friend of Timothy Leary (1920–1996), a prominent advocate of the use of the drug LSD, and protested against the Vietnam War. Although Ginsberg would continue to write poetry for much of the rest of the 20th century, it was for his work in the fifties that he remained most famous. He died on April 5, 1997.

See Also:

Beat Movement • Book Publishing • Burroughs, William • Drugs and Drug Abuse • Kerouac, Jack • Poetry

GOLF

Many of the greatest golfers of the 1950s were American, including Ben Hogan, Sam Snead, and Arnold Palmer. The decade also witnessed a revision in golf rules and the standardization of the sport throughout the world.

American players dominated the golf world in the 1950s. However, most of the successful American golfers did not compete outside the United States. Ben Hogan (1912–1997), the outstanding player of the early years of the decade, won the British Open in 1953 on his only visit to the championship, and it was not until Arnold Palmer (1929–) won the tournament in 1961 and 1962 that American pros began to cross the Atlantic in numbers. In 1953 Hogan lost the opportunity to become the only player ever to win golf's modern grand slam because the British Open did not figure in the scheduling of dates for the American tour. Having added the British Open title to victories in the Masters and the U.S. Open, he was unable to get back to America in time to play in the PGA (Professional Golfers' Association) Championship. In 1957 the U.S. team lost the Ryder Cup to Great Britain for the first time since 1933, but among individual overseas players only Bobby Locke of South Africa and Peter Thomson of Australia could be considered rivals to the best Americans. Neither player ever captured a major in the United States.

President Dwight D. Eisenhower (in white shirt) seated with some of the great golfers of the 1950s: (from left to right) Byron Nelson, Ben Hogan, and Clifford Roberts.

For the majority of the American sports public golf in the postwar era was not considered to be an exciting spectator sport. "Slamming" Sam Snead (1912–2002), the best player after Hogan (*see box*), was a dapper, free-swinging throwback to an earlier age. His trademark was a wide-brimmed straw hat ringed with a tartan band, and his jaunty manner on course made him a crowd favorite. But Hogan had little appeal for a wider audience. He was a somewhat chilly, withdrawn person who scarcely uttered a word to his playing partners. Far from seeking to win popularity, he often seemed to regard the galleries that followed him with disdain.

SNEAD AND HOGAN

Ben Hogan's courage in coming back from a near-fatal car accident in 1949 that left both his legs so severely damaged that he had to learn to walk again added to his reputation. After his victory in the British Open in 1953 he was given a tickertape parade in New York City. A small man with a compact game, he was most people's choice as the greatest golfer of his era and one of the greatest ever. But Sam Snead, a large man with a lazy-looking, natural swing and the driving power that earned him his nickname "Slamming," had supporters who thought that he was the best. Remarkably, Snead never won the U.S. Open, although he finished second on four occasions between 1937 and 1949.

HOGAN: 4 U.S. Open titles, 2 Masters, 2 USPGA, 1 British Open
63 U.S. tour victories, 1938–1959
World Cup individual winner, 1956
USPGA Player of the Year 4 times
Leading money-winner 5 times

SNEAD: 3 Masters, 3 USPGA, 1 British Open
81 U.S. tour victories, 1936–1965
World Cup individual winner, 1961
USPGA Player of the Year one time
Leading money-winner 3 times

Golf and racism

Most Americans associated golf with country clubs for the rich and for whites. President Dwight D. Eisenhower (1953–1961) was famously a member of the exclusive Augusta National Golf Club in Georgia, the home of the Masters, where no women and only white men were allowed to be members. In fact, no black golfer played in the Masters before 1975. Augusta was not alone: Golf clubs throughout America were openly racist. Blacks were only allowed onto courses as caddies, and discrimination was even written into the constitution of the PGA. Article III on membership included a clause stating that "professional golfers of the Caucasian Race, over the age of eighteen (18) years, residing in North or South America ... shall be eligible." That so-called "Caucasian clause" meant that African American players could not make their way onto the PGA Tour and could not be appointed club professionals.

The first African American to win on the pro tour was Charlie Sifford (1922–), a former caddie from North Carolina who won a string of black national championships. In 1952 the heavyweight boxing champion Joe Louis (1914–1981) used his influence to get himself, Sifford, and a few other black friends into the qualifying rounds for the Phoenix Open. They were not allowed to use the locker room at the club, and they teed off together early in the morning in advance of the white pros. Five years later Sifford won the 54-hole Long Beach Open, which was not an official tour event but one that was cosponsored by the PGA. That was a breakthrough, but another 10 years were to pass before Sifford became the first black winner of a full PGA event (the Greater Hartford Open). In 1959 Bill Wright won the U.S. Amateur Public Links title to become the first African American player to win a national championship of any kind open to both whites and blacks.

Television coverage

In 1950 golf was also largely invisible to the public. The first telecast of the U.S. Open, played at the St. Louis Golf Club, Missouri, had been made in 1947, but it had been transmitted only to viewers in the St. Louis area. The 1953 Tam O'Shanter "World Championship" tournament in Chicago was the first to be televised nationally. It was a stroke of good fortune for the television company that the tournament ended with one of the most spectacular finishes in history, with Lew Worsham holing out with a wedge from more than a 100 yards (91m) out on the 18th hole to win the tournament. The U.S. Open was carried on national television for the first time in 1954, and the Masters followed in 1956.

Television and sponsorship were eventually to transform the money-making possibilities of professional golf. However, in the 1950s, even though Americans never ventured overseas because the more lucrative prize money could be won at home, the winnings were still less than handsome. In 1953 the televised Tam O'Shanter tournament was the first to put up a total purse of $100,000, but the average for most events was about $10,000. Lloyd Mangrum (1914–1973) was the leading money-winner on the U.S. tour in 1951, with a year's takings of $26,088. The highest amount won in the decade was $72,835 by Ted Kroll (1919–2002) in 1956.

THE WOMEN'S GAME

The Ladies Professional Golf Association (LPGA) was established in 1950. One of the founder members was Patty Berg (1918–), who had won the first U.S. Women's Open in 1946 for a prize of $5,600 out of a total purse of $19,700, the largest in women's golf. Berg, Babe Zaharias (1914–1956), and Louise Suggs (1923–) were the dominant women golfers of the postwar era. Small prize money and few tournaments made it even harder for women than men to make a living out of tour golf. The $26,774 won by Marlene Hagge (1934–), the leading money-winner in 1956, was almost double the total for most other years of the decade.

Babe Zaharias, a gold-medal winner in the hurdles and javelin and a silver medalist in the high jump at the 1932 Olympics, headed the money list every year from 1948 to 1951. After undergoing major surgery for cancer in 1953, she came back to win five events in 1954, including the U.S. Open. In a short professional career that began in 1947 she won 31 tour events, including the Titleholders Championship three times and the Western Open four times. Louise Suggs won two Opens, four PGAs, four Western Opens, and four Titleholders. The Western Open and the Titleholders were then ranked as "majors" alongside the Open and the PGA.

Suggs was the first woman to win all four majors, but her overall record was bettered by Patty Berg. In two decades on the tour (1941–1962) Berg won 57 professional tournaments, piling up seven victories in each of the Titleholders Championship and the Western Open. She was the leading money-winner in 1954, 1955, and 1957, and twice won six tournaments in a single year (1953 and 1955).

Patty Berg, seen here practicing her swing in 1951, was one of the greatest women golfers of the postwar period.

Arnold Palmer plays at the Phoenix Open in 1964. Palmer burst onto the golfing stage in 1958, when he won his first major title, the Masters. He was to win it four times.

Hogan went into decline after 1953, and until the arrival of Arnold Palmer at the end of the decade there was no young superstar to fill his shoes. There were fine players such as Julius Boros (1920–1994), Dr. Cary Middlecoff (1921–1998), a dentist, and the hot-tempered Tommy Bolt (1916–), but only Boros was able to finish top of the money list on more than one occasion.

Arnold Palmer

In 1951 little-known Al Brosch (1911–1975) set an 18-hole PGA Tour record by shooting a round of 60 in the Texas Open. At once the "round of 59" became the golfing equivalent of the "four-minute mile." In 1954 Sam Snead scored the first 59 in a PGA tournament (a feat since achieved by only three other players: Al Geiberger, Chip Beck, and David Duval). By then Snead was in the twilight of his career. Four years later Palmer announced himself as Snead's successor by winning his first major, the Masters. Palmer was dashing, a working-class boy from Latrobe, Pennsylvania, with a cool haircut and a cigarette dangling from the corner of his mouth. He arrived on the scene just as television was turning from black-and-white to color. He smashed the ball, and his all-or-nothing attitude to shot-making stood out against the careful play of Hogan, Boros, and Middlecoff. He was to bring thousands of new fans to the game—"Arnie's Army"—and lead it into a new era of the commercial exploitation of talent that was to make millionaires of the country's top golfers.

See Also:

Black Americans • Eisenhower, Dwight D. • Games and Pastimes • Leisure Industry • Sports • Sports and TV

RULE CHANGES

In 1951 Francis Ouimet became the first American captain of the Royal & Ancient Golf Club at St. Andrews, Scotland. The same year the R&A and the United States Golf Association (USGA) brought out a revised "Rules of Golf." The result was that only one difference—the size of the ball—remained between golf in the United States and golf in the rest of the world (the ball was 1.68 inches (42.67mm) diameter in America, 1.62 inches (41.15mm) elsewhere). The center-shafted putter was made legal, the penalty for hitting a ball out of bounds was standardized at two strokes (stroke plus distance), and the stymie (an opponent's ball on the green blocking a putter's path to the hole) was abolished. Further standardization was introduced in 1956, when yardage guides adopted by the USGA set holes under 250 yards (229m) as par three and holes over 475 yards (434m) as par five.

The abolition of the stymie was a sad event for old-timers, and there were also many who regretted the virtual disappearance of match-play golf (apart from the Ryder Cup) from the professional game. In 1958 the United States PGA Championship abandoned match-play in favor of a medal event, the last of the four majors to do so.

PANCHO GONZALES 1928–1995

Pancho Gonzales was one of the greatest tennis players of his era. However, he played at a time when there were separate amateur and professional tours, a division that prevented him from winning as many prestigious titles as befitted his talent.

Ricardo Alonzo "Pancho" Gonzales was born on May 9, 1928. He grew up in Los Angeles, where his parents, Mexican immigrants, bought him a tennis racket to keep him "off the streets." In his early teens Gonzales played in a number of local tournaments but was later banned because of persistent truancy from school. After a short spell in the U.S. Navy he returned to tennis to take up a career in earnest.

Gonzales played in his first senior tournament in 1947 at the age of 19. His rise was meteoric. A year later Gonzales won both the U.S. Clay Court Championships and the U.S. National Championships, held on grass at Forest Hills, New York, where he beat Eric Sturgess in the final. The following year Gonzales repeated the feat, adding the U.S. Indoor Championships and the French and Wimbledon doubles titles.

Pancho Gonzales is pictured playing a match on the professional tour in 1956. By this point he was recognized as the best player in the world.

Going pro

Gonzales looked set for many more such victories. However, days after winning his second U.S. title, he quit the amateur circuit to join the pro tour. Gonzales's professional career did not start well. In 1949–1950 he played a grueling series of matches against Jack Kramer (1921–), then regarded as the best player in the world. The pair played 123 times, with Gonzales recording only 27 wins.

After Kramer's retirement, however, Gonzales came to dominate the professional tour, demonstrating his superiority over the greatest players of the era—including Frank Sedgman, Tony Trabert, and Ken Rosewall—by winning the U.S. Professional Championships every year but one between 1953 and 1961. This record of near-invincibility stamped Gonzales as unquestionably the number-one player in the world.

Gonzales spent most of the early 1960s in semiretirement; but when the amateur and professional worlds merged in 1968, he returned to the game. It was in this stage of his career that Gonzales played the match for which he is most remembered. In 1969, at the age of 41, he beat the 25-year-old Charlie Pasarell in the longest singles match ever played at Wimbledon. In a first-round match on Centre Court Gonzales won 22–24, 1–6, 16–14, 6–3, 11–9. The contest lasted five hours and 12 minutes and spread over two days. Gonzales saved seven match points in the final set. Wimbledon fans at last saw fading glimpses of the genius that they had been missing for almost two decades.

Gonzales was one of the great personalities of the game. He was the bad boy of tennis long before Ilie Nastase or John McEnroe. Once, in a match against Ken Rosewall, he drilled a ball at the head of a heckler and walked off court. His legendary temper did not lessen with age: He was disqualified in one match at the age of 44. However, his fiery nature was allied to a fighting spirit that made him a crowd favorite. Gonzales retired from the circuit in 1974 to coach in Las Vegas. He died from cancer in 1995.

See Also:

Connolly, Maureen • Gibson, Althea • Sports • Tennis

GOVERNMENT, LOCAL

A number of changes affected U.S. local government in the 1950s. Among them were the demise of the political machines that had dominated many of the country's major cities and a move away from the amateurism that typified many small-town governments.

On the surface American local government changed little in the 1950s, especially in comparison to the 1960s and 1970s, when new federal programs and more extensive federal involvement greatly reshaped regional politics. However, even in the 1950s some of the catalysts for later change became noticeable, and the United States' urban, suburban, and rural governments were all affected.

Federalism

The basic structure of local government in America was well established by the 1950s. Its key feature was the concept of federalism. In the United States "federalism" refers to the division of power and responsibility among the different levels of government. The U.S. system of local government differs from those of many other countries in that, generally speaking, local governments do not serve as underlings of the federal government in Washington, D.C. Rather, each level of government—national, state, and local—has its own set of responsibilities; other levels have little right to overrule decisions in those areas.

The federal government in Washington has sole control over coining money, for instance, while state governments have control over other issues, such as overseeing the education service and regulating local commerce. In the 1950s the federal government had little authority to order state or local governments to change the curriculum in schools.

In a process that began in the 1930s and accelerated in the 1960s, however, the federal government began to try to influence state and local governments by offering federal money in return for changes in state policy, such as increasing salaries for math teachers or eliminating racial discrimination in highway construction projects. The federal government used such "grants-in-aid" to get the states to participate in the building of the Interstate Highway System in the 1950s and to induce all the states to set a drinking age of 21 in the 1980s.

The types of local government

Below the state level is the local level, which is the most complex level in U.S. federalism. There are a number of different components of local government, the first of which is usually the county. The legislature of each state divides the state into counties, and the county governments then serve as arms of the state government. Counties are typically responsible for issues such as voter registration and property tax collection, carrying out the decisions made by the state legislature on who can vote and how much tax they must

Senator Dennis Chavez of New Mexico is pictured in 1956 after the passage of the Highway Bill that entitled the federal government to raise taxes for a substantial roadbuilding program.

pay. County governments are also responsible for providing basic government services such as the construction of roads, usually through an elected county commission or board, and law enforcement, through an elected county sheriff.

Cities are another major component of local government, and they are profoundly different from counties. While counties are created by the state legislature, cities are created by local inhabitants through a process called "incorporation." If enough voters in an area that is not already part of a city vote to incorporate, they can create a new municipal or city government, with a city charter to serve as a constitution. Within its city limits the new city government will take over most or all of the county's responsibilities for providing services.

Cities of sufficient size may qualify for "home rule." In most state constitutions home-rule designation gives the city government the power to pass ordinances (local laws) and to impose local taxes in addition to standard state taxes, such as an extra sales tax to pay for a city bus system. A home-rule city has considerable freedom and flexibility to run its own affairs, in contrast to county governments, which have little or no ordinance power and little authority to go beyond the narrow limits established by the state governments (*see box opposite*).

A final component of local government is the special district. A special district is usually responsible for a particular issue or service; the most common type of special district is the independent school district (ISD), which is responsible for establishing and running schools in most parts of the United States. The ISD is independent of the city and county government, and is run by a separately elected school board that does not take orders from the city council or county commission.

The ISD is subject to orders from the state legislature, which retains ultimate control over education issues in each state. Other types of special district include water and sewer districts, soil conservation districts, and (especially in the South) mosquito control districts.

Local government in the 1950s

In the 1950s the basic structure of local government was still close to its simplest form, before federal grants-in-aid brought greater influence by national government. As local government scholar Nancy Burns notes: "In the 1950s, the federal government was less involved in local politics than in any later decade." The only exceptions to this generalization were federal programs for "urban renewal," projects intended to tear

Local citizens queue to cast their votes at a polling station in Greensboro, North Carolina, in 1955.

THE MIAMI–DADE COUNTY FUSION

The two most significant types of local government in the United States are the city and the county. In most cases the county is larger than any of the cities that may be located in that county, and the division of labor between the city governments and the county government is usually fairly simple. However, in the case of the nation's largest cities the distinction between the city and the county can be harder to draw. If a city grows to be almost as large as the county itself, then a fusion between the city government and the county government becomes an attractive option.

Such was the case in the late 1950s in south Florida, one of the nation's fastest growing regions. Dade County, located at the southern tip of the state, stretches over a vast area of some 2,000 square miles (5,180 sq. km), the size of the entire state of Delaware. In the first census of the area in 1850 the new Dade County had only 96 inhabitants. It had fewer than 1,000 in 1896, when the city of Miami was founded as the county seat.

However, the area's population surged during the 1920s, when railroads connected sunny south Florida with the rest of the East Coast. A real-estate boom in hotel and vacation properties brought Miami and Dade County to the attention of the rest of the country for the first time. During and after World War II the area again experienced a huge increase in population. The government structure initially established to serve 1,000 people now had to deal with close to one million.

The solution was found in a radical change in the Dade County government. In 1956 the Florida state constitution was amended to give Dade County full home-rule status. The following year a new charter for Dade County established a government that looked much like that of a city. A mayor would be elected countywide, and a 13-member board of county commissioners would be elected by single-member districts. The board would act much as a city council would. The mayor would have the power to veto any ordinance passed by the board, but the mayor's most significant decision would be to appoint a county manager. Based on the model of the city manager, the county manager would be responsible for appointing all the major county officials and for running the business of the county government on a daily basis.

Miami Beach, shown here, is part of Dade County, an area that was granted home-rule status in 1956. The county then elected a mayor, who acted in the same way as the mayor of a large city.

Although the county government took on the appearance of a typical city government, the existing incorporated cities in Dade County, such as Miami, Miami Beach, and Coral Gables, continued to elect their own city councils and provide their own police, fire, and other city services. However, for the inhabitants of unincorporated areas of Miami–Dade County (almost one million-strong in 2004), the county government now functions almost exactly the way a city government would.

down old slums in major cities. Even in the case of urban renewal programs the federal government placed relatively little constraint on the local governments of the areas that received federal money.

The end of part-time government

Change was underway, however, and it was the growth in population in urban areas and especially in the new suburbs that was the cause of much of the transformation of American local government. By the end of the 1950s the United States' largest cities were home to an ever-growing share of the nation's population. Those people were concentrated in a relatively small number of cities. Only 2 percent of the

BASEBALL'S MUSICAL CHAIRS IN THE 1950s

The 1950s are often thought of as a time of stability and tranquillity. In major-league baseball, however, the decade was anything but. Teams with long and rich histories suddenly moved. While the franchise relocations of the 1950s stranded generations of fans without their teams, they also gave major-league baseball a truly national reach for the first time. For good or ill, local governments played the key role in those moves.

The franchise merry-go-round began in 1953, when the Boston Braves moved to Milwaukee. The Braves' time in Boston dated back to 1876, when they had joined the National League as one of its charter members. However, when local governments in the Milwaukee area made an offer to build a new stadium for the team if it would move to Wisconsin, the Braves left their hometown for the Midwest. Their new home park, Milwaukee County Stadium, was the first major-league stadium ever to be paid for completely by public funds. The Braves were "stolen" again in 1966, when governments in the Atlanta area made the team a similar offer.

The St. Louis Browns of the American League (AL) were next to move. Charter members of the AL since 1902, the Browns were a legendarily unsuccessful franchise, both on the field and at the box office. In 1954 the Browns were lured to Baltimore, where the local taxpayers had paid for a new stadium for the NFL's Baltimore Colts in 1950. The Browns became the Baltimore Orioles. After the move they became one of the AL's most successful franchises.

The most famous franchise moves in the 1950s came at the end of the 1957 season, when the New York Giants and the Brooklyn Dodgers, also charter members of the National League, announced that they would both move to California. The Giants had seen their attendance at their Manhattan ballpark, the Polo Grounds, drop to 600,000 in 1956, only half of what it had been for their 1954 championship team. Asked what effect a move would have on the Giants' youngest fans, team owner Horace Stoneham replied, "I feel bad about the kids, but I haven't seen many of their fathers lately."

Mayor George Christopher of San Francisco promised the Giants a new ballpark at taxpayer expense, a promise that would ultimately lead to the establishment of Candlestick Park in 1960. Vice President Richard M. Nixon, in attendance at the first game at Candlestick, pronounced it "the finest ballpark in America." Later fans, cursed by the park's bone-chilling winds and relatively inconvenient suburban location, begged to differ with Nixon's assessment.

Three California baseball fans celebrate the news that the Brooklyn Dodgers will be relocating to Los Angeles in 1958. Los Angeles Mayor Norris Poulson paved the way for the construction of Dodger Stadium.

The Brooklyn Dodgers, the archrivals of the Giants, decamped for Los Angeles, where they would play in the historic Los Angeles Memorial Coliseum for four years. Team owner Walter O'Malley, however, badly wanted a new stadium. He eventually struck a deal with L.A. Mayor Norris Poulson to trade land owned by the team (the grounds of L.A.'s Wrigley Field, a minor-league stadium) for 300 acres (121 ha) of prime real estate just north of downtown L.A. in a location known as Chavez Ravine.

The Chavez Ravine property had been set aside for low-income housing, and the voters of Los Angeles had to approve the Dodgers' deal in a special referendum in June 1958. The motion passed. After receiving the land itself for virtually nothing, the team built Dodger Stadium entirely with the owner's money. Dodger Stadium, which opened in 1962, was the last stadium built with private money until the new San Francisco ballpark, which replaced Candlestick, was built in the late 1990s.

The Dodgers' and Giants' moves brought major-league baseball to the West Coast for the first time. The moves also established a pattern for all major-league sports: It was now the responsibility of local governments to pay for new arenas and ballparks or risk watching another city make their team a better offer.

country's incorporated cities had populations of more than 100,000 people, yet over 40 percent of all Americans lived in such large cities. For most of its history the United States had been largely a rural society; after World War II (1939–1945) it became an overwhelmingly urban and suburban society.

Such demographic changes slowly began to alter the nature of local government, especially for those who served in it. According to scholar Alan Ehrenhalt, a major authority on the subject: "Local government in the 1950s was [still] undeniably a citizen institution. Legislative bodies met infrequently (as little as twice a month even in some large places) and usually at night so that the citizen officeholders could hold down private jobs during the day." The part-time local governments were often dominated by a local elite, centered sometimes around a powerful state senator, party chairman, or city manager. These small groups of influential citizens would usually discuss city business in private in an informal setting.

Such "citizen governments," however, frequently excluded many of the actual citizens. Many people were denied the opportunity to take part in the decision-making process because of their race, gender, social class, or simply because they did not fit in. Importantly, they had no means of appealing against the decisions made by such committees. According to Ehrenhalt, "[T]here were few public hearings and little meaningful debate in the city council or the county commission. The local elite simply did its work and moved on."

In the 1950s most politicians were not professionals. In his survey of the period Ehrenhalt found that most participants in local government "had to make a living some other way. Only at the higher reaches of the system—governors, big-city mayors, some members of Congress—was politics truly a full-time occupation."

In many areas the part-time system gradually began to take on full-time demands as the population grew. For example, in the town of Concord, California, an old farm town that was close enough to San Francisco to serve as a suburb by the 1950s, the population exploded from 7,000 in 1950 to 24,000 in 1955, and to more than 50,000 by 1965. Before the 1950s Concord's old part-time government got by with a city council meeting every two weeks. By the end of the 1950s the city needed a new City Hall to house all the government offices, and the city council hired a city manager to run city services on a full-time basis.

The rise of the suburbs

Population growth was to a large extent channeled into the suburbs. In the 1950s and 1960s some 12 million Americans, mostly white and middle class, moved to the suburbs either from the inner cities or from rural areas. In many cases, such as Concord, the new suburbs were existing outlying towns.

In many other cases, however, a real-estate developer would buy large amounts of land in unincorporated areas and build hundreds or thousands of new homes on land that had never been part of a city. These new developments could then incorporate

THE REVOLUTION OF "ONE MAN, ONE VOTE"

In a series of cases in the early 1960s, including *Baker v. Carr* (1962) and *Reynolds v. Sims* (1964), the U.S. Supreme Court transformed the balance of power that had existed in many local and state governments in the 1950s. Collectively known as "the one-man, one-vote" decisions, the court rulings held that the "equal protection" clause of the U.S. Constitution's Fourteenth Amendment required that each vote in a state, county, or city carry roughly the same power as any other individual vote.

Although it hardly seems revolutionary at first glance, this principle invalidated thousands of electoral districts across the country. In many states, such as Tennessee (the subject of *Baker v. Carr*), electoral districts were rarely reapportioned: The boundaries of the districts for the state legislature stayed the same even as the population shifted dramatically. As the country urbanized in the first half of the 20th century, cities and suburbs were consistently underrepresented in comparison to rural areas. In Tennessee in the 1950s the district that included the city of Memphis had 10 times as many people as some of the more rural districts. In effect that meant that each rural voter had roughly 10 times the voting influence of his or her city-dwelling equivalent.

Other states also used criteria other than population in setting electoral district lines. In the state senate of South Carolina, for instance, each county was a senate district, with each county receiving one senate seat regardless of its population. In the rural counties in particular the state senator was often an all-powerful political boss who appointed all the major offices in his home county while also commanding disproportionate power over the urban counties in the state legislature.

The "one-man, one-vote" decisions laid down a general rule that all electoral districts must be roughly equal in population, and that the district lines must be redrawn as the population grows and shifts. The Tennessee and South Carolina systems were outlawed, and the disproportionate power of rural districts in many states was curtailed. Since the rural areas also tended to be the most conservative, the shift in power to urban and suburban areas brought in new officials and new attitudes to state and local governments.

Richard J. Daley, mayoral candidate in Chicago, celebrates his impending victory in the 1955 election. Daley would be reelected five times, dying in office in 1976.

as a city on their own, although the new suburban cities were made possible by the proximity of the old existing city.

In this way almost all the major American cities came to be ringed by large suburban cities: For example, a resident of White Bear Lake, Minnesota, might drive to work in Minneapolis every day, or a resident of Vashon Island, Washington, might drive to Seattle, only to return to live, vote, and pay taxes back in the sheltered suburb. The Interstate Highway System contributed to the trend by ensuring that the city center was connected to the suburbs by new multilane freeways.

The fall of the machines

In the major cities that the suburbanites had left behind the 1950s were the last great decade of the political machines. In a "machine" government a political party seeks power in order to ensure a steady supply of jobs and money for the party's supporters. In return the supporters keep the machine in power. Critics argue that such a system of government comes at the expense of capable administration and meaningful voter participation. A machine government depends on control of the ballot to ensure that the dominant party nominates only candidates supportive of the machine and on "patronage," meaning the control of the hiring of city employees and the granting of city government contracts. Defenders of political machines argue that while they may be corrupt, that does not necessarily mean that they are inefficient. A common defense of political machines of the early 20th century was that "things got done." Corruption was the price that had to be paid to ensure that wheels were set in motion. Most of the great U.S. political machines grew up in large cities in the late 19th and early 20th centuries, when huge influxes of immigrants were putting great strain on local governments. Some historians maintain that more democratic—and bureaucratic—systems of government would not have been able to deal with the demands of such growth.

Daley's Chicago

The most infamous machine boss of the 1950s was Richard J. Daley (1902–1976), who was mayor of Chicago from 1955 to 1976. The main way in which Daley's machine marshaled votes was through the work of precinct captains, whose job it was to deliver votes in a particular neighborhood. However, outright corruption was also prevalent. In Daley's Chicago votes were counted as many times as might be necessary for the machine to win. One of Daley's predecessors had coined the phrase "Vote early, vote often!"

Victory in a citywide election meant control over 25,000 jobs, which could be given to the party's neighborhood activists, and millions of dollars in city contracts, to be handed out to companies that supported the machine. Machine loyalists were often employed as police officers, building inspectors, and in other vital positions. Opponents of Daley's regime, however, argued that such jobs were often performed with something less than professional competence.

One of the most outspoken critics of Daley's machine was the Chicago columnist Mike Royko (1932–1997), who attacked the politician in local newspaper articles and an unauthorized biography, *Boss* (1971). In one piece Royko chronicled the everyday corruption that was prevalent in Daley's Chicago: "It was a typical night for the Chicago police in early 1960. They were making money. Some were making big money. Others could stop just six or seven good traffic violators in one night—that was an extra $50 in the wallet when midnight came."

Royko took delight in detailing the ways in which the Daley-era police would solicit bribes. One cop's routine was to announce to traffic offenders that he sold pencils for $5, $10, and $25. "The pencils were seldom sold for more than $25," Royko noted, "because that would have meant that someone had been run over, and fixing that required the cooperation of prosecutors and judges and was not something that could be arranged on the scene." But with a little time and with enough of a bribe Mayor Daley's judges and prosecutors were for sale as well.

As the 1950s wore on, however, the machines in Chicago and other major cities came under increasing pressure. That pressure came both from reformers in the political system itself, such as Alderman Dick Simpson in Chicago, and from increasingly hostile coverage by the news media. The machines were also imperiled by the growth of the suburbs, which attracted affluent middle-class taxpayers away from the inner cities, and which provided an example of relatively clean, efficient government.

Machine politics in Utica

Daley's Chicago machine lasted into the mid-1970s, but the machine in Utica, New York, studied by Alan Ehrenhalt, did not survive the 1950s. The Utica machine led by party boss Rufus Elefante thrived for years by requiring all city employees to "contribute" 4 percent of their salaries to the local Democratic Party, which was controlled by Elefante, and by steering Utica city contracts to the many small businesses owned by him. Elefante was also rumored to have had connections to well-known figures in the world of organized crime.

Elefante never ran for office and rarely visited City Hall. Instead, he did all his business at an Italian restaurant called Marino's. If people had queries about the city's refuse collection service, they would approach Elefante at the restaurant rather than go through official channels. Often they would be referred to the associate of Elefante's who was in charge of that particular area (an associate who was usually, conveniently, also having lunch at the restaurant), and the problem would be sorted out, although often at a price.

Gradually, however, Elefante's power was undermined by a succession of reform-minded mayors, each of whom was outside Elefante's control, a hostile press, and a local business community that had tired of the machine's corruption. Eventually Elefante was brought down.

Faced with a middle-class exodus to the suburbs and the beginning of a decline in heavy industry and manufacturing, governments in the large cities of America began to operate less as patronage machines and more as agents of economic development. Keeping and attracting businesses and affluent residents became the central concerns for local officials (*see p. 34*).

The rural elite of the South

Local government in many rural areas, and in particular the South, was dominated by a conservative political elite, the actions of which in many ways mirrored those of the big-city machines. In the rural South the ruling elite stayed in power by a combination of two factors. The first was malapportionment, which was the failure to redraw electoral districts to account for population growth and population shifts. That electoral district lines were not redrawn to reflect the fact that rural areas had lost many inhabitants meant

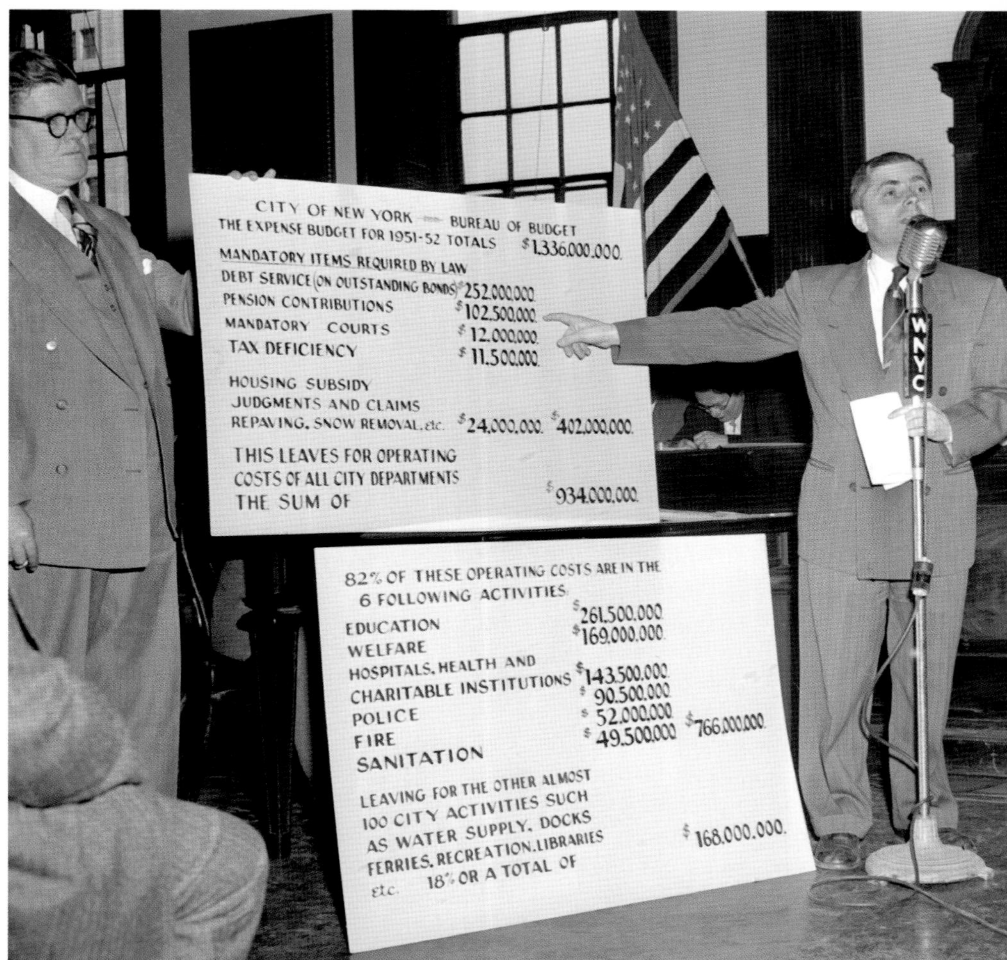

Abe Beame, the budget director of New York City for much of the 1950s, points to a chart detailing the breakdown of the city's expenditure for the 1951–1952 tax year.

African Americans line up to register to vote in Atlanta, Georgia, in 1944. In the 1940s and 1950s black Americans would often be excluded from the electoral process.

that these rural elites retained their political power. The fast-growing cities of the South found themselves with much less political power in the state legislatures than the old rural areas. This situation was only rectified by a series of Supreme Court rulings in the early 1960s (*see box on p. 35*).

Racial discrimination

The second factor that kept the rural elite in power was racial discrimination. Across the South African Americans were denied their right to vote, which was guaranteed, at least on paper, by the Fifteen Amendment to the U.S. Constitution. Those blacks who did try to register to vote in southern states were faced with a series of obstacles: Sometimes the prospective voter would be asked an impossibly difficult question on American government in order to register to vote (the so-called "test of comprehension"); at other times the voter registrar's office would simply close when a prospective black voter appeared; occasionally an African American applicant would be met with outright violence.

The policies of malapportionment and segregation severely limited the opportunities for ordinary citizens to engage in local politics. "In the 1950s in Alabama, an alliance of large landowners made the decisions which controlled the legislature, and often the governor as well," Alan Ehrenhalt argues. "They held the power not because they had any natural flair for politics but because they were the state's traditional governing class.... It was a closed system, and they were the ones who had been inside when the gate was shut." The pattern in Alabama held true for most of the rest of the South as well.

In 1957 the first crack opened in the rural power bloc. The Civil Rights Act made a mostly symbolic gesture toward protecting the right to vote for African Americans. The act did, however, pave the way for more meaningful action in the 1960s, when a combination of new federal laws and Supreme Court decisions shattered the power monopoly of the rural landowners.

See Also:

Baseball • Civil Rights • Politics and Government • Population • Segregation and Desegregation • Suburbs • Supreme Court

BILLY GRAHAM 1918–

Christian evangelist Billy Graham began preaching in the late 1930s and by the late 1940s had become the charismatic chief spokesman for the fundamentalist movement. The 1950s were years of growing fame and influence for him, when he led "crusades" in several major cities.

The son of a dairy farmer, William Franklin Graham, Jr., was born on November 7, 1918, in Charlotte, North Carolina. He was raised as a Presbyterian. After meeting a traveling preacher at age 16, Graham underwent a religious conversion, or, as he described later it, made a "decision for Christ." Thereafter, he attended the fundamentalist Bob Jones College in Cleveland, Tennessee, and then the Florida Bible Institute (now Trinity College) in Tampa. In 1939 he was ordained as a Southern Baptist minister. Four years later he completed a bachelor's degree in anthropology at Wheaton College, Illinois. From 1943 to 1945 Graham was pastor of the First Baptist Church in Western Springs, Illinois. Meanwhile, in 1944, he joined Youth for Christ International, an evangelical organization.

Billy Graham became America's most famous preacher during the 1950s. He held crusades in major cities throughout the decade.

Graham developed a reputation as an inspirational orator. After World War II (1939–1945) he started making radio broadcasts. (His program *Hour of Decision* has been broadcast every Sunday for over 50 years.) In 1949 President Harry S. Truman (1945–1953) invited Graham to the White House. It was an occasion that greatly enhanced his standing, and since then he has formed friendships with nearly every president, especially Richard M. Nixon and George W. Bush.

By the start of the 1950s Graham was internationally famous and widely regarded as the voice of Christian fundamentalism. Yet his messages were largely ecumenical and proposed that all Christian denominations should worship together more often, instead of focusing on the things that set them apart. Although as a fundamentalist Graham believed in the literal truth of the Bible, his sermons were always, for Christians, nonsectarian.

Preacher and businessman

Graham was also virtually unique among prominent evangelists in avoiding scandal. Prudent in his commercial dealings, in 1950 he established the Billy Graham Evangelistic Association (BGEA), thereby separating his personal finances from those of his organization.

Throughout the 1950s Graham made frequent television broadcasts and appeared in person at huge rallies in numerous cities across the United States and around the world. At the latter, which were known as "crusades," he called for repentance and moral renewal. His first large-scale crusade was held in Los Angeles in 1949, and its nightly meetings ran for more than eight weeks. Graham subsequently held crusades in many other major cities, including London, England, for 12 weeks and New York, at Madison Square Garden, for 16 weeks in 1957. However, there was more to the crusades than a rousing sermon. They also featured large choirs and trained teams of counselors to induct potential converts.

In addition to featuring on radio and television, Graham also wrote books. *Peace with God*, published in 1953, sold over two million copies. Since 1952 Graham has also authored a nationally syndicated newspaper column called "My Answer."

See Also:

Book Publishing • Legion of Decency • Magazines • Radio • Religion • Televangelism

GRAND OLE OPRY

By the beginning of the 1950s the Grand Ole Opry *radio show had been a central part of the U.S. country music scene for more than two decades. During the decade it continued to introduce listeners to both new artists and new styles of music.*

Country singer Red Foley records a performance for the *Grand Ole Opry* radio show in the 1950s.

The *Grand Ole Opry* is a weekly Saturday-night radio program of live country music that was first broadcast on WSM in Nashville, Tennessee, on November 28, 1925. Originally entitled the *WSM Barn Dance*, it went out immediately after *The Music Appreciation Hour*, a program of classical works. On December 8, 1928, the *Barn Dance* announcer, George D. "Judge" Hay, introduced that week's edition of the show with the words: "For the past hour, we have been listening to music taken largely from Grand Opera, but now we will present the 'Grand Ole Opry.'" A new title was born.

The show acquired a vast radio audience, and demand for tickets to watch the recording of the program became so great that the original venue had to be abandoned. The *Grand Ole Opry* moved from one place to another until 1943, when it found a long-term home at the Ryman Auditorium at 116 Fifth Avenue North, Nashville. It was transmitted from there until 1974, when it moved to a new custom-built home.

Stars of the 1950s

In the early 1950s one of the most popular performers on the *Grand Ole Opry* was the singer Hank Williams (1923–1953). Williams had made his debut in 1949, when he performed his recent hit "Lovesick Blues." He was called back for so many encores that he was invited to join the permanent *Opry* cast. Williams's appearances on the show over the next few years helped him become hugely popular nationwide, and he had a string of hit singles. However, during this period Williams began drinking heavily and he became extremely unreliable. Eventually, in August 1952, the *Opry* fired Williams, telling him he would be rehired when he sobered up. Instead of heeding the advice, Williams increased his intake of drink and drugs still further. He died of an overdose on New Year's Day, 1953.

Williams was an exponent of a rough-and-ready form of country known as honky-tonk. It was just one of a number of new styles of country music to emerge during the fifties. The trends were reflected by the performers who appeared on the *Opry*. The most radical new style was rockabilly, which fused country with rhythm and blues. The most famous appearance by a rockabilly artist was Elvis Presley's (1935–1977) performance of *Opry* regular Bill Monroe's "Blue Moon of Kentucky" in 1954. It was Presley's only *Opry* appearance; more regular performers in the fifties included Red Foley, Webb Pierce, and Hank Snow.

In 1955 another key moment in the *Opry*'s history occurred when the NBC network produced a pilot show for an *Opry* TV series. Eventually ABC produced a series of shows in 1955 and 1956. This provided a glimpse of the *Opry*'s future. From the mid-1980s onward the *Opry* would be broadcast live on television. At the beginning of the 21st century the show continued to play an extremely important role in the promotion of country music.

See Also:

Country Music • Presley, Elvis • Radio

GUATEMALA

In the early 1950s the Guatemalan government's expropriation of land from the powerful United Fruit Company brought it into conflict with the U.S. government. A CIA-sponsored coup later brought down the regime of Guatemalan President Jacobo Arbenz.

In August 1953 a covert operation by the Central Intelligence Agency (CIA) overthrew the pronationalist Iranian prime minister, Mohammad Mosaddeq, and restored the country's deposed shah (sovereign), Mohammad Reza Pahlavi, to power. The ease with which the CIA reinstated the shah was greeted with jubilation by the U.S. government. It demonstrated the way in which covert operations could be used to remove regimes that were considered a threat to U.S. interests.

In the early 1950s the government of one Central American republic, Guatemala, appeared to be posing just such a threat. Political developments in Guatemala had worried observers in the United States for some time. Following the overthrow of the American-approved dictator General Jorge Ubico in 1944, a reformist-minded ex-schoolteacher, Juan José Arévalo Bermejo (1904–1990), had been elected president in Guatemala's freest elections to date. Arévalo pursued a left-wing social agenda, establishing a code of workers' rights and instigating an education program aimed at lowering the high levels of illiteracy that plagued the country.

However, Arévalo's efforts to improve the working conditions of his people met fierce opposition from the American company that dominated the Guatemalan economy, the United Fruit Company (*see box on p. 43*).

The rise of Arbenz

When Arévalo left office in March 1951, he was replaced by his minister of war, Jacobo Arbenz (1913–1971). Whereas Arévalo's primary aim had been to improve the educational opportunities for his people, Arbenz saw land reform as the key to establishing a fairer Guatemala.

When Arbenz won the presidency, some U.S. politicians initially breathed a sigh of relief. They saw him as a realist as opposed to the idealist Arévalo. Before long, however, the State Department was worried. Arbenz legalized the Marxist Guatemalan Labor Party and announced that the United Fruit Company would have to respect the labor laws set down by the Guatemalan government.

A number of Arbenz's other measures also brought him into conflict with United Fruit. To begin with, Arbenz instigated the construction of a highway to the Atlantic coast. Previously, anyone wishing to transport goods to the coast had been forced to use the rail line belonging to the International Railways of Central America, a subsidiary of United Fruit. The company also owned the major port in the country, Puerto Barrios; but here, too, it found its interests threatened by Arbenz, who announced that a rival state-run port would be built. However, it was Arbenz's plans for land reform that finally forced a confrontation with United Fruit and the U.S. government.

Land reform

Matters came to a head in June 1952, when the Guatemalan national assembly passed Arbenz's land reform bill. Under the so-called Decree 900 the government gained the power to expropriate land from large plantations. Small farms were exempt from this measure: Those less than 223 acres (90ha) in size were unaffected by the law, as were those between 223 and 670 acres (90–270ha), on which two-thirds of the land was cultivated. However, owners of large swaths of land stood to lose much of it.

Despite opposition from large landowners, over the next 18 months some 100,000 Guatemalan families—nearly all Indian—were given 1.5 million acres (605,000ha) of land. All plots were less than 42.5 acres (17ha) in size. The expropriation cost the government $8.3 million, paid in long-term bonds. Arbenz himself gave 1,700

THE "DUCK TEST"

The attitude of many U.S. politicians in the 1950s toward the problem of identifying communist regimes can be summed up by a famous test devised by Richard C. Patterson, a U.S. ambassador to Guatemala. Patterson argued that identifying a communist was easy: All you had to do was use the "duck test." If a bird swam like a duck, looked like a duck, and sounded like a duck, he argued, then it was probably safe to assume that it was a duck. Patterson maintained that the same logic could be applied to the detection of communists in Guatemala. Politicians might claim that they were not communists; but if they behaved like communists, then they probably were.

acres (688ha) of his family's land to be redistributed. However, the landowner who was most affected by the Guatemalan government's move was United Fruit, which owned hundreds of thousands of acres of land.

The battle against United Fruit

In March 1953 a total of 209,842 acres (84,920ha) was expropriated from United Fruit, for which the company was paid $627,572. The size of the compensation immediately became a source of contention. The Guatemalan government had used United Fruit's own valuation of the land, declared the previous year for tax purposes, to work out the amount to be paid. However, United Fruit now disputed the figure, claiming that the land was actually worth far more than the amount declared, and that it had tried to value the land at its true amount but had been prevented from doing so. The U.S. State Department protested on United Fruit's behalf and demanded that the Guatemalan government pay $15.8 million in compensation, a figure that United Fruit believed reflected the land's true worth.

Events in Guatemala were viewed with considerable dismay in Washington, D.C., where Arbenz was seen as both a challenge to U.S. commercial interests in Central America and an ideological threat. Although Arbenz did not see himself as a communist and had no ties to the Soviet Union, to many observers in the United States his political beliefs were indistinguishable from communism.

In October 1953 Jack Peurifoy was dispatched to Guatemala as the U.S. ambassador. Peurifoy was an avowed anticommunist and had served in Greece when the country was under threat of a communist takeover. In December Peurifoy cabled President Dwight D. Eisenhower (1953–1961), claiming that "if Arbenz is not a communist, he will certainly do until one comes along." Peurifoy also spoke about the desirability of the Arbenz administration being out of office by the July 4 celebrations of 1954.

A pretext for action arrived in the spring of 1954. The Guatemalan government was unable to buy weapons from the United States because of an arms embargo that had been in effect since 1948. In the end the Guatemalans turned to the Eastern Bloc. On May 15 a Swedish freighter, the *Alfhem*, unloaded a consignment of Czech arms at Puerto Barrios. Peurifoy and his staff were on the dock waiting for the freighter. Arbenz had made a crucial mistake. The fact that he had bought arms from Czechoslovakia seemed to confirm U.S. suspicions that Arbenz was in league with Communist countries in Europe. Washington seized its opportunity and acted. CIA director Allen Dulles (1893–1969) claimed that Arbenz could use his weapons to attack U.S. interests in the Panama Canal. Such was the fervent anticommunist atmosphere in the United States that nobody questioned why Arbenz would want to do such a thing.

The CIA already had an alternative leader to Arbenz waiting in the wings. Colonel Carlos Castillo Armas (1914–1957) had gone into exile shortly after

This photograph, taken shortly after the coup that took place in June 1954, shows rebel soldiers pointing guns at an effigy of deposed Guatemalan President Jacobo Arbenz.

THE UNITED FRUIT COMPANY

The popularity of bananas with American consumers and the profits that could be made from selling the fruit created one of the most powerful organizations in Central America. The United Fruit Company was formed in 1899, and over the course of the early 20th century it took control of huge tracts of land across the region. In Guatemala the company bought land very cheaply from the government and set up whole communities to service the banana plantations. A local workforce was housed, schooled, and obliged to shop on the plantation, paying United Fruit-determined prices for goods. Wages were notoriously low: In the early 1950s workers went on strike for a wage hike to $1.50 a day. Some 40,000 Guatemalans were employed by La Frutera, or *El Pulpo* ("the octopus"), as the company was sometimes known.

United Fruit's investment went far beyond the plantations themselves. It built and owned the main highways, railroads, and Puerto Barrios, the only port in Guatemala on the Caribbean coast. The company handled cable communications across the region and had its own radio station, Tropical Radio.

In the United States United Fruit had connections at the very top of the Eisenhower administration. Secretary of State John Foster Dulles's (1888–1959) former law firm, Sullivan and Cromwell, represented the company. The head of the CIA, Allen Dulles, had been on United Fruit's board of trustees, while the company's head public relations officer, Ed Whitman, was married to President Eisenhower's private secretary, Ann Whitman.

This photograph shows the hiring hall of the United Fruit Company at Puerto Barrios. Puerto Barrios was the major port on Guatemala's Caribbean coast and was owned by United Fruit.

Former Guatemalan President Jacobo Arbenz (center) talks to reporters in Paris in 1955. After he was deposed, Arbenz sought refuge in Europe.

Arbenz's rise to power. Basing himself first in Nicaragua and then in Honduras, Castillo Armas had assembled a guerrilla force that was armed and trained by the CIA.

The CIA-sponsored coup began on June 18, 1954, when Castillo Armas's troops crossed the border from Honduras into Guatemala. Propaganda played a key role in the coup. Radio broadcasts instigated by the CIA exaggerated the size of the invading force. In reality the rebel army was a hodge-podge group of some 200 men. They were supported by mercenary

OBJECTIVE REPORTING?

Events in Guatemala in the early 1950s were subject to distorted reports in the U.S. press, largely the result of a campaign by public relations consultant Edward Bernays (1891–1995). In April 1951 Bernays was hired by the United Fruit Company to improve the company's image. His huge network of contacts among newspaper owners, editors, and journalists ensured that a steady stream of positive stories about the company appeared in America's newspapers. Such stories typically portrayed any disputes involving United Fruit as battles between communism and American free enterprise. One example was a 1953 photo spread in *Life* magazine that highlighted the dangers of the "Red" land reform. The photo captions talked about the creation of a communist state only two hours' bombing time from the Panama Canal. *Life* further asserted the Guatemalan government was picking on United Fruit because it needed something to hate.

Bernays's campaign was perfectly timed since the American public was growing increasingly terrified of the Soviet menace. Newspaper editors did not want to be seen dissenting from the Cold War rhetoric. There were some journalists who refused to be swept along, however.

Veteran *New York Times* reporter Herbert Matthews (1900–1977) visited Guatemala in 1952. He concluded that Arbenz was simply "young, inexperienced, and enthusiastic" and refused to believe the Guatemalan government posed the communist threat that many other members of the press claimed.

Another *Times* journalist who went against the common view was Sydney Gruson (1916–1998). He filed several stories from Guatemala that irritated President Arbenz and found himself expelled from the country in November 1953. American Ambassador Jack Peurifoy argued for his readmittance. However, Peurifoy did not like the stories subsequently submitted by Gruson. Gruson maintained that Arbenz was supported by other Latin American leaders. While true, this contradicted the official line of the U.S. government. Gruson also claimed that the defining ideology of the Guatemalan government was nationalism and not communism. Such was the reaction from the White House and the CIA that Gruson was banned by his *New York Times* bosses from covering the impending coup.

Public relations expert Edward Bernays, pictured here, was responsible for many of the negative stories about the Guatemalan government that appeared in the American press in the early 1950s.

pilots who bombed Guatemala City from neighboring Nicaragua. The air force was made up of only three airplanes, two of which were soon out of action. However, demoralized by U.S. propaganda, the Guatemalan army did not offer any resistance to the invasion. Arbenz resigned as president on June 27, 1954.

After the defeat of Arbenz, Castillo Armas took over as president. He immediately set about dismantling the reforms made by his predecessor, handing some of the expropriated land back to its former owners. In moves that found favor in Washington, he also banned left-wing political parties, placed restrictions on the activities of labor unions, and actively sought out communist sympathizers. A large number of people suspected of communist activity were tortured and killed. During Castillo Armas's presidency, which lasted until his assassination in 1957, the United States gave $80 million in aid to the country. During the same period the United Fruit Company reestablished its stranglehold on the Guatemalan economy. Castillo was succeeded as Guatemalan president by Miguel Ydígoras Fuentes. Like his predecessor, Ydígoras Fuentes was sympathetic to U.S. interests. He ruled the country until March 1963, when his regime was toppled in a coup.

See Also:

Central America • Cold War • Dulles, Allen • Foreign Policy • Newspapers

H-BOMB TESTS

Scientists detonated the first hydrogen bomb in 1952, creating an explosive force greater than 10 million tons of TNT. A year later the Soviets had their own H-bomb. Together, the Cold War enemies would develop enough such weapons to destroy all life on Earth.

The world entered the nuclear age on July 16, 1945, when U.S. scientists detonated the first atomic bomb at the Alamogordo bombing range in New Mexico. This A-bomb converted a tennis ball-sized mass of plutonium into an explosive force of 20,000 tons (20 kilotons) of TNT. A few weeks later, on August 6, the United States dropped "Little Boy," as the bomb was called, on Hiroshima, Japan, in the hope of bringing an end to World War II in the Pacific. The explosion devastated the city, instantly killing 66,000 of its inhabitants and seriously injuring many more. On August 9 "Fat Man," a larger A-bomb, was dropped on Nagasaki, Japan, killing 39,000 people. The next day the Japanese began negotiations to surrender.

Manhattan Project

The A-bomb had been developed at a military base in Los Alamos, New Mexico, as part of the top-secret Manhattan Project. Costing over $2 billion, the project collected many of America's best scientists. The project's director of scientific operations, physicist J. Robert Oppenheimer (1904–1967), personally recruited the scientists, and among them were some 20 who had either won or would go on to win the Nobel Prize for either physics or chemistry. These Nobel laureates included Luis Alvarez (1911–1988), Hans A. Bethe (1906–), Niels Bohr (1885–1962), Enrico Fermi (1901–1954), and Richard P. Feynman (1918–1988). Other notable scientists who worked on the Manhattan Project were John von Neumann (1903–1957), Edward Teller (1908–2003), and Stanislaw Ulam (1909–1984), as well as around 80 others.

The end of the war put military planners in a difficult situation over what to do with the vast resources for building the A-bomb. Teller suggested that the scientists should continue their research into nuclear explosions to build a device

In 1946 the United States carried out an A-bomb test on the Bikini Atoll in the Pacific. It was meant in part as a signal to the Soviets that the United States was continuing to move further ahead in the new Cold War arms race.

THE DIFFERENCE BETWEEN AN A-BOMB AND AN H-BOMB

Both A-bombs and H-bombs create their immense explosive force from the energies within the nuclei of atoms. However, they work in very different ways. Basically, the atomic bomb uses nuclear fission, while the hydrogen bomb uses nuclear fusion.

In the A-bomb the nuclear core of a heavy atom splits into two or more smaller nuclei. In practice these heavy atoms are usually uranium or plutonium, while the two atomic fragments are lighter metals, such as silver. Since the total mass of the final fragments is less than that of the original atom, this "missing mass" is released as energy. The energies are typically huge, as predicted by the equation $E=mc^2$ (where "E" stands for energy, "m" for mass, and "c" for the speed of light), meaning "energy equals mass multiplied by the speed of light squared." Albert Einstein developed this equation in the early 20th century long before work began on the Manhattan Project in the early 1940s.

Teller's H-bomb, which followed the A-bomb in the early 1950s, relied on two nuclei of hydrogen, the lightest atomic element, to fuse into helium, the next lightest. This helium nucleus is less massive than the total of the two original hydrogen nuclei and again releases energy. This is the same chain reaction that occurs continually in the sun.

H-bombs are about 100 to 1,000 times more powerful than A-bombs, mainly because hydrogen is about 200 times lighter than uranium or plutonium, making it easier to store. Moreover, the fusion reaction is very efficient at merging most of the hydrogen atoms into helium, whereas the fission reaction misses many heavy nuclei. On the other hand, H-bombs are more difficult to ignite than A-bombs, and an atomic detonator is the only practical way of exploding an H-bomb.

The spectacular explosions from H-bombs are caused by the same nuclear reactions that happen over and over again in the sun.

In early 1950 Eleanor Roosevelt, widow of President Franklin D. Roosevelt, hosted a TV show discussing the future of and moral justification for nuclear weapons. Among her guests were Manhattan Project scientists Hans A. Bethe and J. Robert Oppenheimer, both of whom opposed the H-bomb.

of unprecedented destructive power. Teller claimed that his "Super" would be hundreds of times more powerful than the atomic bombs dropped on Japan. The new bomb would fuse hydrogen into helium, a chemical process similar to that which occurs inside the sun. Whereas scientists detonated the A-bomb with conventional explosives, they would need an A-bomb to trigger the fusion reaction inside Teller's Super (*see box*).

Initially the U.S. government was unwilling to supply the money and labor to build the Super. It was focused more on postwar reconstruction in Europe and Japan. However, on August 29, 1949, an event occurred that changed this view: The Soviets detonated their own A-bomb. One month later President Harry S. Truman (1945–1953) announced that the USSR had caught up with the United States in the arms race. Americans were shocked, and Teller responded by pushing for more resources for his Super project.

Not everyone supported Teller. Oppenheimer and others who had worked on the Manhattan Project called the Super a "weapon of genocide" that "should never be built." On the advice of his military, however, Truman announced on January 31, 1950, that work on the project would continue.

"Mike" passes the test

Just after dawn on November 1, 1952, U.S. scientists detonated their first hydrogen bomb, nicknamed "Mike." With an explosive force of 10 million

INVENTORS OF THE H-BOMB: FERMI, TELLER, AND ULAM

Although Edward Teller is known as the "father of the H-bomb," Stanislaw Ulam also played an essential role in its development. Both Teller and Ulam immigrated to the United States from Eastern Europe in the 1930s. Teller was an atomic physicist, while Ulam was a mathematician.

Teller first got interested in the H-bomb after a conversation with Italian physicist Enrico Fermi in 1941. Fermi, a Nobel Prize-winner who had immigrated to the United States before the start of World War II, speculated that an atomic bomb might set off a thermonuclear reaction in the isotope deuterium to create a much larger explosion. At first Teller thought it impossible, yet after working on some calculations, he became convinced.

Nearly 10 years later, after the Soviets had developed their own A-bomb, President Truman gave the go-ahead for the H-bomb. However, calculations by Ulam showed that Teller's original design could not work. For several months the project was stuck. Then, in early 1951 Ulam suggested that the atomic-bomb detonator should compress the nuclear fuel while setting off the bomb. This design led to the first hydrogen-bomb-testing device, known as "Mike," in 1952.

Enrico Fermi, one of the 20th century's greatest physicists, sits at the control panel of a particle accelerator ("atom smasher") in 1951.

TURNING H-BOMBS INTO WEAPONS

After successfully exploding the first H-bomb, the next step for the Americans was to create an H-bomb that could be dropped from an aircraft. U.S. scientists completed such a bomb, called "Bravo," in Operation Castle. On March 1, 1954, Bravo vaporized several miles of coral reef at Bikini Atoll in the Marshall Islands. To the surprise of the scientists Bravo's immense explosive force of 15 megatons was more than three times the expected blast. On a ship 30 miles (48km) away physicist Marshall Rosenbluth (1927–2003) described the explosion: "There was a huge fireball with turbulent rolls going in and out.... It spread until the edge looked as if it was directly overhead. It was a much more awesome sight than a puny atom bomb."

The main difference between Bravo and Mike was that Bravo used a solid nuclear fuel rather than liquefied hydrogen. This meant that the bomb was smaller and lighter because it did not need a bulky cooling facility. The solid nuclear material was powdered lithium deuteride, a chemical compound of lithium and deuterium. (In the energetic explosion the lithium also converts some deuterium into tritium to help the fusion reaction.) Weapons designers packed this powder around a plutonium detonator to make a relatively small and compact device about the size of a conventional bomb.

Following the successful detonation of Bravo, the U.S. military put its efforts into building lightweight, solid-fuel H-bombs for battlefield munitions. Throughout the 1950s these were carried by the B-52 bomber. First introduced in 1955 as an atomic-bomb carrier, these huge aircraft had eight jet engines and were 160 feet (49m) long. Each bomber could deliver several H-bombs to targets many thousands of miles from where it took off.

Another military use of H-bombs was as a warhead on an intercontinental ballistic missile (ICBM). These rockets can transport the nuclear device across continents in less than an hour. American scientists had developed their first ICBM, called Atlas, by 1957.

tons (10 megatons) of TNT its fireball expanded to 3 miles (4.8km) across and shone as brightly as 1,000 suns. It gouged a crater 2 miles (3.2km) wide and several hundred yards deep, completely vaporizing its test island at Enewetak Atoll in the South Pacific. Mike's destructive force was more than 500 times greater than than that of the atomic bomb dropped on Hiroshima.

Mike was not suitable for military use, however, mainly because it weighed 70 tons (70 tonnes) and was larger than a bus. In particular, it needed a cryogenic refrigeration plant to liquefy the hydrogen nuclear fuel. This fuel was stored around the detonator, a stick of plutonium. Conventional explosives encasing the hydrogen started the reaction by compressing both the hydrogen and plutonium (*see p. 46*). The plutonium then exploded like an atom bomb, which started a thermonuclear reaction (fusion) in the hydrogen. This fusion reaction spread through the nuclear fuel in an uncontrolled explosion.

For Mike and all later H-bombs a particular type of hydrogen had to be used to create the right kind of thermonuclear reaction. Hydrogen atoms are naturally found in three different forms, or isotopes, that have the same chemistry but different masses. The two heavier forms—deuterium and tritium—make particularly good nuclear fuel. In the nuclear reaction two nuclei form the cores of either deuterium or tritium atoms, fusing into the nucleus of a helium atom. Scientists cannot use normal hydrogen because the mass of two such atoms is less than one helium atom, unlike its heavier isotopes.

The Soviet–American arms race

On August 12, 1953, about a year after the explosion of Mike, the Soviets detonated their own thermonuclear device at a secret base in Kazakhstan. Their bomb was called *sloika* (meaning "layer cake"), for its design of separate folds of uranium and lithium deuteride.

While the Soviet's first hydrogen bomb had a comparatively small explosive force of 440,000 tons (400 kilotons) of TNT, it was small enough to fit inside an aircraft. In other words, it was ready to use as a weapon. Two years later, on November 22, 1955, the Soviets exploded their first megaton-sized hydrogen bomb. The United States and Soviet Union were now on an equal footing.

Aftereffects of nuclear testing

The Bravo explosion (*see box*) alerted the world to another effect of nuclear weapons: radioactive fallout. Ash from the blasted coral reef fell on a Japanese fishing vessel, the *Lucky Dragon* sailing 80 miles (128km) downwind from the test site. The 23 crewmen became severely ill from radiation sickness, and one person later died. In response the Japanese media demanded that the Americans "Tell us the truth about the ashes of death." Today several islands and areas used for nuclear testing in both the United States and the former Soviet Union are still highly radioactive.

See Also:

Cold War • Japan • Los Alamos • Nobel Prizes • Nuclear Power Program • Oppenheimer, J. Robert • Physics • Science and Technology • Soviet Union • Spies and Spying • Teller, Edward

HAITI

After years of coups and political unrest in Haiti the 1950s brought at first some stability and much-needed economic growth under the presidency of Paul Magloire and then a long period of repressive dictatorship under "Papa Doc" Duvalier.

In 1492 Christopher Columbus landed on a Caribbean island that he called Hispaniola. The indigenous people of the island were the Taino Indians. By the early 16th century nearly all had either died of disease or been killed by the Spanish. Gradually French settlers arrived and imported Africans to work as slaves cultivating sugarcane.

The western third of the island formally became a French colony in 1697. In 1804 the colony was declared independent as Haiti. It was the world's first black republic and only the second colony, after the United States, to win independence. Yet for most of the next 150 years the Caribbean state endured revolutions and counterrevolutions, coups, and foreign domination. Haiti was occupied by U.S. Marines from 1915 to 1934.

At the beginning of the 1950s Haiti was governed by Dumarsais Estimé, who had been placed in power by the military four years earlier. Estimé oversaw the introduction of various reforms such as the introduction of income tax and the creation of labor unions, and he promoted many fellow blacks. This made him unpopular with the mulattos (descendants of black slaves and white slave owners), and in 1950 the military intervened to depose him. Colonel Paul Magloire (1907–2001), who had become wealthy with the help of his mulatto friends, led the coup.

The rule of "Iron Pants"

Magloire, or "Iron Pants" as he was known, ruled over a period of peace and growing wealth for Haiti. With the aid of foreign investment and good world prices for coffee—one of Haiti's main crops since the 17th century—he was able to introduce numerous economic and social reforms. Roads were built, towns were improved, and the country's first major dam was constructed. The vote was given to women, and for the first time the electorate was able to vote for the president directly.

In October 1950 Magloire was elected president with 99 percent of the vote. However, although black, he also did much to maintain the mulattos' superior position in Haitian society. He joined them in cultivating a luxurious lifestyle and organized glittering social events. Among them were celebrations in 1954 of the 150th anniversary of Haiti's independence from France, culminating in a reenactment of the final battle against the French.

Magloire was very popular with President Dwight D. Eisenhower (1953–1961) and others in the U.S. government. At a time when the Cold War was gathering pace, Magloire's anticommunism was much appreciated, as was his obvious ability to have and give other people a good time. Haiti became an attractive destination for American tourists and well-known figures in the literary and entertainment worlds such as Truman Capote and Irving Berlin.

However, by 1954 there were signs of corruption within the government. When that same year Hurricane Hazel struck the island, causing enormous damage, the theft of the relief funds that were subsequently provided was seen as part of a general pattern of corruption and embezzlement by members of the Haitian government.

In December 1950 Colonel Paul Magloire (left) delivered his inaugural address as the new president of Haiti, ushering in a brief period of stability and prosperity.

FRANÇOIS "PAPA DOC" DUVALIER AND HAITIAN VOODOO

Born in Port-au-Prince, François Duvalier (1907–1971) was one of a tiny minority of Haitians to be educated. He trained as a doctor and during the 1940s was employed on a U.S.-funded public health project to eradicate the common tropical disease yaws. He also became increasingly involved in the Noiriste (black pride) movement that was partly inspired by Jean Price-Mars's book *Ainsi parla l'oncle* ("Thus Spoke the Uncle"), published in 1928. This led Duvalier to a study of voodoo, which he would later use to great effect.

Duvalier wore dark suits and spectacles. Calling himself "Papa Doc" (implying that he would look after the interests of Haitians), he gave no indication of the ruthless side of his character. When elected president in 1957, he consolidated his position by using the dreaded Tontons Macoutes. They were to help keep Duvalier in power for 14 years by creating a reign of terror, during which thousands of Haitians were killed or forced to flee the country. Duvalier also kept the mass of the uneducated population in awe of him by posing in top hat and tails as Baron Samedi, the voodoo spirit of the dead.

The origin of Haitian voodoo belief stems from Africa. Traditionally, voodooists believe in many spirits, some of whom are more malevolent than others. They are called up in ceremonies led by a priest or priestess that involve singing, drumming, dancing, and the ritual sacrifice of animals. It is thought that the spirits possess people who are in a trance state, enabling them, for example, to give advice to others, perform notable physical feats, or cure a medical complaint.

During the centuries when African slaves worked on the plantations of Haiti, great efforts were made to convert them to Christianity. It appeared that some conversion had occurred because the slaves adopted icons of the Catholic saints in place of voodoo sacred objects, but this did not mean that they had given up their old beliefs. There were numerous attempts to suppress voodooism in the 19th and 20th centuries, but the majority of Haitians continued to be voodooists—a fact that Papa Doc exploited.

In 1964 Duvalier had himself elected president for life. The election was followed by the publication of a version of the "Lord's prayer" that began "Our Doc, who art in the National Palace for Life, hallowed be Thy name.... Thy will be done at Port-au-Prince and the provinces...."

By the time he died, Duvalier had done little to improve the circumstances of the poor, although he had given more power to the black middle class. He had also amended the constitution to ensure that he would be succeeded by his son, Jean-Claude "Baby Doc."

Haitian President Francois "Papa Doc" Duvalier came to power in late 1957 and ruled the country as a dictator for the rest of his life. He eliminated all political opposition in part by playing on the superstitious fears of voodoo that many Haitians believed in.

Following the overthrow of President Magloire, demonstrators took to the streets in 1957. The protests led to a short-lived military rule before the rise of "Papa Doc" Duvalier.

In 1956 strikes and demonstrations were organized by Magloire's opponents as a dispute took place over when his term of office should end. The army withdrew its support, and Magloire fled abroad, taking a large fortune with him. He was to live in exile for 30 years, only returning to Haiti from New York after the fall of the Duvalier regime, which ruled the country from 1957.

The Duvalier regime

Following Magloire's departure there was almost a year of unrest and political chaos, with a series of provisional presidents. Finally, in September 1957 presidential elections were held in which the main candidates were Louis Déjoie, who was supported by the mulattos, and François Duvalier (*see opposite*), who spoke on behalf of the black middle class and rural poor, promising to end the privileged status of the mulatto minority. Duvalier secured twice as many votes as Déjoie, and on October 22, 1957, he began his reign as president. He was soon to become a feared dictator with the nickname "Papa Doc."

Members of the mulatto business community were the first to discover that Duvalier was not the quiet country doctor he appeared to be. The mulattos attempted to make life difficult for Duvalier's government by organizing a commercial strike in which shops and offices in the capital, Port-au-Prince, were closed. Duvalier responded by calling in the "cagoulards," hooded thugs from the slums, to force the mulattos to reopen.

Over time the cagoulards evolved into the Tontons Macoutes, named after a character in a Haitian folk story, Uncle Knapsack, who stuffs children into his bag at night and takes them away forever. Also known as Volontaires de la Sécurité Nationale (VSN; National Security Volunteers), the Tontons Macoutes were a private militia. Receiving no pay, they were allowed to use violence—or the constant threat of violence—to take what they could from the population as long as they were totally loyal to Duvalier. They dressed in denim jackets, jeans, red neckerchiefs, and sunglasses, and their constant presence at Duvalier's side meant that he was secure in his position as president.

By 1960 Duvalier had nothing to fear from the army. His political opponents had been imprisoned, as had the country's leading newspaper editors, while support for him had grown among black Catholics, who resented the power of European clerics within the church. There was no one to challenge his hold on power throughout the 1960s, although the living standards of the Haitian population continued to fall. By the time of Duvalier's death in 1971 Haiti was the poorest nation in the Americas.

See Also:
Cold War • Cuba • Foreign Policy • Organization of American States

BILL HALEY AND HIS COMETS

In 1954 Bill Haley and His Comets recorded the song "Rock around the Clock," one of rock 'n' roll's earliest and biggest hits. Although the band's popularity waned toward the end of the decade, a large number of their supporters remain loyal even today.

Bill Haley (1925–1981) was born in Michigan but grew up in Pennsylvania. There he performed with a country band at school dances. Leaving school at age 15, he found work bottling water before recording his first record, "Candy Kisses," at 18. He then began traveling as a musician and got work as a yodeler for country bands. Success eluded Haley, however, and he returned to Pennsylvania, becoming a disc jockey for a local radio station. He performed on air with his new band, The Four Aces of Western Swing. Haley disbanded the group in 1950 and formed The Saddlemen with Al Rex (string bass), Billy Williamson (steel guitar), and Johnny Grande (accordion and piano). Within a couple of years the band had a hit with "Rock the Joint."

Bill Haley, on guitar, leads the pioneering Comets at a concert in 1957, when the band was still very popular.

Experimenting with different musical styles and rhythms, The Saddlemen crafted a new sound that fused country with rhythm and blues (R&B). But their name was not considered hip enough for their pioneering music. They changed it, following the suggestion that with a leader named Haley, they should be called the Comets for the famous Halley's Comet.

Comets' first hit

By this time Marshall Lytle had replaced Rex, and drummer Charles Higler had joined the band. Bill Haley and His Comets had their first success in 1953 with the Top 20 hit "Crazy Man Crazy," written by Haley after he overheard the phrase at one of their high school shows. It was also during this period that they made their first appearance on *Bandstand*, the television show that would later be known as *American Bandstand.*

In 1954 the band released "Thirteen Women." The single flopped, but not long afterward the flip side of the record, "Rock around the Clock," began to gain airplay. Their next single, "Shake, Rattle, and Roll," was a Top 10 hit, becoming the first million-selling rock-'n'-roll record. "Rock around the Clock" was reissued, this time also reaching the Top 10, but it was not until it was used in the movie *Blackboard Jungle* in 1955 that it hit number one on the popular music chart, staying there for eight weeks.

In 1955 three members left the band: Lytle, Joey D'Ambrosio (tenor sax), and Dick Richards (drums)—the latter two had only been with the group a short time—decided to form their own band. Haley recruited Ralph Jones (drums) and Rudy Pompilli (tenor sax); he also persuaded Al Rex to rejoin. Finally, Haley added Frank Beecher to play electric guitar. With Haley himself the band now comprised seven members, and it would stay with more or less the same personnel for the rest of the decade.

Haley's fame grew when he starred in a movie, *Rock around the Clock*, in 1956. The movie was a worldwide hit, creating intense excitement in theaters, with young people jiving in the aisles and ripping up their seats. It was even banned in some cities. The same year the band had another Top 10 hit with "See You Later Alligator," but it was to be their last. The fans increasingly turned to younger, new rockers such as Elvis Presley. Haley continued to tour and play revival gigs until the 1970s.

See Also:

American Bandstand **• Country Music • Movie Industry • Presley, Elvis • Radio • Rock 'n' Roll • Teenage Culture**

HARLEM GLOBETROTTERS

During the 1950s the Harlem Globetrotters included some of basketball's all-time greatest players, from Wilt Chamberlain to Marques Haynes. On the court the team's amazing combination of outstanding skill and comic antics inspired awe and laughter around the world.

Before the formation of the National Basketball Association (NBA) in 1949 and the surge in popularity of professional basketball in the 1950s the Harlem Globetrotters, with their combination of slapstick comedy, trick shots, and athletic genius, were the most successful professional sports team in the United States.

The team did not start in Harlem but in Chicago. In 1926 Abe Saperstein, a 24-year-old businessman, gathered and coached a group of young basketball players he called the Savoy Big Five. When he began taking the team on tour, he changed its name first to the Saperstein's New York Globetrotters and later to the Harlem Globetrotters.

The players' distinct uniforms were based on the U.S. flag, but it is their theme tune that is perhaps most recognizable. Called "Sweet Georgia Brown," it was originally written in the 1920s by Kenneth Casey and Maceo Pinkard with help from Ben Bernie. However, it was the 1949 version, with whistling and bone-cracking by the group Brother Bones and His Shadows, that the Globetrotters adopted in 1952.

Outstanding sportsmen

In their first 23 years the Globetrotters won 93 percent of their games. In the 1930s they were so superior to Midwest teams that they took to clowning as a way of keeping the crowds coming. The mixture of clowning and outstanding play remain their trademark.

Led by Goose Tatum and featuring in the 1950s stars such as Wilt Chamberlain, Marques Haynes, and Meadowlark Lemon, the Globetrotters, with their razzle-dazzle dribbling, passing, and shotmaking, were pure showbusiness. They shot sitting down, riding piggyback, and standing on their heads. They bounced the ball off the floor into the basket. When critics moaned that their clowning demeaned the game, the Globetrotters replied by playing no-nonsense basketball for the whole game, as they did when they defeated a Canadian all-star team, 120–20.

In 1949 the Globetrotters drew 22,000 fans to Chicago Stadium to see them beat the mighty Minneapolis Lakers. That was the largest indoor crowd ever to have watched a basketball game. Yet for the first few years of the 1950s the Globetrotters were used by the NBA in prematch games to bring in the fans for league encounters.

Global superstars

The team made its big money from international touring. In 1950 gross receipts from a 215-game tour of North America, Europe, and North Africa reached more than $3 million, allowing Saperstein to put Goose Tatum on an annual salary of $25,000, making him one of the country's top-paid sportsmen. In 1951 the State Department declared the Globetrotters "ambassadors of good will," and on their European tour that year they played in West Berlin, watched by 75,000 spectators. During the tour they also played their most unusual game, when they performed in front of only one spectator, the pope.

In the 1950s the Globetrotters had some of the greatest players of all time, including Marques Haynes, who was with the team from 1947 to 1953 and from 1972 to 1979.

See Also:

Basketball • Black Americans • Chamberlain, Wilt • Games and Pastimes • Olympic Games • Russell, Bill • Segregation and Desegregation • Sports • Sports and TV

HEALTH AND HEALTHCARE

After World War II there was an enormous expansion in the health industry. Effective new vaccines were introduced against diseases such as polio, and the federal government invested heavily in new hospitals and medical research.

Americans in the 1950s enjoyed better health than ever before. Average life expectancy for both men and women in the United States rose from 62.9 years in 1940 to 69.7 years in 1960. A speaker at the centennial celebrations of Mount Sinai Hospital in New York City in 1952 described "the marked improvement in the health of the population," measured by longer life expectancy, and remarked that it largely reflected higher standards of living. These improved standards were the result of better housing, better nutrition, and better sanitation, as well as advances in bacteriology.

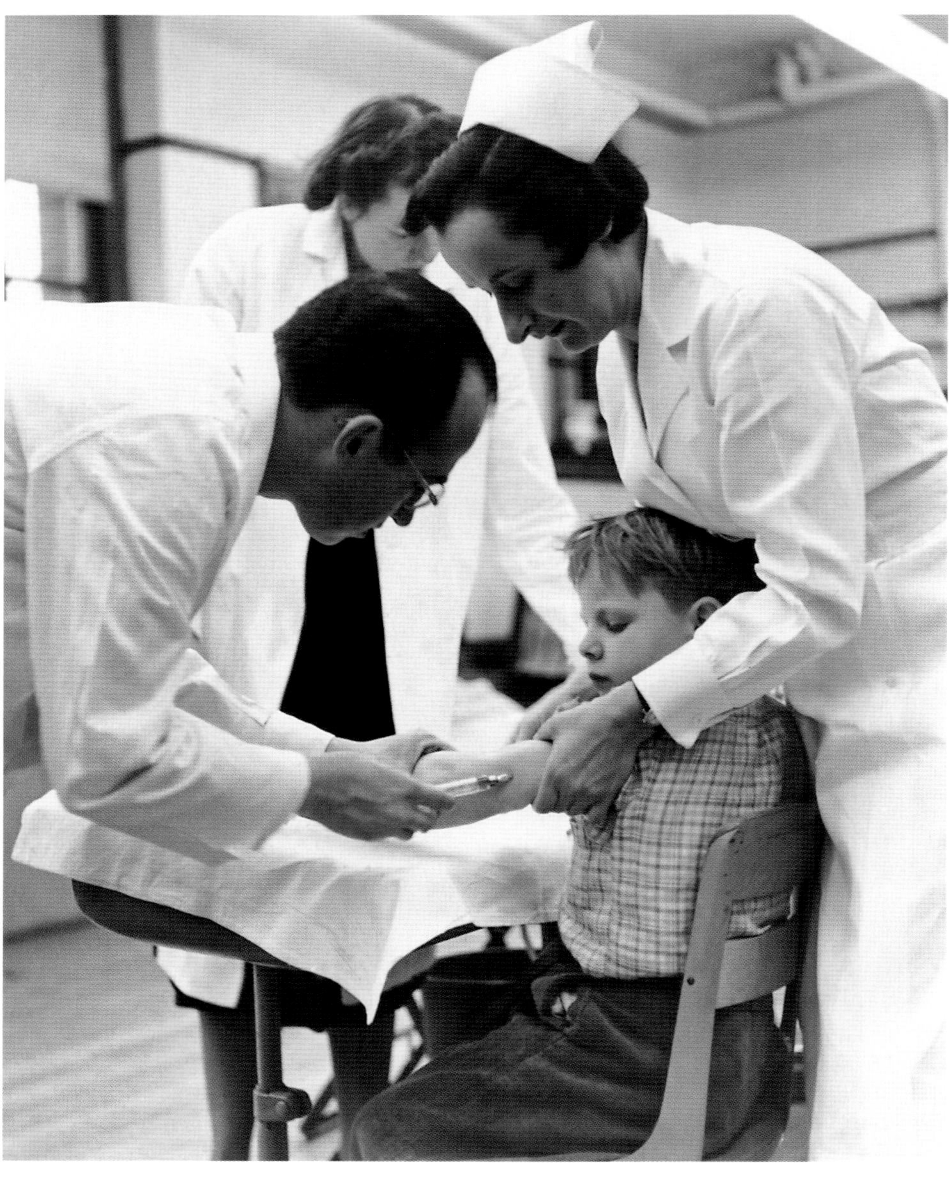

Dr. Jonas Salk inoculates a boy as two nurses assist him. Salk developed a polio vaccine that could be injected, and in 1954 it was tested on 1.8 million children.

Health of a nation

In the 1950s health matters in general consumed more and more of the nation's interest. A number of polls of newspaper readers taken in the early part of the decade showed that the most widely read columns were those devoted to medicine and health. It was a period of history when doctors were held in very high esteem. Their judgments and clinical advice largely went unquestioned by patients. In 1931, 48 percent of the population visited a doctor at least once a year; by the early 1950s, 72 percent did so, and the average number of visits doubled. Between 1945 and 1960 admissions to hospitals increased by 58 percent. To meet that rising demand, the health industry expanded rapidly, in manpower terms by more than 50 percent. In 1940 there were one million people employed in the health industry; by 1960 there were three million.

By today's standards the range of medical treatments available was limited. When World War II (1939–1945) ended, the average urban family spent only $150 a year on healthcare. There was no birth-control pill, and abortions were illegal. It was expected that children would contract mumps, chickenpox, and measles as a matter of course. Pollution of the environment as a factor in health and well-being was barely on the national agenda. Health and safety regulations in the workplace were in their infancy, as was product labeling of food. The explosion in government health regulations did not start until the mid-1960s.

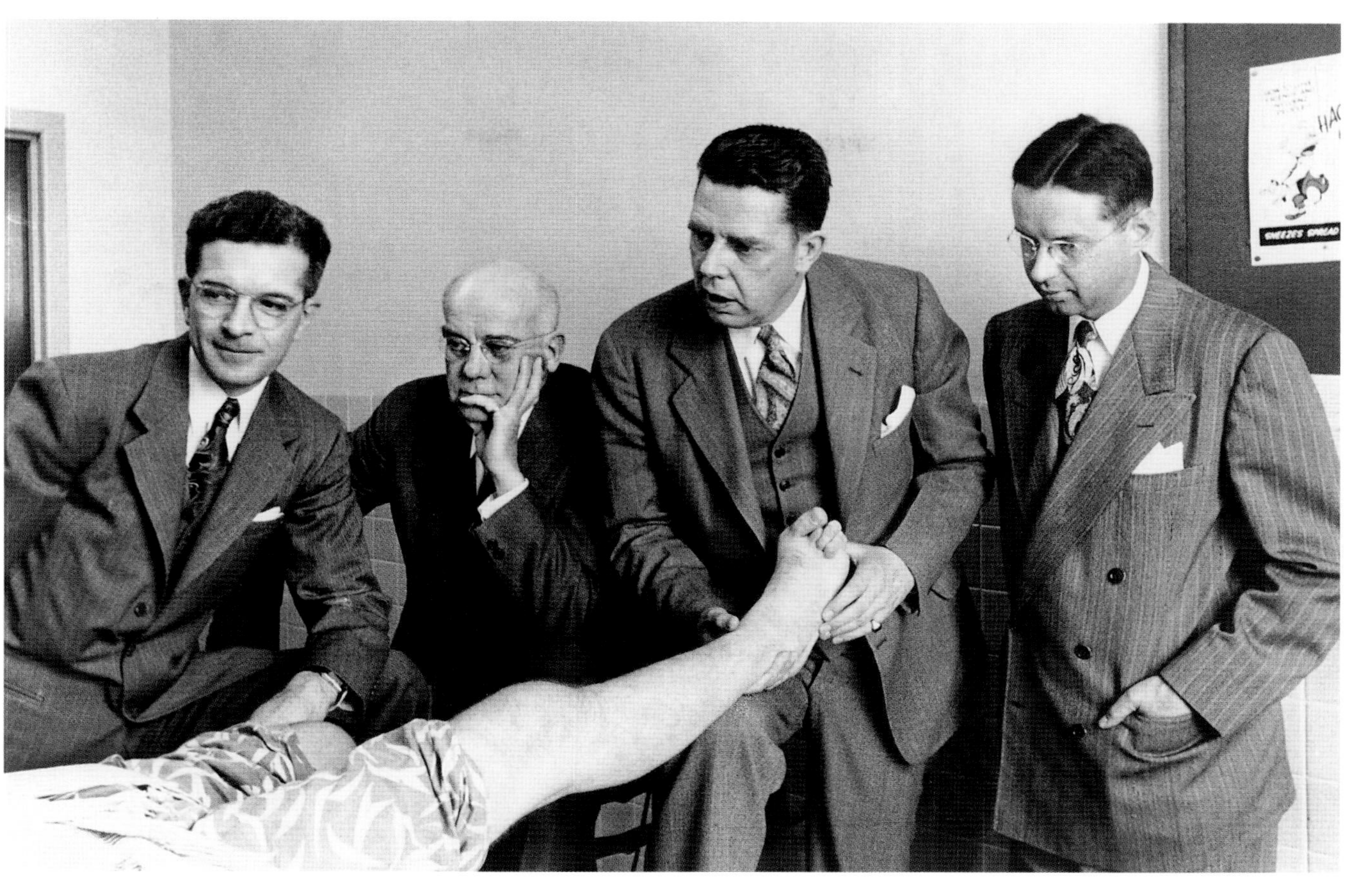

Doctors from the Mayo Clinic in Rochester, Minnesota, examine a patient. The team carried out research into cortisone and discovered its effect as a painkiller.

Pharmaceuticals

The 1950s witnessed a revolution in the pharmaceutical industry. During World War II antibiotics had been used extensively for the first time for wounded soldiers. As a result, the pharmaceutical industry, which had strong links with the nation's universities and their biomedical departments, experienced enormous growth. In 1956, 80 percent of the drugs prescribed by physicians had been on the market for less than 15 years. Medicinal drugs came to be part of everyday life. Those drugs included the two great breakthroughs of the 1940s: penicillin and streptomycin. Penicillin was effective against diseases such as pneumonia, syphilis, and tetanus, while streptomycin was used against tuberculosis. New drugs developed during the 1950s included antihistamines, cortisone, an array of new antibiotics, and tranquilizers.

In fact, the 1950s were the new era of "wonder drugs" based on cortisone and related steroids. During the 1930s and 1940s Philip S. Hench (1896–1965) and Edward C. Kendall (1886–1972) had done pioneering work at the Mayo Clinic in Rochester, Minnesota, on cortisone (a hormone from the cortex of the adrenal gland) and its beneficial effects as a painkiller. In 1949 the American chemist Percy Julian (1899–1975) discovered a cheap way to make artificial cortisone using soybeans. It soon became easily available and was used for pain relief by sufferers from rheumatoid arthritis. Another breakthrough was the introduction of the drug isoniazid in 1952, which improved the treatment of sufferers from tuberculosis.

Vaccines

In the 1950s vaccines were introduced to control diphtheria and whooping cough, diseases that had killed significant numbers of children little more than a generation earlier. Jonas Salk (1914–1995) developed a vaccine against polio that could be injected, and a nationwide vaccination program was set up in 1955. Research was also undertaken to find vaccines for mumps and measles. A vaccine against measles was developed by John Enders (1897–1985) at Harvard University in 1958 but was not introduced until the 1960s.

Two American scientists, Solomon Berson (1918–1972) and Rosalyn Yalow (1921–), pioneered a new technique called radioimmunoassay (RIA) to trace and measure hormones in the body. That led to a range of improved treatments for hormonal disorders. In 1952 an American GI, George Jorgensen, created a national sensation when he had a highly publicized sex-change operation. Jorgensen, later known as Christine, was given a female physiognomy by Dr. Christian Hamburger at the Serum Institute in Denmark, using hormone therapy and plastic surgery.

However, there were some areas of healthcare in which there was little progress made during the decade. For example, despite advances in the understanding of tobacco's harmful effects, the campaign against smoking did not gain real momentum for another 20 years. In the 1950s doctors were happy to endorse cigarette brands, and the American Medical Association (AMA) continued to publish cigarette advertisements in its journal.

Heart disease

Heart disease was the nation's number-one killer. One of the most significant and highly publicized medical breakthroughs of the decade was open-heart surgery, which allowed the replacement of narrowed, hardened arteries by artificial valves and the fitting of pacemakers to control the pulse rate. In 1952 a team of surgeons at the University of Minnesota Hospital stopped a patient's circulation for the first time to close a hole in the heart. It was a seven-minute operation during which damage to the brain was prevented by lowering the patient's body temperature. The key to open-heart surgery was the development by the American surgeon John H. Gibbon, Jr. (1903–1973), of the world's first heart-lung machine, which enabled doctors to arrest the action of the heart and isolate it from the rest of the circulatory system. Using the machine successfully for the first time in 1953, Gibbon closed a hole in an 18-year-old girl's heart in an operation that lasted less than half an hour.

The decade also saw the first successful kidney transplant (1954) and the introduction of hemodialysis on an artificial kidney machine (1956). However, it was not until the 1960s that kidney transplantation had a high success rate; during the 1950s nearly all kidney-transplant patients died within a year of the operation.

Mental health

There were also some advances in mental healthcare during the 1950s. Psychoanalysis—a therapeutic method of treating mental disorders—had been

Rosalyn Yalow, along with Solomon Berson, pioneered techniques in tracing hormones in the body. Her work helped improve treatments for patients with hormone disorders.

developed by the Austrian neurologist Sigmund Freud (1856–1939) in the early part of the 20th century. The study of pyschiatry became popular during World War II as thousands of physicians were given the task (for which many of them were unprepared) of helping servicemen cope with the trauma of military action and, after the conflict, with the strain of returning to civilian life. By the 1950s psychiatry had come of age. Increasing numbers of people who could afford to do so paid weekly visits to their psychiatrists, or "shrinks" as they became known. The number of psychiatrists increased at twice the rate of population growth at a time when the number of physicians was barely managing to keep pace with demographic changes.

In 1949 the Mental Hygiene Division of the U.S. Public Health Service was reorganized as the National Institute of Mental Health to conduct research on mental illness. A year later the Psychiatric Foundation, the National Mental Health Foundation, and the National Committee for Mental Hygiene merged to form the National Association for Mental Health, which worked to improve attitudes toward mental illness. Over the next 10 years more and more old people came to spend their last years in mental institutions. Even so, the widespread use of a variety of medical treatments for mental disorders meant that in 1956, for the first time, more people were released from mental hospitals than were admitted. However, communities had neither the expertise nor the resources to help people released from mental institutions adjust to the outside world. The nature of conditions such as schizophrenia (severe mental illness characterized by delusions) and episodes such as psychoses (severe mental derangements) were the subject of controversy and heated debate. Many of the beliefs and attitudes of that period seem very outdated today. For example, the McCarran–Walter Act of 1952 to control immigration provided for the exclusion of "aliens afflicted with psychopathic personality" from admission to the United States, while the American Psychiatric Association declared homosexuality in particular to be "psychopathic."

The most controversial method used to treat mental illness was a lobotomy—the severing of nerves in the frontal lobes of the brain—which, although usually done without the patient's consent, permanently dulled sense perceptions. In 1949 neurologist António Egas Moniz (1874–1855) was awarded the Nobel Prize for physiology or medicine for the treatment of schizophrenia by prefrontal lobotomy. Widely condemned today as barbaric, the practice had largely come to an end by the close of the 1950s.

Also highly controversial was electroconvulsive therapy—the passing of an electric current through the brain—which continued to be used to treat people suffering from severe depression. However, the introduction of tranquilizing drugs in the mid-1950s to control patients in mental institutions extended the range of psychiatric practice. A new medical discipline, psychopharmacology (medicine that uses drugs to affect the brain),

MENTAL HEALTH AND CRIME

In 1951 Monte Durham, who had a long history of mental illness, was convicted of housebreaking. He was acquitted on appeal in 1954 on grounds of insanity. The case established a precedent known as the "Durham rule." Abe Fortas, who was Durham's defense counsel and later became a Supreme Court justice, said that the significance of the Durham case was that "the law has recognized modern psychiatry. ... [*Durham*] is a charter, a bill of rights, for psychiatry." In 1957 the Court of Appeals for the District of Columbia declared that for a defendant with "a mental illness which makes it likely that he will commit other violent acts when his sentence is served, imprisonment is not a remedy." The remedy was compulsory hospitalization until it was deemed safe to release him.

In 1955, in a health message to the nation, President Dwight D. Eisenhower talked about the rising problem of juvenile delinquency in the language of mental health. He recommended a program of grants to states amounting to $5 million a year. He justified the expenditure as "a vital part of our attack on a serious health and social problem." Delinquents were portrayed as deviants from the social norm, sick people whose illness could be detected early, diagnosed, and treated. That approach had its critics, however, who argued that the cause of delinquency was not so much the criminal bent of individuals as social conditions such as poverty and poor education. That was also the position taken by the National Institute of Mental Health, which awarded money to community projects like the Henry Street Settlement in New York City.

was developed. It was founded in the belief that drugs were useful in the treatment of mental illness, and that psychiatric disorders were diseases that were entirely curable by drugs.

Health insurance

Advances in healthcare cost money, and the public grew ever more concerned about the cost to individuals. In 1945 the country had no national healthcare program, and very few Americans had private health insurance. Medical care was so expensive that millions of people relied on faith healers and home remedies. President Harry S. Truman (1945–1953) was a strong believer in national healthcare. In his State of the Union Address in 1948 he said that his aim was to enact "a comprehensive insurance system to protect all our people equally against insecurity and ill health." He endeavored to introduce a medical insurance program throughout his term in office. However, his attempts were attacked by the AMA as "socialized medicine" and defeated in Congress, much to the relief of private health insurers such as Blue Cross.

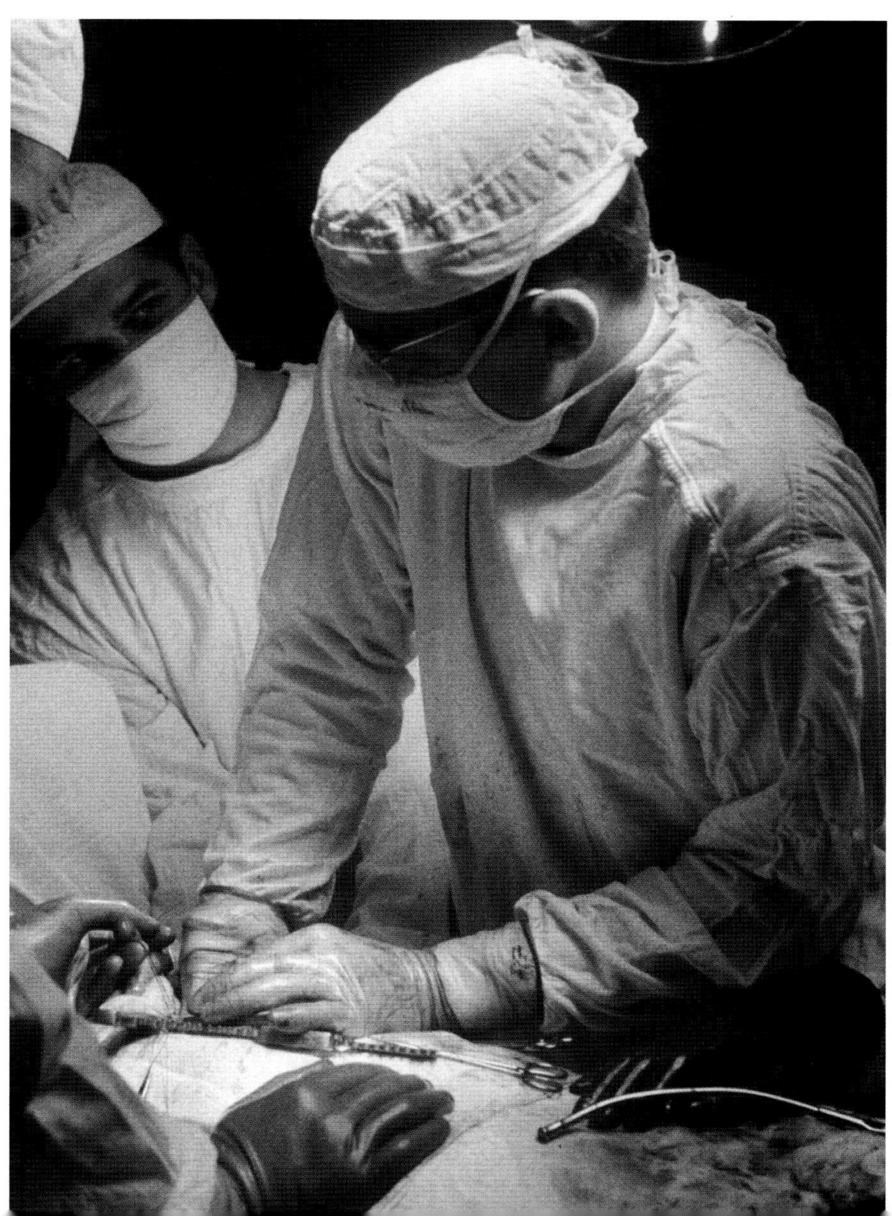

Surgeons perform a heart operation in 1959. During the 1950s surgeons pioneered open-heart surgery, which allowed them to carry out hole-in-the-heart operations.

A NEGLECTED GENERATION

The 1959 Senate hearings on the difficulties faced by America's retired people produced powerful testimony demonstrating that the high cost of medical care was their single most worrying problem:

"I live with my wife and my income is $1,500 a year. Well, we are old people and we don't require much.... But what do we do if something happens and we need medical care.... I will have to seek some charity institution and submit to the humiliation of what they call a necessity, and pronounce to the whole world that I am only a pauper, a beggar. Now if I alone were involved in this personally, I might suffer it. I would take it and swallow it. But if my children are brought into that, then I say, 'No, never.' I would rather die than submit to that humiliation and that degradation."

A retired working man from Florida

"We cannot get medical care because we cannot afford to pay $5 and $7 for a doctor. They also would not come at night. They say go to the clinic. We go there in the morning. We stay in line like a lot of cattle. We pay $1.75 or $2 for a ticket to get in.... Then they write out a prescription ... $11 prescription. How in the world can I pay $11 for a prescription."

A 75-year-old woman from Boston, Massachusetts

"Do these 150,000 members of the medical association have more power than the 16 million people on old age pensions, which are all voters, mostly, and citizens of the United States? What kind of democracy do we call this? ... Most of our European states have a government health bill ... and here, the richest country in the world does not take proper care of the old people."

A retired decorator from Oakland, California

Robert Felix of the National Institute of Mental Health appears before the Senate Committee on Labor and Public Welfare in 1955 to argue for more training for mental health workers.

Instead, during Truman's term of office Congress supported spending on hospitals and medical research. Congress passed the Hill–Burton Act in 1946 to provide federal money for hospital construction and modernization. In addition, the National Heart Act of 1948 and the Omnibus Medical Research Act of 1950 helped establish new research institutes. The federal government put a great deal of money into biomedical research. By 1965 the government was paying for two-thirds of national expenditure on biomedical research, which had been expanding at the rate of 20 percent each year. Furthermore, charitable institutions such as the Ford Foundation and large corporations

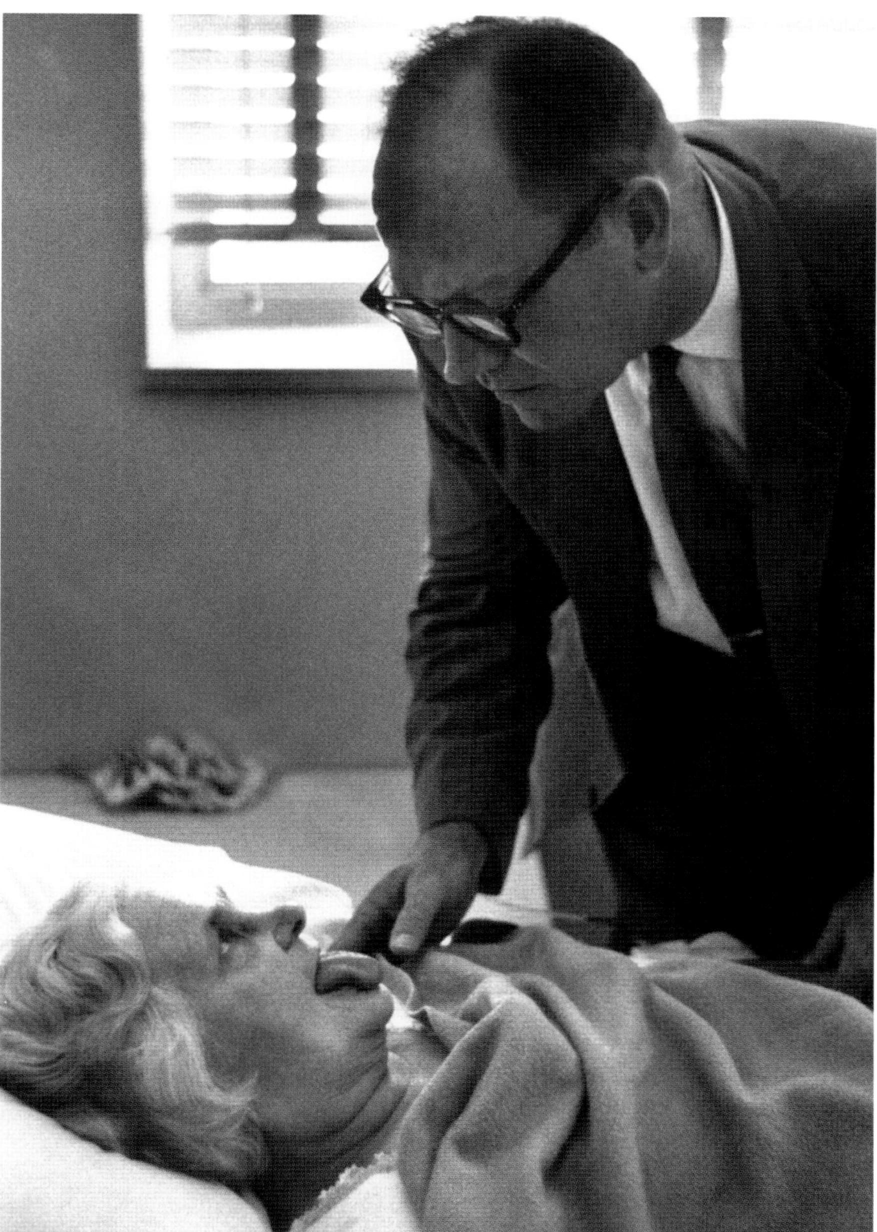

A doctor visits an old lady in the hospital in 1959. As the number of patients over 65 increased, the question of who should pay their expenses became a political issue.

such as General Motors contributed funds toward medical research, especially into cancer.

The AMA's campaign against Truman's vision of "socialized medicine" turned out to be the most expensive lobbying campaign in American history. In 1949 alone it spent $1.5 million. In the 1950 mid-term elections some doctors even promoted conservative candidates by dropping leaflets from helicopters and writing to their patients with political advice. In the 1952 election campaign both the Republican and Democratic candidates for the White House, Dwight D. Eisenhower (1890–1969) and Adlai Stevenson (1900–1965), joined the outcry against "socialized medicine." The Republican platform condemned "federal compulsory health insurance, with its crushing cost, wasteful inefficiency, bureaucratic dead weight, and debased standards of medical care." The campaign ensured that a national health insurance plan was off the immediate political agenda.

Elderly patients

Eisenhower became president in 1953. Unlike Truman, he was opposed to any sort of compulsory medical insurance bill. "It is unfortunately a fact," he said in his State of the Union Address in January 1954, "that medical costs are rising and already impose severe hardships on many families. The federal government can do many helpful things and still carefully avoid the socialization of medicine."

However, the growing number of elderly Americans rekindled the issue of a national health insurance program. On the one side there were 16 million voters over the age of 65 (also the lowest income group in the country) and on the other side the doctors and their allies. Various conferences on aging held throughout the decade were evidence of a growing public awareness of the plight of the nation's elderly. In 1955 a governors' conference recommended a huge program of assistance covering many areas, including welfare, housing, medical care, and mental health. The White House ignored the call from the Republican senator from Michigan, Charles Potter, who was supported by 54 senators, for a national commission of investigation. Yet as the decade went on, the call for some sort of insurance plan, backed by liberal, activist Democrats such as Senators Hubert Humphrey and Paul Douglas, became too insistent to be ignored.

Opponents of government health provision put their faith in the growth of the healthcare profession (doctors, nurses, researchers, and hospital administrators) as the way to distribute services more fairly. They believed that medicine should be part of the free-enterprise system and be regulated by supply and demand. Doctors, according to them, were no different from other small businessmen. They argued that the way forward for healthcare in America was to increase the supply of medical resources rather than subsidize access to them.

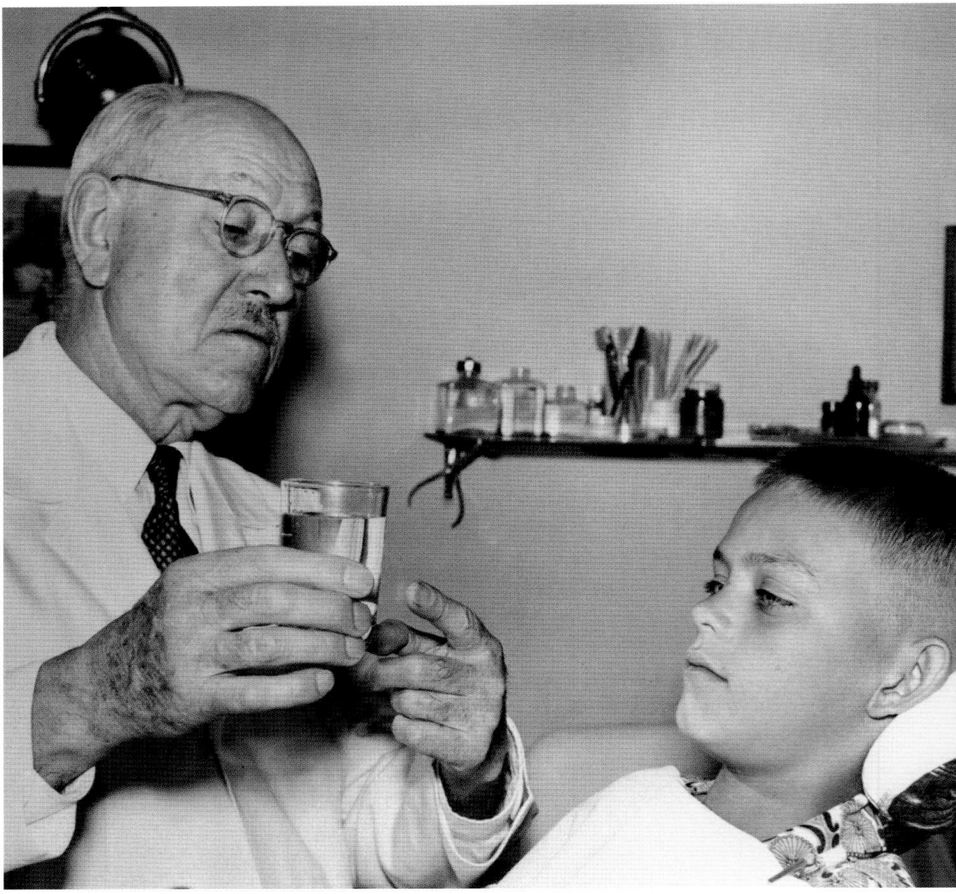

Dr. Frederick S. McKay, a dentist from Colorado Springs, Colorado, explains to a young patient how fluoride in drinking water contributes to good dental health, 1952.

Some Democrats, meanwhile, were still working on a plan of their own. In 1952 Oscar Ewing, head of the Federal Security Agency, had proposed making healthcare a benefit for older people under existing Social Security. A bill to give the elderly 60 days of covered hospitalization a year without raising payroll taxes for Social Security was introduced in the lower house every year from 1952 to 1955. However, even Adlai Stevenson, the leading Democrat, continued to oppose the idea of national medical insurance, and the bill got nowhere.

Forand Bill

In 1956 the union organization the AFL–CIO had been instrumental in securing legislation authorizing Social Security benefits for the permanently disabled. After that success labor leaders turned their attention to national health insurance for the retired. The AFL–CIO came out in favor of national cover for the elderly for hospitalization, nursing home care, and surgery and doctors' fees. The proposal was taken up by the Democrat Aime Forand, a member of the House Ways and Means Committee.

Over the next three years support for the Forand Bill increased. Despite receiving neither support from the party leaders nor coverage in the media, it was the subject of more congressional mail than any other bill. The bill was supported by organized labor, Democratic politicians, and the Democratic Advisory Council, as well as the AMA and its associates in the American Dental Association, the American Hospital Association, and the American Nursing Homes Association. A genuine grass-roots crusade for care for the elderly sprouted. "I want to pay tribute to the AMA," Forand said in 1960, "for the great assistance they have given me in publicizing this bill of mine. They have done more than I ever could have done."

In 1959 a subcommittee of the Senate Committee on Labor and Public Welfare held public hearings across the country that publicized the bill. There emerged a distressing picture of millions of elderly men and women living on the edge of poverty, unable to afford medical expenses (*see box on p. 58*). The committee's report had a dramatic effect. The three northern senators seeking the 1960 Democratic presidential nomination—Hubert Humphrey, Stuart Symington, and John F. Kennedy—all announced their support for a revised Forand Bill. The government opposed the bill on the grounds that health insurance should be voluntary and proposed its own plan. Both Eisenhower's plan and the Forand Bill were rejected, but a compromise bill, the Kerr–Mills Bill, which gave states matching funds, was signed into law in 1960.

One of the few Republicans to support some sort of compulsory insurance was Vice President Richard M. Nixon (1913–1994). Nixon had his sights on the White House and knew that this bill would be popular. A poll taken in Minnesota in 1960 showed that 55 percent of people supported the Forand Bill, and the Survey Research Center found a ratio of 3:1 support for the statement that "the government ought to help people to get doctors and hospital care at low cost." A Gallup poll in 1961 indicated that 67 percent of people were in favor of a health insurance program for the elderly, today known as Medicare. Medicare became part of the Democratic platform and was a key issue at the 1960 election. The foundations of the Medicare Act of 1965 had been laid.

See Also:

Antismoking Campaign • Birth Control • Drugs and Drug Abuse • Medicine • Polio Vaccine • Schools and Universities • Science and Technology

LILLIAN HELLMAN 1905–1984

Lillian Hellman, partner of the crime writer Dashiell Hammett, earned a reputation as one of America's best playwrights of the 1930s and 1940s. During the 1950s, however, she fell foul of the House Un-American Activities Committee and was blacklisted.

Lillian Florence Hellman was born in New Orleans, Louisiana, on June 20, 1905. When she was five, her father, a shoe salesman, moved the family to New York City. Hellman's childhood was subsequently disrupted since the family split its time between the two cities. Her mother's family was wealthy, and Hellman's antipathy toward her relatives would later become the theme of her most successful play, *The Little Foxes* (1939).

Hellman studied at both New York University and Columbia between 1922 and 1924 without graduating. After working as a book reviewer for the *New York Herald Tribune*, she moved to Hollywood in 1930, where she worked as a script reader.

Playwright Lillian Hellman was a supporter of leftist causes and faced questions about her political views from the House Un-American Activities Committee in the 1950s.

The Children's Hour

In 1930 Hellman met the writer Dashiell Hammett (1894–1961), who would have a great influence on her. He suggested that she write a play based on the events of a scandal in a Scottish boarding school. The resultant drama, *The Children's Hour* (1934), with its candid treatment of lesbianism, was a Broadway hit. Two movie adaptations, written by Hellman, followed.

Hellman was unusual in being a female playwright in a male-dominated world. She was also openly left-wing in her political views and a supporter of the Soviet Union, which she believed represented a real opportunity for an egalitarian society. An initial defender of the USSR's pact with Nazi Germany in 1939—as illustrated in her play *Watch on the Rhine* (1941)—Hellman eventually acknowledged the necessity of U.S. involvement in World War II (1939–1945).

In 1951 Hammett, as chairman of the Civil Rights Congress, was jailed for several months for refusing to reveal who had put up the bail money for some communists on trial for conspiracy. Hellman's relationship with Hammett and her outspoken views brought her to the attention of the House Un-American Activities Committee (HUAC). In 1952 she was subpoenaed to appear before the committee, which wanted her to name theater colleagues who might have communist associations. Hellman refused to give any names, and as a result, her own name was added to the Hollywood blacklist. Her situation worsened when she received a tax bill that forced her to sell her home.

A successful revival of *The Children's Hour* eased Hellman's financial situation. In 1951 she wrote *The Autumn Garden*. It was followed in 1954 by a highly successful adaptation of *L'Alouette* ("The Lark") by Jean Anouilh and in 1956 a less successful musical version of Voltaire's *Candide* with Leonard Bernstein. Hellman also began to teach classes on playwriting, fiction, and poetry at Harvard, Yale, and the City University of New York.

Hellman and Hammett lived together following Hammett's release from jail and his heart attack in 1955. Hellman took care of him until his death in 1961. Controversy dogged the end of her own life. She tried to sue another left-wing writer, Mary McCarthy, after McCarthy accused her of lying in her autobiographies. Hellman died in Martha's Vineyard, Massachusetts, on June 30, 1984.

See Also:

Blacklist • House Un-American Activities Committee • Literature • Soviet Union • Theater

ERNEST HEMINGWAY 1899–1961

At the start of the 1950s the novelist Ernest Hemingway had not published anything of note for several years. However, by the end of the decade, with his career reborn, he had won both the Pulitzer Prize and the Nobel Prize for literature.

Ernest Miller Hemingway was born in a wealthy suburb of Chicago on July 21, 1899. Soon after graduating from high school, he volunteered as an ambulance driver in Italy during World War I (1914–1918). Later he reported from the Spanish Civil War (1936–1939) and World War II (1939–1945). He worked as a journalist before achieving success with his novel *The Sun Also Rises* in 1926. In 1929 he published *A Farewell to Arms*, a love story set against the backdrop of World War I. By the end of the decade he had become one of the most popular writers in America.

Hemingway (right) talks on the set of the movie of *The Old Man and the Sea* with the producer Leland Hayward. The movie, starring Spencer Tracy, was released in 1958.

At the beginning of the fifties a decade had passed since Hemingway had published a successful novel. He was considered by many people—critics and the public alike—to be a writer on the wane. At the start of the decade he returned to Europe with his fourth wife, Mary. He had been working on the final draft of *Across the River and into the Trees* (1950); and when his agent secured $85,000 for the serialization rights, the couple traveled to Venice and Paris.

The Old Man and the Sea

The novel received very poor reviews on its publication in April, and Hemingway retired to the Finca Vigía, his home outside Havana, Cuba. He set to work on the short novel that was to restore his reputation: *The Old Man and the Sea* was completed by May 1951. The rest of Hemingway's year was dogged by tragedy. His mother died in June, followed by his ex-wife, Pauline, in October. The heaviest blow was the sudden death of his mentor and publisher, Charles Scribner, in February 1952, to whom he dedicated *The Old Man and the Sea*. Although Hemingway was on the verge of a comeback, there is no doubt that these personal losses damaged his fragile psychology.

Life magazine paid $40,000 for the serial rights to *The Old Man and the Sea*. When it published the novella in its entirety in its September 1, 1952, issue, the magazine sold five million copies. The Book of the Month Club bought the book, and Scribner's sold out of its first print run. The novella

AMERICA'S MOST FAMOUS NOVELIST

Hemingway occupies a unique position in American literary history. He was not only the most famous American writer of the last century, but he was also almost unique in being both a critical and popular success. His novels, with their innovative sparse style and clarity of language, were huge bestsellers. When *For Whom the Bell Tolls* was published in 1940, it sold half a million copies, and *Life* magazine published five million copies of its issue with the complete *The Old Man and the Sea* in 1952. While the public enjoyed Hemingway's novels, literary critics were devoting entire books to the study of his fiction by the 1950s.

Hemingway's fame rested as much on his lifestyle as his novels. He was an attractive man whose adventures, whether deep-sea fishing in Cuba, big-game hunting in Africa, or war reporting from Spain, seemed glamorous. *Life* and *Look* magazines both featured articles on Hemingway the man. He knew movie stars such as Gary Cooper and Ava Gardner as well as writers like F. Scott Fitzgerald. When news of his death was announced in July 1961, television stations interrupted their programming, and the news made headlines in the papers.

Hemingway gets ready to go shooting in Torcello in northern Italy in 1948. He was passionate about hunting and fishing.

was as popular with the public as it was with the critics. A movie, starring Spencer Tracy as Santiago, the old Cuban fisherman, was made in 1958.

Hemingway was now one of the most famous writers in the world. He won the Pulitzer Prize for his novella in May 1953, having earlier been denied it for *For Whom the Bell Tolls* (1940). The next month he and Mary left Havana for Europe and Africa. Hemingway visited Spain for the first time since the civil war and was warmly welcomed. He arrived in Kenya in September for a five-month safari.

On January 21, 1954, the Hemingways embarked on an aircraft tour of Africa. Two days later their plane crashed, and newspapers erroneously reported Hemingway's death. The couple set off again in another plane that crashed in flames on takeoff. Hemingway survived but was badly injured and burned. On October 28 he learned that he had been awarded the Nobel Prize for literature. He declined to travel to Stockholm to accept the prize because of his poor health.

Depression

For the rest of the decade Hemingway suffered from worsening health. High blood pressure, diabetes, and the effects of his plane crash compounded his inherited depression, which had claimed his father's life in 1928. The late 1950s were characterized by short bursts of writing and longer periods of paranoid depression.

In 1957 Hemingway started work on a series of sketches about Paris in the 1920s after he rediscovered papers stored at the Ritz Hotel since 1937. He delivered *A Moveable Feast* to his publishers in 1960, but it was published posthumously in 1964. His family and friends grew increasingly concerned about his health.

The revolution in Cuba in January 1959 forced Hemingway to relocate to Ketchum, Idaho. In the summer he returned to Spain to cover a bullfight—one of his lifelong passions—but his behavior had become increasingly erratic. Commissioned to write a 35,000-word piece for *Life* magazine, Hemingway worked on it over the winter of 1959 and in May 1960 submitted his finished article of 120,000 words.

Following hospitalization for his severe depression and two failed suicide attempts, Hemingway shot himself on July 2, 1961. He was buried in Sun Valley, Idaho.

See Also:

Book Publishing • Cuba • Literature • Magazines • Nobel Prizes • Pulitzer Prize

HIGH NOON

The 1952 movie High Noon *was a western that challenged the stereotype of a cowboy hero. The tense tale of an honorable man fighting alone for his principles is less an account of the "Old West" and more an unflattering portrayal of American society in the 1950s.*

The film *High Noon* was one of the most successful westerns to be made in the 1950s. The movie stars Gary Cooper (1901–1961) as retiring marshal Will Kane and Grace Kelly (1928–1982) as his Quaker wife, Amy. Their wedding is interrupted by news that Frank Miller, a murderer arrested by Kane five years earlier, has been released from jail and is returning to Hadleyville on the noon train, bent on revenge. Kane and Amy hurriedly leave town but only travel a little way before Kane's integrity forces him to turn back, overriding his wife's objections, to face his enemy.

In *High Noon* Gary Cooper plays the dignified marshal, Will Kane, while Grace Kelly plays his young Quaker wife, Amy. Cooper won his second Oscar for this role.

Noon strikes, the train arrives, and the middle-aged lawman finds himself abandoned: forsaken by his pacifist wife for breaking his promise never to touch a gun again and spurned by the townspeople, his pleas for help rejected through cowardice, resentment, and self-interest. With help from Amy, who has returned to his side, Kane wins a gunfight with Miller and his gang. The townspeople rush to applaud their marshal, only to see him throw his badge away and, without a word, leave town with his wife.

High Noon has little action until the final gunfight, focusing instead on the psychological state of its hero. After the movie was poorly received by preview audiences, it was reedited to include frequent closeups of Cooper's rugged face, catching each flash of anxiety and fear as the minutes tick toward noon. The tense atmosphere is further heightened by the sorrowful title song, "Do Not Forsake Me, Oh My Darlin'," which is sung repeatedly by Tex Ritter.

McCarthy hearings

Writer Carl Foreman (1914–1984) based the screenplay on "The Tin Star," a story by John Cunningham. Critics have variously interpreted the movie as a statement of approval for the United States's return to conflict in the Korean War (1950–1953), an allegory for the Cold War, and a comment on social decay in America. More usually, however, *High Noon* is regarded as a parable for the anticommunist witch hunts of the time, of which Foreman was himself a victim. While the movie was in production, he was subpoenaed to appear before the House Un-American Activities Committee (HUAC). Foreman refused to answer the committee's questions and was subsequently obliged to relinquish his credit as associate producer on the film.

High Noon won four Academy Awards in 1952: best actor (Cooper), song, scoring, and editing. It was also nominated for best picture, director, and screenplay. In addition, it won the New York Film Critics Circle Award as best picture of 1952 and launched Grace Kelly's movie career. In 1998 the American Film Institute named *High Noon* its top western, ranking it at number 33 in its list of the 100 greatest American movies of all time.

See Also:

Blacklist • House Un-American Activities Committee • Movie Industry • Oscars • Western Movies

HIGHWAY NETWORK

When President Eisenhower took office in 1953, he was determined to expand the nation's interstate system. The Federal-Aid Highway Act of 1956 authorized the biggest public works project in history and changed the face of America.

The building of the highway network was the largest civil engineering operation of its kind in the world. It had an enormous effect on the economy, the environment, and transportation. Since the majority of the network was financed by the federal government, it was also a significant political event because it represented a shift of power from the states to Washington, D.C. For ordinary Americans the new network would change the way they lived.

Origin of the interstate highways

Although some Americans acknowledged as long ago as the late 19th century that an integrated interstate road system was needed, the idea did not really begin to take shape until 1923, when General John Pershing, the chief of staff of the Army, submitted a report to Congress detailing possible routes for a nationwide system of express highways.

Interest in an interstate highway system was renewed during the Great Depression of the 1930s. At that time, however, politicians were primarily concerned with tackling severe unemployment; the issue of urban traffic congestion was secondary. President Franklin D. Roosevelt (1933–1945) tried to solve both problems by using the construction of a network of toll superhighways to create jobs. He envisaged a simple network of three east–west and three north–south routes. The Federal-Aid Highway Act of 1938 called for a study of the feasibility of such a plan. The Bureau of Public Roads (BPR) submitted its report, "Toll Roads and Free Roads," in 1939. It advised that a toll network would not be viable and instead advocated the construction of a network of nontoll interregional highways.

The interchanges of the highway network built in the 1950s needed to be several stories high where multiple roadways met.

In 1941 Roosevelt appointed the National Interregional Highway Committee to investigate the need for a system of national highways. As America joined World War II, however, civilian road planning was largely put on hold, and the report commissioned in 1941 was first presented to Congress in 1944. Called "Interregional Highways," it called for 39,000 miles (63,000km) of limited-access freeways to connect major military installations and cities with populations of more than 300,000.

The report led Congress to authorize designation of a 40,000-mile (64,000-km) network, to be called the National System of Interstate Highways, as part of the Federal-Aid Highway Act of 1944. The system would connect the principal metropolitan areas, cities, and industrial centers, serve national defense, and link with cross-continental routes. However, despite the act's ambitious intentions, no funds were specifically allocated to individual states for the construction of the proposed network; it was simply expected that states would use the bulk of their regular federal aid funds for road construction. Many states, however, did not want to divert their funds from local projects, and without targeted federal assistance little progress on the interstate system was achieved. In addition, by 1950 the United States was at war in Korea, and once again civilian road planning became a lesser priority than spending on defense.

Federal funding

The Federal-Aid Highway Act of 1952 authorized the first funds specifically for construction of the interstate system. It

THE EVOLUTION OF SERVICE STATIONS

In the 1950s some oil companies began employing women attendants to work at their service stations in the hope of attracting customers.

Gasoline was originally sold at country stores; with the invention of the gas pump, however, dedicated filling stations appeared, and they soon started selling other goods, including liquor. As cars became more common in the early 20th century, service stations began to offer the repair and maintenance of automobiles.

In the 1920s large oil companies that owned service stations sought distinction from their competitors by creating their own architectural trademarks along the roadside. The Pure Oil Company, for example, adopted a cottage style for its gas stations in 1925. In the 1930s and 1940s Sinclair Oil Company stations were built in the mission style, while art deco filling stations were also increasingly popular. Texaco adopted the so-called International style of modernism for its stations. In the 1930s industrial designer Walter Dorwin Teague created the "Type EM": a square building with porcelain-enameled steel facing, a style that was used until the 1950s.

There were also bizarre architectural styles, such as a service station in the shape of an iceberg situated on Route 66 in Albuquerque, New Mexico. Meanwhile, leading architect Frank Lloyd Wright (1867–1959) believed that filling stations would replace the old general store as the social center of town. One of his stations, built for Phillips 66 in 1956, is still in operation in Cloquet, Minnesota.

With increased prosperity after World War II larger service stations were built to include restaurants and accommodation. In the 1950s "megastations" began to appear. One of the first and largest was called "Little America." Located in Wyoming, it was a complex of 55 gas and diesel pumps with a 300-capacity coffee shop, a 150-room motel, and a cocktail lounge.

provided for federal funding for states on a 50 percent matching basis. By that time, however, several states had already constructed toll superhighways. The first segment of the Pennsylvania Turnpike opened to traffic in 1940. In its first year of operation some 2.4 million vehicles—as many as 10,000 each day—traveled the 160-mile (260-km) route. In 1948 the New Jersey Turnpike Authority was created to oversee construction of a high-speed expressway due for completion in 1951, and the New York State Thruway Authority was created in 1950 to build the nation's longest toll superhighway system.

Support from Eisenhower

President Dwight D. Eisenhower took office in January 1953. By that time the states had completed about 6,200 miles (10,000km) of improvements to the nation's roads at a cost of around $100 million (half of this sum had come from the federal government).

Eisenhower was a longtime advocate of an interstate highway network. In 1919, as a young officer in the U.S. Army, he had taken part in the military's first transcontinental motor convoy. Around 280 soldiers drove motorcycles, trucks, and other vehicles from Washington, D.C., to San Francisco, California, in order to test the feasibility of transporting a military unit across the country using the road network instead of trains. For thousands of miles the roads were narrow and unpaved, and nearly all the vehicles broke down at one time or another. In all, the excursion lasted 62 days. It was a grueling exercise that Eisenhower never forgot.

Toward the end of World War II, when Eisenhower, as supreme commander of the Allied forces in Europe, witnessed the multilane autobahn network in Germany, he recalled his 1919 journey and the abysmal state of

American roads. Not only had the autobahns helped the Germans transport military units efficiently, they also enabled the Allied troops to conquer the country more quickly.

By the time Eisenhower became president, the United States was under threat of nuclear attack from the Soviet Union. American cities in particular were in far greater need than ever before of having an efficient means of evacuation in case the Soviets launched a nuclear strike. A highway system similar to the German autobahns would also help the military transport equipment more rapidly in the event of an attack.

Eisenhower appointed a committee to work out a plan for financing a network. The committee submitted its report in early 1955, but there was further debate and compromise before legislation finally passed Congress virtually unopposed. Eisenhower signed the Federal-Aid Highway Act and the Highway Revenue Act of 1956 on June 29.

The Interstate Highway System

The Federal-Aid Highway Act gave the network the official title of the National System of Interstate and Defense Highways, stressing the importance of national defense. It authorized construction of 41,000 miles (65,970km) of toll-free highways. With its connection to the most densely populated areas of the country the system would serve 90 percent of cities in the United States with populations of more than 50,000 people, 65 percent of the urban population, and 50 percent of the rural population.

The federal share of funding, which had been increased to 60 percent with the passage of the Federal-Aid Highway Act of 1954, was raised again to 90 percent. The estimated total cost was $27 billion, with completion scheduled within 13 to 15 years. The 1956 act also created the Highway Trust Fund to allocate funds to the individual states for planning, construction, and rights-of-way.

The Highway Revenue Act established funding through federal excise taxes on the users of the system. The main excise tax was on gasoline, but there were also taxes on diesel, on tires weighing more than 40 pounds (18kg), and on heavier trucks and trailers. Taxation on fuel has remained the main contributor to funding, although percentages varied from 97 percent in 1957, down to 57 percent in 1980, and up again to 71.6 percent in 1987.

Criteria for the highways

The 1956 legislation, however, did not provide a definitive blueprint for the interstate highway network; it was meant to evolve instead through the planning and design process. Uniform design standards were to be agreed on by the American Association of State Highway Officials (AASHO) and the BPR (today known as the Federal Highway Administration; FHWA).

The BPR had overwhelming power. It had the authority to condemn and purchase land in both urban and rural areas. Public hearings were decreed in and around metropolitan areas, but they were more public presentations than consultations since they were held after the routes had been planned.

Design standards were obligatory to create a system that was intended to be "a credit to the nation." Engineers sought to balance the requirement for high-speed travel with maximum safety. The initial concept was for four traffic lanes, 12 feet (3.7m) wide, with limited access. Specific design standards grew from these basic objectives: Shoulders and medians were wide, ditches were gradual to minimize impact in the event of vehicles leaving the roadway, and cloverleaf interchanges were incorporated to enable traffic to move at a constant speed. In rural areas margins were set at 150 to 300 feet (46m–91m), but in urban areas right-of-way margins were not specified because of their potential cost. Curvatures, elevation, sight distance, and gradients were to be determined by the design speeds of 70 mph (113km/h) in flat areas, 60mph (97km/h) in "rolling" areas, 50 mph (80km/h) in mountainous areas, and at least 50 mph (80km/h) in urban areas. The criteria to determine the speed limit was based on topography (the physical or natural features of the landscape) only, with no consideration given to variations in population and traffic density. This led to later controversy over speed limits.

Commercial activities were barred from interstate route rights-of-way, but air space and subterranean space were allowed for parking. Route numbering guidelines specified even numbers for routes running east–west and odd numbers for routes running north–south. Existing toll roads and bridges could be included in the system, depending on minimum design criteria. In 1957 about 2,100 miles (3,380km) of toll roads were accepted for eventual connection with the network.

The Pennsylvania Turnpike, opened on October 1, 1940, was the nation's first major highway and toll road. It served as a model for the Interstate Highway System of the 1950s.

CONSEQUENCES OF THE HIGHWAY NETWORK

The expressway built through Boston greatly improved the flow of traffic but also caused environmental and urban-development problems.

By the 1960s cars, buses, and trucks had become the dominant means of transporting people and goods across the United States. This meant that the new highway network directly contributed to the demise of rail as the primary method of goods transportation. In 1950 the railroads carried 1.4 billion tons of goods, while trucks carried 800 million tons. By 1970 truck handling had grown to 1.9 billion tons, while rail handling remained almost the same at 1.5 billion tons.

The carryover effect of the Interstate Highway System was not confined to transportation, however. As transportation patterns changed, so did lifestyles, consumption patterns, and culture. The highway network greatly affected the areas through which it passed. In major cities large areas were cleared and whole neighborhoods uprooted for highways; in rural areas the decrease in traffic on existing routes led to the decline of neighboring cities and towns. State governments were eager to take advantage of federal funds for interstate highways to the detriment of local routes and interests.

Some observers claim that President Eisenhower was proud of his role in creating the system but ultimately disappointed by its outcome. He was apparently under the impression that the highway network would be predominantly a rural project and was largely unaware of highway construction in urban areas. Later, in his memoirs he tried to minimize his role in fostering the Interstate Highway System.

Missouri was the first state to award construction contracts, but the 8-mile (13-km) stretch Topeka–Valencia in Kansas was the first section of interstate highway completed, in September 1956.

Legacy of the highways

In the 1960s the automobile industry and the highway network came under close public scrutiny. The main concern was safety. In 1966 President Lyndon Baines Johnson (1963–1969) signed the National Traffic and Motor Vehicle Safety Act and the Highway Safety Act, which sought to reduce injuries and fatalities from traffic crashes and improve highway safety. That year there were close to 50,000 deaths on the nation's highways, and highway design was largely blamed for that figure. Some deadlier highways had acquired nicknames, such as "Dixie Die-way" for the Detroit–Miami route.

Concern also turned to the environment, with cars being blamed for air, water, and noise pollution and for blighting the landscape. The Highway Beautification Act of 1965 called for control of outdoor advertising and the screening or removal of certain junkyards along highways. However, while the effect of the highway network on the environment and on American culture and lifestyles has always been a matter of controversy, the immense economic influence of the highways is undeniable. The scope of industries and services related to the automobile alone—manufacturing, sales and services of cars, construction, servicing and maintenance of roads, and roadside services (*see box on p. 66*)—has grown immensely. In 1963 one in six jobs was in an auto-related occupation. The Department of Transportation, created in 1966, became the fourth-largest federal department. In 1990 the highway network was renamed the Dwight D. Eisenhower National System of Interstate and Defense Highways in recognition of the president's role in the development of the highways. And in 1994 the American Society of Civil Engineers declared the network as one of the "Seven Wonders of the United States."

See Also:

Air Travel • Automobile Culture • Automobile Industry • Civil Engineering • Economy • Eisenhower, Dwight D. • Environment • Pollution • Suburbs

ALGER HISS 1904–1996

A State Department official during the presidency of Franklin D. Roosevelt, Alger Hiss was denounced in the late 1940s as a Soviet spy and imprisoned in 1950 for perjury. His case continues to provoke passionate debate more than 50 years later.

Alger Hiss was born on November 11, 1904, in Baltimore, Maryland. He attended Johns Hopkins University and Harvard Law School, and then became law clerk to Supreme Court Justice Oliver Wendell Holmes. From 1933 he served in various capacities in the administration of Franklin D. Roosevelt (1933–1945) and attended the 1945 Yalta Conference as an adviser to the president. Hiss served as temporary secretary-general of the United Nations at its founding conference before becoming president of the Carnegie Endowment for International Peace.

Alger Hiss has become an iconic figure over whom liberals and conservatives continue to clash in their differing interpretations of the effect of the Cold War on American society.

Whittaker Chambers

In 1948 Hiss's career in public service received what turned out to be a fatal setback when Whittaker Chambers (1901–1961), a former editor of *Time* magazine and a self-confessed former communist, repeated in public an allegation that he had previously made before the House Un-American Activities Committee (HUAC). He stated that in 1938 Hiss had given him classified documents to hand over to the Soviet Union. Hiss sued Chambers for libel, but the proceedings in this case were subsumed when Hiss was indicted for perjury: He was charged with having lied when he stated under oath that he had never passed documents to Chambers or met him after January 1937. Prominent among those who pursued Hiss was Richard M. Nixon (1913–1994), a young congressman seeking to make a name for himself. Hiss pleaded not guilty, and his first trial in 1949 ended in a hung jury. There was a retrial, and in 1950 Hiss was found guilty and sentenced to five years in prison.

Hiss served three and a half years in jail, and after his release in 1954 he worked as a stationery salesman. He continued to proclaim his innocence until his death on November 15, 1996.

The evidence—documents and microfilm—used to convict Hiss has never been successfully linked to him except by Chambers's testimony, so one of the crucial questions in the case has been the mental health of Chambers and therefore his reliability as a witness. When Soviet archives were searched in the 1990s, no reference was found to Hiss. However, transcripts of cables between U.S. and Soviet agents released in 1996 suggested that Hiss had been an agent codenamed "Ales."

The lack of hard evidence meant that opinions about Hiss tended to divide along party political lines: Republicans thought he was a communist, while Democrats suspected the charges had been trumped up to denigrate the memory of Roosevelt's New Deal legacy, which Hiss represented. The affair was damaging to President Harry S. Truman (1945–1953), who took numerous testimonials to Hiss at face value. The case sparked further charges of communist influence in the U.S. government by Senator Joseph McCarthy, and in the 1952 elections many voters turned to the Republican Dwight D. Eisenhower partly out of fear that the Democrats had been infiltrated by communists.

See Also:

House Un-American Activities Committee • McCarthy, Joseph • Nixon, Richard M. • Spies and Spying

HOCKEY

In the 1950s hockey consolidated its finances around a core of six major teams before the expansion of the NHL in the years that followed. The decade also saw television extend the sport's fan base and players flex their negotiating muscles for the first time.

Hockey fans look back on the 1950s as the golden age of the "Original Six." However, the six teams that made up the National Hockey League (NHL) from 1943–1944 to 1966–1967 were not actually the original NHL (which was founded by four Canadian teams in 1917), and the decade was really golden only for two all-conquering teams: the Detroit Red Wings and the Montreal Canadiens. The players themselves were mostly all Canadian, whichever team they played for. For the teams at the bottom of the league—the Chicago Blackhawks and the New York Rangers—it was a distinctly dark era. Between them the Red Wings and the Canadiens won every league title and all but one Stanley Cup; the Rangers made the postseason playoffs three times, Chicago only twice. Between 1942 and 1951 the Toronto Maple Leafs had won the Stanley Cup six times, but in the fifties they entered a period of decline and failed to win it again until 1962.

The Chicago franchise was so fragile that the owners of the other clubs came to its rescue in successive years (1953–1955) with an aid package that made players from their teams available to the Blackhawks. That the franchise survived owed something to a change of front-office management. Jim Norris and Arthur Wirtz, long associated with Detroit, took over the Blackhawks in 1952. In 1955 Norris bought the Buffalo Bisons of the American Hockey League (AHL), starting a farm system (using minor teams to train players for the majors) for the first time in the club's history.

Twice NHL expansion was rumored: in 1952, when the Cleveland Barons of the AHL were on the brink of entering

Bernie Geoffrion of the Montreal Canadiens disengages himself from Detroit Red Wings goalie Terry Sawchuk and Benny Woit (5) in a 1955 game.

Montreal Canadiens goalie Jacques Plante gets ready for action against the New York Rangers in a game from 1957. In 1959 he became the first goalie to wear a mask.

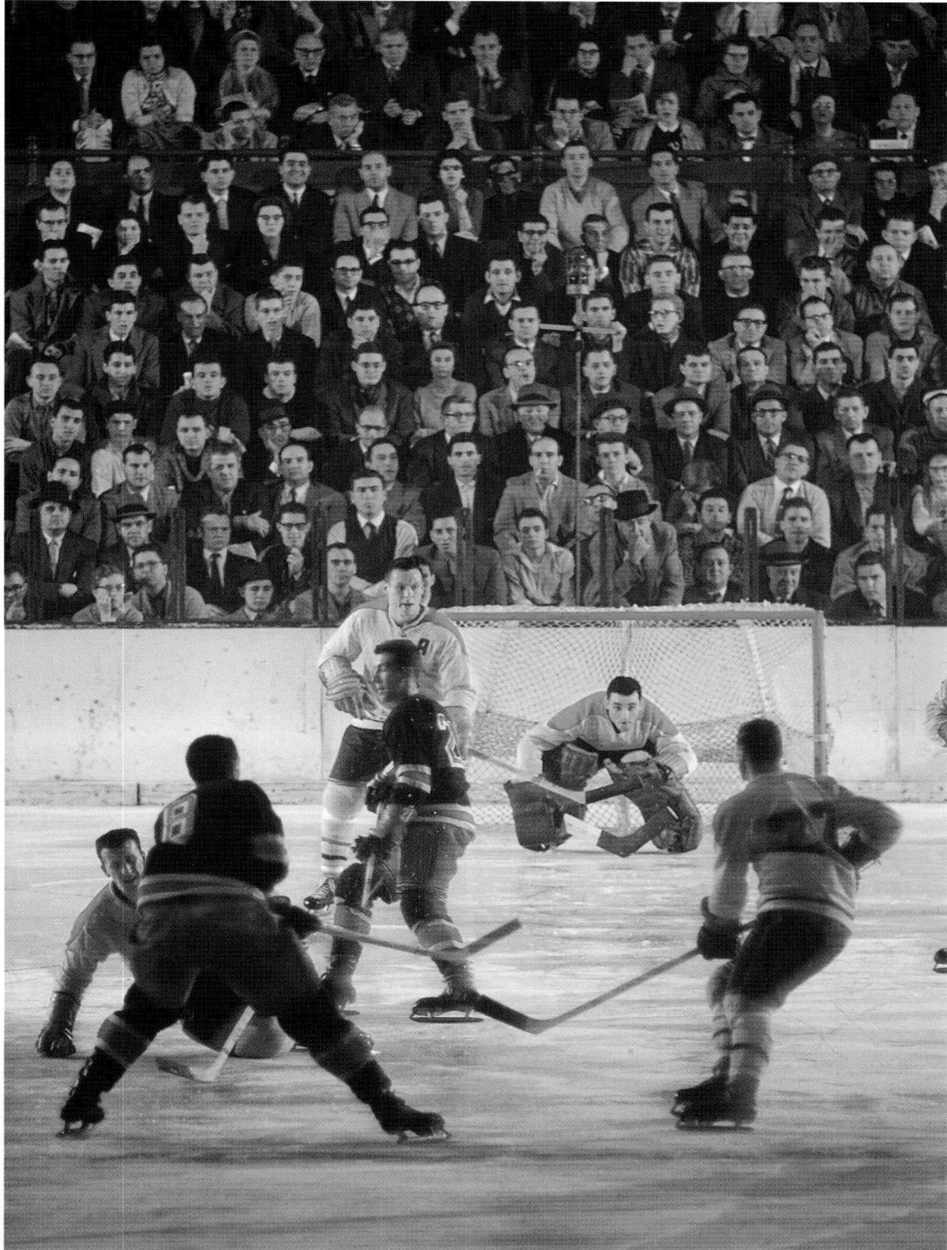

the league, and in 1959, when it was thought that backers from Los Angeles and San Francisco, following in the wake of baseball's Dodgers and Giants, might buy in teams from elsewhere. Cleveland's backers were unable to come up with the $425,000 deposit required by the NHL to demonstrate financial solidity, and expansion to the West Coast was put back for a decade. In 1953 the over-ambitious Barons filed a "challenge" for the Stanley Cup, but it was rejected on the grounds that Cleveland had no authority to represent the AHL, and that the AHL was, in any case, inferior to the NHL.

Television

The televising of NHL games began in 1952–1953 with the Saturday night broadcast of *Hockey Night in Canada* from the "home" of hockey, the Maple Leaf Gardens in Toronto. Fears about television's effect on live attendances meant that the telecast began at 9:30 P.M., when the second period was already underway. The fears proved unfounded. Every Toronto game in the decade sold out well in advance. The veteran Canadian commentator Foster Hewitt (instantly recognizable by his his high-pitched, nasal voice and his famous catchphrase, "He shoots, he scores!"), moved over from radio to television. In 1957 he made way for his son, Bill. By that year, when CBS began showing Saturday afternoon games from the four American cities in the NHL, all six NHL franchises had opened their arenas to television. One effect was the introduction of the rule that home teams would wear colored uniforms, visiting teams white ones. Television was also responsible for the use of hand signals by referees, the white-and-black striped shirts of referees and linesmen, and the wearing of players' numbers on their skates.

Television was also a factor in the formation in 1957 of the Players' Association (NHLPA), with the perennial all-star left-winger Ted Lindsay (1925–) of Detroit as its first president. In a New York court the NHLPA filed suit against the league and the club owners, claiming they operated a monopoly and seeking higher pensions and a bigger slice of television revenues. In Toronto the NHLPA sought legal recognition as a labor union under the Ontario Labour Relations Board and free agency for the players after five years with a club. Its cause was injured by the decision of the Detroit players to withdraw from the union, and at a meeting in February 1958 the owners refused to recognize the union. Although the owners made certain concessions—increased pensions, a larger share of playoff revenues for the players, and a minimum salary of $7,000—they remained all-powerful. During preseason training in 1959 the Leafs players threatened to strike for higher salaries. The Toronto general manager and coach, Punch Imlach, said that if they did, he would replace them with players from the minor leagues. The players signed without striking.

STATISTICS

LEAGUE CHAMPIONS		STANLEY CUP		
1950	Detroit	1950	Detroit d. New York	4–3
1951	Detroit	1951	Toronto d. Montreal	4–1
1952	Detroit	1952	Detroit d. Montreal	4–0
1953	Detroit	1953	Montreal d. Boston	4–1
1954	Detroit	1954	Detroit d. Montreal	4–3
1955	Detroit	1955	Detroit d. Montreal	4–3
1956	Montreal	1956	Montreal d. Detroit	4–1
1957	Detroit	1957	Montreal d. Boston	4–1
1958	Montreal	1958	Montreal d. Boston	4–2
1959	Montreal	1959	Montreal d. Toronto	4–1

ART ROSS TROPHY (Leading Points Scorer)		Goals	Assists	Total
1950	E. Lindsay (DET)	23	55	78
1951	G. Howe (DET)	43	43	86
1952	G. Howe (DET)	47	39	86
1953	G. Howe (DET)	49	46	95
1954	G. Howe (DET)	33	48	81
1955	B. Geoffrion (MONT)	38	37	75
1956	J. Beliveau (MONT)	47	41	88
1957	G. Howe (DET)	44	45	89
1958	D. Moore (MONT)	36	48	84
1959	D. Moore (MONT)	41	55	96

HART TROPHY (Most Valuable Player)			
1950	C. Rayner (NY)	1955	E. Kennedy (TOR)
1951	M. Schmidt (BOS)	1956	J. Beliveau (MONT)
1952	G. Howe (DET)	1957	G. Howe (DET)
1953	G. Howe (DET)	1958	G. Howe (DET)
1954	A. Rollins (CHI)	1959	A. Bathgate (NY)

The most important rule change of the decade, introduced in 1956–1957, allowed a player serving a two-minute penalty to return to the ice if the opposing team scored. The most visible changes on the ice were the "platooning" of goaltenders, which became commonplace after the Leafs played both Al Rollins and Turk Broad in 1950–1951, and the introduction of protective face masks for goaltenders. After his face was cut in a game against the Rangers on November 1, 1959, Montreal's Jacques Plante (1929–1986) decided to wear a mask. Other goaltenders, such as Terry Sawchuk (1929–1970) of Detroit and Gump Worsley (1929–) of New York, dismissed the innovation, but Plante persisted over the objections of the Montreal coach, Toe Blake, who feared the mask might impair vision. Plante was vindicated, playing for 11 straight Montreal victories and going on to claim his fifth consecutive Vezina Trophy as the NHL's top keeper. Don Simmons of Boston soon followed Plante's example, and the Rangers made masks compulsory throughout their farm system.

Winning streaks

Winning streaks were a feature of the era, the most impressive being the still-unbeaten run of seven consecutive league titles won by the Detroit Red Wings from 1949 to 1955. In 1950–1951 the Red Wings compiled a record 101 points (over a 50-game season) and followed that performance with 100 points the next season. Toronto was unlucky that 95 points—the highest total in the club's history—was only good enough for second place in 1950–1951, although they won that year's Stanley Cup, beating Montreal in the only final series in which every game was decided in overtime. Detroit won a record 15 games in a row at the end of the 1955 season before being stopped by the Canadiens in the third

Coach Toe Blake sips from the Stanley Cup after the Montreal Canadiens won a 4–1 victory over the Detroit Red Wings in April 1956.

THE ST. PATRICK'S DAY RIOT

Fights and brawls are part and parcel of professional hockey, but no episode has quite matched the drama of March 13, 1955, when Canadien Maurice "Rocket" Richard lost his cool in a game against Boston. After being high-sticked by Hal Laycoe, the Rocket went after the Bruins' defenseman, continuing to attack him with his stick. Twice he was restrained by officials and twice broke away to attack Laycoe again. After being pinned to the ice by Cliff Thompson, Richard got to his feet and landed two punches on the linesman. That was not the first time that the NHL's bad boy had attacked an official, and the league president, Clarence Campbell, suspended Richard for the rest of the season.

Richard, though the holder of the record 50 goals for a season, had never won the scoring championship. Suspension ended his hopes (in the remaining few games of the season he was overtaken by his teammate, Bernie Geoffrion) and dealt a blow to the Canadiens' gallant attempt to dethrone Detroit as league champions; even without Richard they finished only two points behind the Red Wings. It was all too much for Montreal's fans. Four days after the Laycoe incident the Red Wings played the Canadiens at the Montreal Forum. Campbell turned up for the game and was pelted with eggs, tomatoes, and pickled pigs' trotters.

With Detroit leading 4–1, a teargas bomb exploded behind a goalnet. Campbell ordered the game to be stopped and awarded to Detroit. Outside an angry mob gathered, throwing rocks through the windows of the Forum and setting cars and shops on fire. Sixty rioters were arrested, and the next day Richard appealed for calm over the radio. Without Richard the Red Wings beat Montreal 6–0 in the final game of the season to take the championship. And to add insult to injury, they went on to beat the Canadiens in the Stanley Cup final in a seven-game thriller.

Detroit Red Wings (left to right) Ted Lindsay, Gordie Howe, and Sid Abel are pictured together in 1950. Their partnership was so efficient it was called the "production line."

game of the Stanley Cup final series. As the Red Wings fell away in the second half of the decade, the Canadiens got better and better, winning the Stanley Cup every year from 1956 to 1960.

The Red Wings were led by the famous "production line" of Ted Lindsay, Sid Abel (1918–2000), and Gordie Howe (1928–), the highest-scoring unit in history. Howe, generally considered the greatest player ever before Bobby Orr and Wayne Gretzky came along, won four scoring titles in a row between 1951 and 1954. In Maurice "Rocket" Richard (1921–2000), like Howe a right-winger, the Canadiens had the most flamboyant and quick-tempered star in the NHL. No other player could lift fans off their seats like Richard on a forward rush. Montreal's ace-in-the-hole was Doug Harvey (1924–1989), a smooth-stickhandling, unflappable, attacking defenseman who won the first four of his seven James Norris trophies from 1955 to 1958.

If they had had Harvey in their lineup, Detroit might have remained unstoppable. At the end of the 1954–1955 season the Canadiens offered him to the Red Wings in exchange for the goalie Terry Sawchuk. Detroit, despite having Glenn Hall to replace Sawchuk, rejected the offer. "With Harvey," Lindsay said, "we could have won seven or eight Stanley Cups. But Jack Adams [the Detroit owner] wouldn't make the deal.... What a mistake that was!" The next year Adams traded Sawchuk to the Boston Bruins.

See Also:

Sports • Sports and TV • U.S.–Canadian Relations

JIMMY HOFFA 1913–1975

As president of the International Brotherhood of Teamsters, Jimmy Hoffa helped make the truckers' union one of the most powerful labor organizations in the United States. However, his connections with organized crime led to his downfall—and to his mysterious disappearance.

James "Jimmy" Riddle Hoffa was born on February 14, 1913, in Brazil, Indiana. On the death of his father, a coal miner, in 1920 his family moved to Detroit, Michigan, and it was there that Hoffa, having left school at 14, began his working life as a warehouseman. He became involved in union activities and organized his first strike in 1933.

Hoffa rose quickly through the ranks of the Teamsters union, which represents truckers, and soon became famous for his skill both as an organizer of strikes and as a negotiator with management. In 1940 Hoffa was appointed chairman of the Central States Drivers Council and two years later president of the Michigan Conference of Teamsters. In 1952 he became the union's international vice president and in 1957 its leader when his predecessor, Dave Beck, was charged with misusing union funds. In the same year Hoffa himself was acquitted of trying to bribe an official of a Senate investigating committee. As president, he succeeded in negotiating national agreements on pay and conditions for his members.

Jimmy Hoffa is pictured in 1959, when he was at the height of his power as president of the Teamsters union but already under severe pressure for his links to organized crime.

A pattern of violence

Having begun his career in the 1930s, when strikes were ruthlessly broken by physical violence, Hoffa was willing to use and condone violence himself, leading to associations with organized crime that eventually proved disastrous. In the 1950s he invested Teamsters pension funds in Mafia business projects and allowed the Mafia to set up "paper locals"—union branches with no members but staffed by the Mafia, who used their position to gain control of trucking routes and the businesses they served as well as access to union funds. It was those activities that led to Hoffa being targeted by Robert F. Kennedy, chief counsel of the Senate Rackets Committee (1957–1959), which investigated the influence of organized crime in labor unions. As U.S. attorney general (1961–1964) Kennedy continued to pursue Hoffa, and in 1964 he was convicted of tampering with a jury, fraudulent use of the Teamsters' pension fund, and conspiracy. After losing a series of appeals, he went to prison to begin a 13-year sentence in 1967.

Despite his incarceration, Hoffa refused to resign as president of the Teamsters until 1971, and in December that year his sentence was commuted by President Richard M. Nixon (1969–1974) on condition that he did not engage in any union activity until 1980. On his release, however, Hoffa tried to reestablish his union powerbase, both openly through legal action and covertly by attempting to use his influence.

Hoffa's Mafia associates, however, were better pleased with his more compliant successor as Teamsters president, Frank Fitzsimmons, and did not want Hoffa to return. Some of them (it has never been established who) lured Hoffa to a meeting in Detroit on July 30, 1975, at which he was kidnapped and presumably murdered. His body has never been found, and he was legally declared "presumed dead" in 1982.

See Also:

American Federation of Labor–Congress of Industrial Organizations • Industry • Labor Relations • Law and Order

BILLIE HOLIDAY 1915–1959

"Lady Day," as Billie Holiday was universally known, was perhaps the greatest American female jazz singer. Her short life was marked by drug abuse and racism, yet her voice produced some of the most beautiful renditions of jazz songs ever recorded.

Billie Holiday was born Eleanora Fagan Gough on April 7, 1915, in Philadelphia. Her mother, Sadie Fagan, was not married to her father, Clarence Holiday, a jazz guitarist, and the couple parted shortly after Billie's birth. As a child she was left with relatives while her mother searched for work. She was later to claim in her autobiography, *Lady Sings the Blues* (1956), that she endured beatings and was raped at the age of 11.

Holiday played hooky from school so often that in 1925 she was ordered to spend a year in the Baltimore House of the Good Shepherd for Colored Girls. She only completed fifth grade. At the age of 12 she started to work as a prostitute in a Baltimore bordello. She also sang to clients and listened to recordings of the two singers she was to credit as being her greatest influences, Louis Armstrong (1901–1971) and Bessie Smith (about 1894–1937).

Becoming a star

Determined to have a career in music, Holiday moved to New York City in 1927. Initially she worked as a maid, prostitute, and waitress. Following a raid by the vice squad, she spent a short time in a workhouse. On her release she changed her name, taking her father's surname and the Christian name Billie for the silent movie actress Billie Dove. Holiday had no formal musical training, but by the age of 15 she was singing in a Harlem nightclub.

In 1933 Holiday made some recordings with swing musician Benny Goodman and others. Her career as the leading jazz singer of her time was truly launched on July 2, 1935, when she recorded a session with the pianist Teddy Wilson. During the years 1935–1942 Holiday made more than 100 records, among them hits such as "They Can't Take That Away from Me" and "Easy Living."

While Holiday's recordings at this time were all made with small jazz groups, she sometimes appeared on stage with big bands. In 1937 she briefly joined the Count Basie Orchestra. She then became one of the first black singers to perform with the Artie Shaw Orchestra. Touring the South with the band, she had to endure much racial discrimination.

By 1939 Holiday was a star. Her voice was small, with only an octave range, but audiences loved the sense of intimacy it conjured up. She was able to take a song and make it her own. A good example was her rendition of the Gershwin brothers' "Summertime" (1936), which she transformed from a peaceful song to one of foreboding.

While Holiday's singing career blossomed, her personal life was turbulent. She did, however, form a close platonic friendship with the saxophonist Lester Young (1909–1959). Young invented the name "Lady Day" for Holiday and "Duchess" for Sadie, Holiday's mother, with whom she had also become close. Holiday

Billie Holiday performs in New York City in 1950. From around 1940 she was usually accompanied by a small combo, but she made a few earlier appearances with big bands.

"STRANGE FRUIT"

In 1939 Holiday became resident singer, accompanied by Frankie Newton's Orchestra, at the Café Society in New York City. It was here that she first sang "Strange Fruit." The song was written by Lewis Allan (the pseudonym of Abel Meeropol, a Jewish teacher and activist who later adopted the sons of Ethel and Julius Rosenberg). "Strange Fruit" was a harsh, metaphorical account of southern lynchings of black men. Holiday's heart-wrenching rendition silenced audiences. It brought to the fashionable jazz audiences of the Café Society the cruel reality of the racism faced by all black musicians. Columbia Records refused to record it, and it was eventually produced by Milt Gabler's Commodore label, with backing from Newton.

"Strange Fruit" provoked strong reactions. Some saw it as signaling the start of Holiday's decline as an artist. For others it was one of the most significant songs ever written and recorded about racial prejudice.

Holiday appears in concert in 1954. By the 1950s Holiday's personal problems were beginning to take their toll, and the quality of her performances varied considerably.

called Young "Prez"—short for president—because she had such a high regard for him. The two collaborated on several hits, including "I'll Get By" and "Mean to Me."

During the 1940s Holiday's career was blighted by her marital difficulties and her worsening drug problem. In 1941 she embarked on the first of her marriages to men who abused her. She had smoked marijuana as a child, and her husband now introduced her to opium and heroin. One result was the coarsening of her voice, which became more haunting. By 1947 Holiday's drug problem was so serious that she entered a clinic in an attempt to end her addiction. Soon after, federal agents arrested her for drug possession, and she spent almost a year in a federal reformatory. She lost her cabaret license, which meant that on her release she was no longer able to appear in the popular clubs of New York City.

Between 1952 and 1957 Holiday recorded for Verve Records and produced some of her finest work. Critics consider her 1952 recording of "These Foolish Things" better than that of 1936. Her sense of timing and phrasing remained unchanged. However, drugs continued to take their toll. In February 1956 Holiday was arrested again for drug possession. She stopped taking heroin but drank more, and her voice slowly deteriorated.

The final years

Holiday was still able to rise to the occasion, and in late 1957 she sang "Fine and Mellow" on *The Sound of Jazz* telecast to great acclaim. Her final album, *Lady in Satin*, was released the following year, and she sounded much older than her years. Her last performance was on May 25, 1959, at the Phoenix Theater in New York City.

Holiday had remarried but was living alone when, on May 30, 1959, she collapsed into a coma. She recovered consciousness in the hospital and suffered a final humiliation when she was arrested for possession of drugs. She died in the hospital on July 17. Asked why jazz musicians died young, she had said, "We try to live a hundred days in one day.... Like myself, I want to bend this note, bend that note, sing this way, and get all the feeling, eat all the good foods, and travel all over in one day, and you can't do it."

See Also:

Armstrong, Louis • Jazz • Popular Music

BUDDY HOLLY 1936–1959

Buddy Holly rose to fame as one of the earliest stars of rock 'n' roll. His promising career as a guitarist, singer, and songwriter was cut short when he died in a plane crash at age 22, but his influence on popular music remains strong to this day.

Charles Hardin Holley, nicknamed Buddy, was born on September 7, 1936, in Lubbock, Texas. Holly (as he later became) started playing country music from a young age and began performing in local clubs as early as 1953. But a new wave was developing in music. Elvis Presley (1935–1977), less than two years older than Holly, had become the newest, brightest star in the business after switching from his country roots to the new genre of rock 'n' roll. After hearing Presley, Holly became a rock-'n'-roll devotee. He opened for Presley's show when he came to Lubbock in 1955 and later that year performed in a concert featuring Bill Haley and His Comets. Holly's move from country music to rock 'n' roll was cemented when he added a drummer to his band and began using a Fender Stratocaster electric guitar instead of an acoustic one.

Less than two years after his first hit record, "That'll Be the Day," Buddy Holly was killed in an airplane crash, leaving behind a string of rock-'n'-roll classics.

First contract

Holly gradually played bigger club dates and radio broadcasts. His first recording contract was with Decca Records in Nashville in 1956. The single releases were disappointing, however, and the contract was not renewed. The contract itself featured a misspelling of his surname, dropping the "e" in Holley. The singer adopted the new spelling and continued using it throughout his career.

In February 1957 Holly went to Clovis, New Mexico, to work with independent producer Norman Petty. They recorded "That'll Be the Day"; but because Holly had originally recorded the song with Decca, he needed to release the new version under a different name. Teaming up with Jerry "J.I." Allison on drums, Niki Sullivan on rhythm guitar, and Joe B. Mauldin on bass, Holly formed the Crickets. Under Petty's guidance they experimented with recording techniques and crafted a sound that set them apart from other bands.

"That'll Be the Day" was released on the Brunswick label in May 1957 and sold more than one million copies by September. Holly also signed a separate contract with the Coral label, Brunswick's sister company, and released some records as a solo artist. The popular duo the Everly Brothers convinced Holly to upgrade his onstage wardrobe and to change his half-metal glasses for the thick, black-framed spectacles that became his trademark.

Holly—with and without the Crickets—had further success with songs such as "Oh Boy" and "Peggy Sue." The band went on several tours and appeared on *American Bandstand* and *The Ed Sullivan Show.* At the end of 1957 guitarist Sullivan left the band, citing exhaustion. The three-man Crickets went on to record such hits as "Maybe Baby" and "It's So Easy."

Toward the end of 1958 Holly ended his business relationship with Petty and left the Crickets. He moved to New York City with his wife to pursue a solo career. In early 1959 his single "It Doesn't Matter Anymore/Raining in My Heart" was released, and he joined the "Winter Dance Party" tour through the Midwest. The tour also included the singers Ritchie Valens and J.P. "The Big Bopper" Richardson. Holly was killed on February 3, 1959, when his tour plane crashed near Clear Lake, Iowa, minutes after takeoff. The pilot, Valens, and Richardson also lost their lives. In 1971 Don McLean's hit song "American Pie" called that day "the day the music died."

Despite his short recording career, Buddy Holly left an enduring rock-'n'-roll legacy. His work inspired and influenced many performers, including the Beatles, the Rolling Stones, Roy Orbison, and Eric Clapton.

See Also:

***American Bandstand* • Country Music • Haley, Bill, and His Comets • Popular Music • Presley, Elvis • Recording Industry • Rock 'n' Roll**

HOMOPHILE GROUPS

At a time when homosexuals were widely regarded as being mentally ill, a few small homophile groups began a campaign in support of their rights. The campaign was, however, very low-key and encouraged homosexuals to behave as "normally" as possible.

During the 1950s gay men and women suffered harassment, discrimination, and even persecution in both their public and private lives. Homosexuality was widely perceived to be a mental illness, and sex between men was illegal across the United States. Gay men were often subject to entrapment by the police, their lives ruined after being named and shamed in the local press.

In the largest cities, such as New York and San Francisco, there were vibrant homosexual subcultures, often closely associated with artistic and bohemian circles. The vast majority of gay men and women, however, kept their sexual identity secret and so were largely invisible as homosexuals within society. Disclosure of their sexuality could easily have resulted in the loss of their job, estrangement from friends and family, and violent harassment at the hands of homophobic members of their community.

Homosexuals demonstrate in Washington, D.C., in the early 1960s. In marked contrast, the homophile groups of the 1950s did not campaign openly for homosexual rights.

"Act normal"

In the late 1940s and 1950s a few gay men and women began to form so-called "homophile" societies. The aims of these societies were to protest about laws that, they argued, oppressed a minority, and to offer support and counseling to other homosexuals. Among the first and most important of these were the Mattachine Society, founded in Los Angeles in 1950, and the lesbian Daughters of Bilitis, founded in San Francisco in 1955.

Unlike the outspoken, militant "queer" campaigners of today, the members of the homophile movement tended to be moderate, cautious, and socially conservative. They encouraged gay people to "act normal." Men, they believed, should dress and act "like men" and women "like women": If they fitted in with mainstream society as much as possible, homosexuals would become accepted by other Americans as being "just like them." In support of their argument, they pointed to the work of sexologist Dr. Alfred Kinsey (1894–1956), whose pioneering research suggested that homosexuality was both widespread and psychologically "normal."

"Security risks"

In the early 1950s the homophile societies tended to be extremely secretive. The leaders of the Mattachine Society, for example, worked under assumed names. Many, too, were communists, or at least were leftist. Supporters of McCarthyism—the anticommunist hysteria fueled by Senator Joseph McCarthy—frequently portrayed homosexuals as both sexual and political subversives who threatened the fabric of American society. Typical McCarthyite views were expressed by Paul Coates, who wrote in a Los Angeles newspaper in 1953 about the close link between "sexual deviates" and "security risks," and homosexuals banding together to wield "tremendous political power."

Such attacks taught the homophile societies the value of being more open. At the same time, the communist leaders of the Mattachine Society were forced out, and their positions were taken by more politically neutral members. There was also a renewed emphasis on the development of a homosexual community by reaching out to gay men and women across the United States through magazines such as the Mattachine monthly *ONE Magazine*, which was founded in 1953.

Toward gay liberation

Throughout the 1950s homophile groups remained very small. Only the Mattachine Society came close to being a national movement. In the early 1960s a more militant Gay Liberation movement would arise. Abandoning the cautious approach of the homophile groups, it would adopt the civil rights activism of the period.

See Also:

Birth Control • Kinsey, Alfred • McCarthy Hearings • Women's Movement

J. EDGAR HOOVER 1895–1972

J. Edgar Hoover was director of the Federal Bureau of Investigation (FBI) from 1924 until his death. During the 1950s he concentrated increasingly on monitoring political dissidents, allowing crime bosses to operate relatively free of scrutiny.

John Edgar Hoover was born in Washington, D.C., on January 1, 1895. He studied law at night at George Washington University while working as a messenger in the Library of Congress. After receiving a masters degree in 1917, he was admitted to the bar and took a job as a file reviewer in the Justice Department. In 1919 Attorney General A. Mitchell Palmer put Hoover in charge of the department's General Intelligence Division. In that year and early 1920 labor unrest led to a widespread panic (the "Red Scare") that communists would overthrow the government. Hoover gathered information that could be used to target and deport suspected communists.

By the 1930s J. Edgar Hoover had established the FBI as a professional crime-fighting force, but his legacy was tarnished by his politically motivated misuse of power later in his career.

In 1924 Hoover became director of the Bureau of Investigation (it became the FBI in 1935). Inheriting a demoralized workforce that had fallen into disrepute following the corrupt administration of President Warren G. Harding (1921–1923), Hoover set about reorganizing the bureau on a thorough, professional basis. He hired agents on the basis of merit, not connections, and made sure that they received rigorous training at the FBI National Academy. He also established a modern forensic laboratory and a fingerprint file, which became the largest collection of such data in the world.

During Prohibition (1919–1933) the FBI made efforts to combat organized crime, and Hoover used his flair for publicity to ensure that the agency received maximum credit for its (in truth rather limited) success in bringing big-time gangsters to justice. In the late 1930s President Franklin D. Roosevelt (1933–1945) gave the FBI responsibility for investigating foreign espionage in the United States. From the start of the Cold War in the late 1940s the FBI maintained intensive surveillance of communists and other left-wing activists in the United States. Hoover reportedly supplied Senator Joseph McCarthy (1908–1957) with much of the information on which the senator based his accusations about government officials being communists. The association ended in 1954, when McCarthy made the mistake of showing an internal FBI document as part of a public presentation. The FBI also provided information to the House Un-American Activities Committee (HUAC).

Compromised by blackmail

Hoover's position in the FBI was unassailable because he used FBI surveillance to collate secret dossiers—which he kept himself—about politicians, including almost every president, that he could threaten to reveal if necessary. At the same time, however, the Mafia was able to operate with minimal interference from the FBI. Since Hoover's death it has been claimed that this was because from the early 1950s he was being blackmailed by crime boss Meyer Lansky, who allegedly had evidence of Hoover's homosexuality.

Although his public reputation suffered badly—his authoritarianism and persecution of reformers such as Martin Luther King, Jr., became notorious—Hoover held onto his post until his death on May 2, 1972.

See Also:

Federal Bureau of Investigation • House Un-American Activities Committee • Law and Order • McCarthy, Joseph • Politics and Government

LENA HORNE 1917–

A singer and actress with a huge following in the 1940s and 1950s, Lena Horne became the first African American to be given a long-term contract at a major Hollywood studio. She also became a champion of both left-wing political causes and the civil rights movement.

Born on June 30, 1917, in Brooklyn, New York City, Lena Calhoun Horne often accompanied her actress mother on tour. At the age of 16 she became a chorus girl at Harlem's Cotton Club, and within two years she was starring in her own shows as a singer. She spent the next five years performing at nightclubs, in all-black cast revues on Broadway, and on tour with a predominantly white swing band, thereby becoming one of the first black women to work successfully with both black and white performers. However, racial segregation made touring an unpleasant experience. Horne could not stay in the same hotel as the white musicians in the band, could not sit with them on the stage between songs, and had to change on the tour bus because she was prohibited from using the dressing rooms.

Lena Horne was one of the most popular singers and actresses of the 1950s. She won the acclaim of New York drama critics for her performance in 1957 in the musical *Jamaica*.

Movie career

In 1938 Horne made her first appearance in a movie, the independent all-black *The Duke Is Tops*. Four years later she moved to Hollywood and signed a seven-year contract to make movies with MGM. Her contract stipulated that she would not play the role of a servant or African native because she believed it "essential ... to try to establish a different kind of image for Negro women." She turned down the studio's suggestion that she change her name and learn Spanish in order to pass as a Latin American.

Horne featured in 13 MGM movies, usually in specially designed sequences that were independent of the plot and could easily be cut when the films were shown to southern audiences. The notable exceptions were *Cabin in the Sky* and *Stormy Weather*, which were made in 1943 with all-black casts, Realizing that Hollywood would only offer her bit parts, Horne decided to concentrate on her singing career.

A friend of Paul Robeson (1898–1976), the black singer and actor who was virtually ostracized in the United States for voicing his political views, Horne was blacklisted for her left-wing links in the fifties. As a result, she was prevented from working in Hollywood, in movies, radio, or television. She was also included in *Red Channels*, a publication that listed "subversives" in the entertainment industry. Meanwhile she worked as a singer in nightclubs and in 1957 made one of her best albums, *Lena Horne at the Waldorf-Astoria*.

Civil rights campaigner

Horne was an active participator in the civil rights movement and took part in the March on Washington led by Martin Luther King, Jr., in 1963. She also performed at rallies for the National Council of Negro Women.

Horne enjoyed huge success in 1981 with *Lena Horne: The Lady and Her Music*, which became the longest-running one-woman show in Broadway history. It won several awards, including a Tony Award and a citation from the New York Drama Critics Circle. She continues to make occasional screen appearances and is still recording.

See Also:

Black Americans • Blacklist • Broadway • Civil Rights • Movie Industry • Musical Theater • Robeson, Paul • Segregation and Desegregation

HORSE RACING

The 1950s were a turbulent decade for horse-racing enthusiasts in the United States. Having experienced a rebirth in the years around World War II, the sport struggled to maintain popularity as corruption, competition, and missed media opportunities all had an effect.

By the beginning of World War II (1939–1945) horse racing was established as one of the United States' most popular sports. The 1930s had seen major changes in the sport to place it in such a strong position. The U.S. government reversed many of the controls that had been placed on race betting in the first decades of the 20th century, which had resulted in widespread track closures. It also took steps to control corruption, and the first photo-finish camera was installed at Hialeah Race Track in Florida on January 16, 1936, putting an end to disputed finishes. The race season was extended through winter—mainly in the sunshine states of California and Florida—so that race enthusiasts could follow their sport year-round. Furthermore, impressive thoroughbred horses such as the famous Seabiscuit gave particularly exciting races, and horses and riders became national heroes.

The onset of war with Japan in 1941 threatened the sport. Problems for U.S. horse racing were not as severe as those faced in Europe, where war was actively being fought; indeed, all of the U.S. tracks stayed open throughout the conflict. However, there were major challenges within the sport: There were wartime restrictions on horse food, transportation, materials for building and repairing grounds, and travel. When the war finished in 1945, the American people demonstrated their joy by flooding back to the grounds, providing a massive surge in betting revenues. The future of the sport looked bright.

Business and corruption

By 1950 horse racing was entering one of its most exciting periods. All racing speed records held prior to 1945 were smashed, and racecourse owners increased both the number of racing days and the number of races held each day. New tracks went into development. In Jamaica, Queens, New York City, for example, the venerable

The size of the crowd in this image of a race at New York's Aqueduct Racetrack in June 1952 shows the enormous popularity of racing during the early 1950s.

Eddie Arcaro sits on Native Dancer, winner of the American Derby at Washington Park, Illinois, August 1953. Trainer Bill Winfrey stands on the right.

Aqueduct Racetrack underwent a major rebuilding program. The New Aqueduct was opened in 1959 at a cost of $33 million—a reflection of how much money was pouring into the sport during the decade.

As revenues from betting increased, horse racing became more of a business than a sport, with individual horses generating more than $1 million for their owners through race wins. The weighting of horses became a particularly difficult issue. In flat racing superior runners are given a weight handicap of around 10 pounds (4.5kg) by sewing weights into the saddle pad. The purpose of the weights is to ensure that less capable horses have a significant chance of winning and therefore that the race result is less certain (an open race outcome is essential for betting). As the purses in horse racing became larger in the 1950s, however, more owners argued against weight restrictions or searched around for races where there would be less of a weight handicap. Another problem was "ringing"—fraudulently entering a horse in a race when it was of a better class than the race allowed. However, the Thoroughbred Racing Protective Bureau, an investigative organization established in the late 1940s, had this problem under control by the mid-1950s, and ringing was almost entirely stamped out.

Glory days

Horse racing in the 1950s concentrated on shorter, faster races rather than long tests of endurance, and this made for exciting viewing. Certain horses attained the status of national heroes. One such horse was Native Dancer, who in three years of racing lost only one race out of 22. Owned by Alfred Vanderbilt III of the powerful New York Vanderbilt family, Native Dancer became famous for his dramatic racing style, often coming from the back to take first place just as he crossed the finishing line. Nicknamed the "Gray Ghost," Native Dancer appeared on the cover of *Time* magazine and was twice named "Horse of the Year" (in 1952 and 1954). Much of his popularity derived from his frequent television appearances as his races were broadcast across the nation. *TV Guide* actually ranked Native Dancer's popularity alongside that of TV host Ed Sullivan.

STIMULANTS

A problem that worked its way into horse racing in the 1950s was the use of illegal stimulants. A few unscrupulous jockeys or owners were discovered to have given their mounts chemical stimulants to improve performance. The racing industry was particularly sensitive to the issue after the case of Tom Smith (former trainer of the legendary horse Seabiscuit), who was suspended from racing for a year by the Jockey Club after he had allegedly given the horse Magnific Duel eight squirts of the stimulant ephedrine using a nasal spray. Magnific Duel subsequently won his race at the Jamaica Park track in New York on November 1, 1945. In the late 1940s and early 1950s racing authorities introduced mobile testing laboratories. The labs took samples of a horse's saliva for analysis just before each race, and this action effectively brought the problem under control.

SWAPS AND NASHUA

Probably the most famous rivalry between two horses in the 1950s was between Swaps and Nashua. Both horses were born in 1952, Swaps coming from California and Nashua from Kentucky. In 1955 they began their racing careers and quickly achieved fame with superb performances and record-breaking times. The two horses finally competed against each other in the 1955 Kentucky Derby, in which Swaps just took the finishing line ahead of his rival. By this point there was huge interest throughout the United States in the battle between the two horses; so when they met again later that year at Washington Park in Chicago, the race was broadcast to the nation by CBS. This time it would be Nashua who took the trophy home by six lengths, although many people have pointed to the fact that Swaps was suffering from an injured hoof, which slowed his performance. Despite the defeat—his first in nine races as a three-year-old—Swaps went on break more records and win more trophies, as did Nashua. Nashua was crowned Horse of the Year in 1955, and Swaps took that title a year later.

Kentucky Derby winner Swaps, ridden by Willie Shoemaker, stands before the Winner's Circle at Hollywood Park, California, in 1955.

As well as great horses, there were great races. One of the biggest races on the calendar was (and still is) the Kentucky Derby at the Churchill Downs track in Louisville. By 1950 the Kentucky Derby was almost 80 years old, and the decade was a successful one for both the race and the track. The first national TV broadcast of the Derby went out on May 3, 1952. A film patrol system, which recorded all races on film stock, was installed in 1954, thereby allowing officials to watch replays in the event of a dispute.

Winners of the Kentucky Derby during the fifties included Count Turf (1951), Determine (1954), Needles (1956), and Tim Tam (1958). The Derby was also the one race that Native Dancer lost (in 1953), although only by a fraction: In fact, there were allegations that the overwhelming favorite had been physically pushed into second place by another horse. The race was won by Dark Star, who never had another win.

Decline

Although racing began the 1950s in a promising fashion, it did not end the decade in the same way. Once the postwar euphoria had died away, there began a steady decline in the fortunes of U.S. racecourses. There were some signs of trouble early in the decade. The Centennial Racetrack in Littleton, Colorado, opened on July 4, 1950, with predictions that it would bring in an income of $400,000 on every racing day. By the end of that year, however, the figures revealed that the course was only taking $50,000 each racing day. Other racetracks were experiencing similarly disappointing results by the end of the fifties.

The economy was booming, and Americans were finding alternative ways to spend their money than horse racing, such as on an increasing range of consumer goods. There was also growth in many other gambling activities, such as casinos and dog racing. Arguably the most crucial factor in the decline, however, was the failure of the horse-racing community fully to embrace television. It was reasoned that if potential betters were at home watching the races on television, they would not be down at the track parting with their money (offtrack betting did not begin to be legalized in the United States until the 1970s). The reasoning was flawed. Other sports, such as baseball, embraced television enthusiastically and greatly increased their popularity. Across the Atlantic in the United Kingdom, which was committed to televised racing, the sport went from strength to strength. Although racing attendance was still significant in 1959, horse racing in the United States was facing a steady decline in popularity.

See Also:

Games and Pastimes • Leisure Industry • Sports • Sports and TV

HOUSE UN-AMERICAN ACTIVITIES COMMITTEE

The House Un-American Activities Committee was a government body that aimed to combat communism. It is most famous for its investigations into communist infiltration of the movie industry. As a result of the committee's activities many people lost their livelihoods.

The House Un-American Activities Committee (HUAC) was an investigative body of the U.S. House of Representatives. In the late 1940s and early 1950s its investigations into communist influence in American politics and society riveted the nation. HUAC's activities were very controversial. To its supporters HUAC played an important role in the fight against communism. Critics, however, saw its investigations as irresponsible witch hunts that condemned the innocent and the guilty alike.

The House Un-American Activities Committee of the late 1940s was a continuation of a House special committee, informally known as the Dies Committee (*see box opposite*), that was charged with investigating communist and Nazi influence in the United States in the late 1930s as World War II (1939–1945) loomed. As a "special committee," the Dies Committee had no legislative responsibilities. Its job was not to propose or pass laws but simply to hold fact-finding hearings and report the results to the House of Representatives.

The Dies Committee met frequently in 1938 and 1939, then less so in 1940 and 1941. Following the American entry into World War II in December 1941 the committee's activities lapsed almost completely: It was not disbanded but met very rarely. The committee was revived in 1946, but what really returned the now permanent House Un-American Activities Committee to prominence was the Republican victory in the 1946 congressional elections. Having been out of power for 14 years, the new Republican majority was eager to use its control over Congress to exert its authority and create a new political climate. Newly elected representative Richard M. Nixon (1913–1994), a Republican and staunch anti-communist elected from a district that had previously supported the Democrats, was the prototypical new member of HUAC. Nixon and his fellow committee members pushed for a broad investigation of communist influence in American life.

Attack on Hollywood

In October 1947 HUAC began hearings into the role of communists in Hollywood and the American entertainment industry in general. It was fertile ground. The Depression of the 1930s had led many in Hollywood to join left-wing groups, including the Communist Party of the United States. In addition, during the early 1940s, with the United States and the Soviet Union fighting together against Nazi Germany, major Hollywood studios had produced movies and documentaries sympathetic to America's wartime communist ally.

Several prominent directors and writers were called before HUAC to testify about their political beliefs and

Members of the House Un-American Activities Committee, including future President Richard Nixon (far right), visit the house of committee chairman J. Parnell Thomas (second left).

THE DIES COMMITTEE

The first incarnation of what would become the House Un-American Activities Committee was known as the Dies Committee for its first chairman, a conservative Democrat from East Texas named Martin Dies (1901–1972). In 1938 Dies and other members of the House of Representatives pushed for a committee that would investigate the "extent, character, and objects of un-American propaganda activities." The committee would target both foreign agents and their American sympathizers. The House Special Committee to Investigate Un-American Activities and Propaganda, under Dies's leadership, came into being in August 1938.

The particular phrase "un-American" was employed for more than one reason. On the surface, the very broad nature of the term "un-American" meant that it could apply equally to either of the great perceived foreign menaces of the late 1930s: communism and Nazism. Dies did lead inquests into the extent of Nazi influence and the possibility of Nazi sabotage in the United States. However, the committee undoubtedly saw communism as the more serious threat, a reflection of the chairman's own political tendencies. Dies had modeled the committee on earlier short-term investigations into communist propaganda and espionage in the United States in the early 1930s.

The other great advantage of the use of the term "un-American" was that it allowed Dies to attack his own political opponents. Dies himself stood at the far right of the Democratic Party and had become a fierce opponent of the liberal social policies pursued by President Franklin D. Roosevelt (1933–1945) as part of his New Deal program. During the course of its attempts to combat communism the Dies Committee investigated a number of New Deal programs. One example was the Federal Theatre Project, in which government funds were used to put on plays. Hallie Flanagan, the head of the program, was subpoenaed to appear before the committee and answer charges that the project was a hive of communist activity. By investigating programs associated with the New Deal, the Dies Committee was able to suggest that there was something intrinsically "un-American" about Roosevelt's policies. The taint of a connection with communism and "un-American" beliefs dogged the New Deal ever after, even though Dies's investigations uncovered no evidence of links to communism.

Congressman Martin Dies, Jr., was the head of the House Special Committee to Investigate Un-American Activities and Propaganda.

affiliations. A few, such as director Elia Kazan (1909–2003), agreed to cooperate with the committee. Asked in 1952 to "name names," Kazan implicated a number of people who had shared his interest in communism in the 1930s. However, others called before the committee refused to do so. In 1947 one group of screenwriters and directors defied HUAC by citing their First Amendment rights to free speech and freedom of association.

The group included director Edward Dmytryk, screenwriters Ring Lardner, Jr., and Dalton Trumbo, and John Howard Lawson, the first president of the Screen Writers Guild. The group later became known as the Hollywood Ten. When asked whether he had ever been a member of the Communist Party, each claimed the right not to answer. The Hollywood Ten were held to be in contempt of Congress for refusing to testify; and although they appealed to the federal courts for help, a U.S. Court of Appeals upheld their contempt charges.

The members of the Hollywood Ten were sentenced to prison for up to a year. The jail sentences were to prove to be only the beginning of their misfortunes, however. As well as losing their short-term freedom, the defendants also lost their long-term livelihoods. The major Hollywood studios agreed to suspend the contracts

ACHIEVEMENTS AFTER THE BLACKLIST

Kirk Douglas plays the title role in the movie *Spartacus*. The screenplay was the work of blacklisted writer Dalton Trumbo.

The 1947 HUAC hearings into communist influence in Hollywood ensnared some of the movie industry's biggest names. Among others, the director Edward Dmytryk and screenwriters Dalton Trumbo and Ring Lardner, Jr., were called to testify about their membership in the Communist Party in the 1930s.

Dmytryk, Trumbo, and Lardner refused to testify and became members of the famed Hollywood Ten, who were sent to prison for contempt of Congress. Perhaps worse, they were also placed on the blacklist of people who could not be hired by the Hollywood studios. The career of some members, such as screenwriter Alvah Bessie, never fully recovered after the blacklisting.

Midway into his prison term Dmytryk agreed to cooperate with HUAC. He was released early from jail and removed from the blacklist. He went on to direct two of the most famous World War II movies of the 1950s: *The Caine Mutiny* (1954) and *The Young Lions* (1958).

Trumbo and Lardner were steadfast in their refusal to betray their friends. After being released from prison, each endured long sentences on the blacklist. As writers, however, they could work under assumed names. Trumbo even won an Oscar after writing under the name Robert Rich (*The Brave One*, 1957).

Finally, in the early 1960s the blacklist system began to crack. In 1960 Trumbo was openly credited as the screenwriter for two major movies: Otto Preminger's *Exodus* and Stanley Kubrick's *Spartacus*. In the climax to the latter movie the followers of the rebel slave leader Spartacus refuse to betray him, even though it costs them their lives. The scene was a thinly veiled attack on those people who gave up their friends to HUAC.

One director who did "name names" was Elia Kazan, who appeared before HUAC in 1952. Consequently, Kazan was never blacklisted. He directed several of the most iconic films of the 1950s: *A Streetcar Named Desire* (1951), *Viva Zapata!* (1952), and *On the Waterfront* (1954). Significantly, the hero of the latter film, the dockworker Terry Malloy, is someone who betrays his colleagues for the common good.

In spite of his great artistic and commercial success, Kazan was treated as a pariah by many in Hollywood. In 1999 Kazan—then in his nineties—was honored with a lifetime achievement award at the Oscars. Even a half-century after the HUAC hearings such an honor was still resented by many within the movie industry. The awards ceremony was picketed by protesters, and many inside the auditorium refused to applaud the controversial director.

of the Hollywood Ten and further declared: "We will not knowingly employ a communist or a member of any party or group which advocates the overthrow of the government of the United States by force or by any illegal or unconstitutional method." In practice this meant that anyone who refused to testify before HUAC could not expect to work in the movie business. This also applied to anyone implicated by the testimony of another or anyone even suspected of past communist sympathies.

HUAC renewed its investigation into communists in Hollywood in 1951 and continued the inquest until 1954. Pioneering TV comedienne Lucille Ball (1911–1989) made a vague confession of past left-wing activities and was treated leniently by the committee. However, a number of other major actors, including Sam Jaffe, Lee Grant, and Zero Mostel, invoked their Fifth Amendment rights against self-incrimination. They joined the hundreds of actors, directors, writers, and technicians on the blacklist, the list of people who would not be hired by the studios. The blacklist cost the American entertainment industry the services of some of its most talented writers and performers.

The pressure from HUAC also caused the major studios to shy away from any projects that might have been seen to contain a liberal message or offer any form of social criticism. Out of a need for self-preservation the studios also began to produce rabidly anticommunist movies in order to prove their patriotism.

Communists in government

As well as targeting the entertainment industry, HUAC also pursued alleged communist spies and sympathizers in American government itself. The most famous such case was triggered by the testimony in 1948 of journalist Whittaker Chambers (1901–1961), who had been an active member of the Communist Party of the United States in the 1930s, but who had later turned against his former comrades. Chambers enthusiastically "named names" of fellow communists for the committee. One of the people he implicated was State Department official Alger Hiss (1904–1996), who had held very sensitive and powerful government positions in the 1930s and 1940s. Chambers accused Hiss of having been a spy for the Soviet Union. Chambers also testified that he had liaised between Hiss and the KGB, the Soviet intelligence agency.

When Hiss was called before HUAC, he vigorously denied the accusations made by Chambers. Hiss also sued Chambers for libel. During the proceedings of that suit Chambers produced copies of secret State Department documents that he claimed to have received from Hiss. Chambers also led HUAC investigators to a trove of documents and microfilms that he had hidden in a hollowed-out pumpkin at his rural Maryland home. Although he was never convicted of espionage, Hiss was convicted of perjury in 1950. He continued to claim his innocence until his death in 1996. However, evidence discovered shortly before Hiss died suggested that Chambers's accusations had been true (*see box on p. 88*).

Education

From 1952 to 1954 HUAC also investigated possible communist influence in American universities. Many colleges responded by requiring professors and other employees to take loyalty oaths foreswearing any involvement in communism. University employees were also strongly encouraged to cooperate with the HUAC investigation. Over the course of HUAC's inquest into American higher education some 100 faculty members were fired for refusing to testify before the committee or for having been implicated by the testimony of others.

By the early 1950s, however, HUAC began to be overshadowed by investigations in the Senate, which had been the primary investigative house of Congress for much of the country's history. Jealous perhaps of HUAC's prominence, the Senate established a Permanent Subcommittee on Investigations as part of the Senate Committee on Government Operations. This provided the opening for ambitious Wisconsin Senator Joseph McCarthy (1908–1957), whose accusations of

Members of the Hollywood Ten enter the federal court in Washington, D.C., to answer charges of contempt of Congress for their refusal to cooperate with the HUAC hearings.

EVIDENCE AFTER THE TRIAL: THE VENONA DECRYPTS

The politically explosive clash between Alger Hiss, a high-ranking State Department official who played a key role in Franklin D. Roosevelt's administration, and his HUAC accusers played out without a key piece of evidence that was kept secret at the time. Hiss was accused of being a spy for the Soviet Union; and although he was never convicted of espionage, he was sent to prison for perjury for his denials to HUAC and in court. Hiss maintained his innocence throughout the ordeal.

Even as HUAC investigated possible communist influence in American politics and society, the Central Intelligence Agency (CIA) had amassed a mountain of relevant information through the Venona Project. "Venona" was the CIA codename for a program of codebreaking that intercepted and decrypted communications between the Soviet Embassy in Washington, D.C., and its government in Moscow. Although the Venona Project could not crack all the Soviet codes, it did gather a tremendous number of partial decrypts, like small pieces of a huge puzzle.

The Venona intercepts were kept classified for the entirety of the Cold War but were finally released to the public in 1995 and 1996. An intercepted message from 1945 was especially damning for Hiss: It referred to a Soviet spy codenamed "Ales" who had accompanied President Roosevelt to the Yalta Conference and was still passing key secrets to the Soviets. Hiss had been on the Yalta mission, leading CIA officials of the time to conclude that he was the spy mentioned. In 1988 a KGB defector had already claimed that Hiss was the spy "Ales."

For his part, Hiss continued to claim his innocence, going so far as to ask the Russian government to make public any information it had on the case. In 1992 the head of the Russian military intelligence archives denied that his government had any evidence that Hiss had ever been in the service of the Soviet Union. Hiss died in 1996, shortly after the release of the Venona materials. Although Hiss still has his defenders, Venona has led many scholars to conclude that HUAC was right about Hiss after all.

Whittaker Chambers (far right) testifies before HUAC. The evidence given by Chambers centered around the allegation that State Department official Alger Hiss was a spy.

communist influence in America were so wild that they made the excesses of HUAC seem almost mild by comparison. The Senate hearings spear-headed by McCarthy took away much of the attention that had been focused on HUAC. The extreme nature of McCarthy's attacks eventually led to him being discredited, however. In particular, a televised investigation into possible communist activity in the Army revealed the tenuous nature of McCarthy's allegations. McCarthy was censured by the Senate, and the momentum for further investigations from any organization began to fade.

Although it met rarely after the mid-1950s, the House Un-American Activities Committee was not formally disbanded. It was renamed the House Internal Security Committee in 1969 and then was quietly abolished in 1975.

Although the committee had its successes, such as the Alger Hiss affair, the HUAC era is now generally seen as a dark episode in American history. HUAC attempted to protect the United States from the twin evils of communism and Nazism, ideologies associated with the suppression of free speech. To do so, however, it effectively made the expression of certain political views a crime and destroyed the livelihoods of many U.S. citizens.

See Also:

Ball, Lucille • Blacklist • Hiss, Alger • McCarthy, Joseph • McCarthy Hearings • Movie Industry • Nixon, Richard M. • *On the Waterfront* • Spies and Spying

HOUSING AND HOUSEHOLD APPLIANCES

In the 1950s there was a significant transformation in housing as a result of suburbanization. Middle-class whites left the cities and moved into new, modern homes in the suburbs that they equipped with the latest electronic household appliances.

The years following World War II (1939–1945) witnessed an unprecedented housing boom across the United States. Both private and federal projects sought to meet the huge demand for good, affordable housing created by the burgeoning population and the return of millions of servicemen to civilian life. For many Americans the ideal was still the self-owned, detached single-family house with a large backyard, and as a consequence during the period low-density suburbs continued to sprawl outward from the big cities. Pre-fabrication of materials, low-cost construction methods, and the increasing popularity of the pared-down "Contemporary" architectural style, together with generous federal subsidies, helped achieve a profound transformation in housing.

The new suburbs

The suburbanization of the cities had begun at the beginning of the 20th century, as the prosperous white middle classes left the cramped and heavily commercialized city centers to live in outlying communities, where idyllic houses with mansard roofs and Gothic cupolas nestled among lawns and shrubberies. Such housing was made affordable by the availability of plentiful cheap land and the use of inexpensive construction methods and materials. Expanding networks of roads and railroads enabled commuters to reach their jobs back in the city.

In order to meet the country's expanding housing needs, the federal authorities increasingly encouraged home ownership. In 1939, for example, the government introduced tax deductions for mortgages, and through the GI Bill of 1944 it offered returning servicemen cheap mortgages. Such measures encouraged construction companies to invest heavily in vast new suburban, or "tract," developments, complete with roads, parks, swimming pools, and community schools. One of the most notable development companies of the period was Levitt and Sons, whose "Levittowns" rapidly became a byword for American 1950s suburbia (*see p. 90*). The first Levittown was finished in 1951.

In terms of increasing levels of home ownership federal policies were undoubtedly successful. In 1940, 43.6 percent of householders owned their own home. By 1950 this figure had leaped to 55 percent, and by 1960 it had reached 61.9 percent. The vast majority of these houses were of the type that symbolized the "American dream"—detached, single-family units. In 1950, 73 percent of householder-owned homes were of this kind; in 1960, 78.3 percent.

This photo shows a typical suburban house in Cold Spring Harbor, Long Island, in 1952. Increasingly the prosperous middle classes moved to the outlying city communities.

LEVITTOWNS

The New York City entrepreneur William J. Levitt (1907–1994) founded his construction company in 1929. Initially he specialized in building luxury houses, but during World War II the company won government contracts to build standardized mass-produced homes for naval workers. After the war Levitt turned his company's expertise to producing similar homes for civilians, creating vast suburban estates that were christened "Levittowns" after the company owner.

The first Levittown—on Long Island, east of New York City—was begun in 1947 and completed in 1951. During this period 17,450 homes were built using an industrialized construction process that was broken down into 27 steps, each performed by a member of the crew. At one point as many as 30 houses were being built every day. Similar developments followed in Bucks County, Pennsylvania, and in New Jersey.

A contemporary aerial photograph of the Long Island Levittown suggests the somewhat monotonous layout of the streets and houses. Indeed, most of the houses were very simple—in outline little more than rectangular boxes with pitched roofs—but Levitt also provided less conventional housing units, sometimes featuring the flat roofs and plate-glass windows characteristic of the "Contemporary" style. Most of the houses incorporated garages or carports, open planning, and smart, streamlined, and fully equipped kitchens, the last often the main selling point for the house.

The Levittown houses were hugely popular. Hoards of potential buyers flooded to view the model show houses, and in 1949, 1,400 contracts were signed on one day for properties in the Long Island development. Mortgages were offered on very lenient terms. The complete price for a high-end "Country Clubber" home in Pennsylvania was $17,500, with a monthly all-inclusive mortgage payment of $100. There was a modest down payment of $2,600, but veterans had to pay even less—$1,000—or even nothing at all. Levitt, however, refused to sell his homes to African Americans, a policy that led to protracted courtroom battles.

The Levittowns were among the most successful responses to the acute postwar housing shortage. Despite criticisms of the uniformity of the projects, other studies, notably Herbert Gans's book *The Levittowners* (1967), noted the homeowners' feeling of pride in their houses and their heightened sense of privacy, security, and well-being.

A homeowner opens a window in a recently constructed house in Levittown, Pennsylvania, in 1953.

An apartment block in Marseilles, France, designed by Le Corbusier. Le Corbusier's ideas about public housing were extremely influential among American architects.

Levittowns and other similar suburban developments were often exclusively white. Many middle-class, white Americans moved to the suburbs not only because they wanted space and greenery and a more healthful, crime-free environment, but also because they did not want to live in "black" or "mixed" inner-city neighborhoods, which were largely the result of the mass migration of African American families from the South to the cheaper districts of northern cities during the early 20th century. After the Supreme Court outlawed school segregation in 1954, increasing numbers of whites relocated to the suburbs. It became a cliché for white families to claim that they were moving to the suburbs "for the kids," meaning that they did not want their children to go to mixed-race schools. Moreover, in many new suburbs, including the Levittowns, African Americans were simply excluded from buying homes. In addition, they found it hard to get the cheap mortgages provided by the Federal Housing Administration, which ran an elaborate and discriminatory credit-rating system that included ethnicity as one of its factors. Under the system the elderly and families headed by a woman were also similarly penalized.

While the new suburbs were enthusiastically adopted by the white middle classes, they also increasingly attracted criticism. The monotony of the housing, the sometimes poor construction standards, and the lack of civic amenities and community spirit were commonly voiced concerns. Another was the rigid conformism that critics claimed prevailed, a conformism that chimed well with the political and social McCarthyism of the era. More recently criticism has also focused on the harmful effects on the urban environment that such suburbs helped create: discrepancy between prosperous suburbs and run-down city centers, and the overdependence on the automobile as a means of getting suburban homeowners to their place of work.

Public housing

While postwar federal government saw the encouragement of private ownership as a priority in meeting the national housing shortage, it was also aware that it had a duty to provide low-cost public housing for low-income families. The traditional working-class tenement blocks of cities had long ceased to be adequate in terms of both their quality and their capacity to house the rapidly increasing urban population. In 1949 a revision to the Housing Act called for "a decent home and a suitable living environment for every American family" and introduced an ambitious federal program under which 800,000 new public homes were to be built by 1955.

As in Europe, where wartime bombing campaigns had destroyed millions of urban homes, the authorities attempted to meet the acute shortage in cheap public housing through the construction of high-rise concrete apartment blocks. Such blocks took their inspiration from the ideas of European modernists, notably the Swiss architect Le Corbusier (1887–1965). During the 1930s Le

Corbusier conceived the idea of industrially produced, high-density *machines à habiter* ("machines for living in") and in the postwar period designed the enormously influential Unité d'Habitation ("Housing Block") in the southern French city of Marseilles. With its balconies, flat roof, standardized dwelling units, and communal facilities, it became the prototype for many collective housing projects across the world.

During the 1950s the federal Public Housing Authority initiated numerous high-rise housing projects across the country, sometimes leveling whole urban neighborhoods in the process. Among the most famous of these developments were the Pruitt-Igoe apartment blocks in St. Louis, Missouri, designed by the Japanese-American architect Minoru Yamasaki (1912–1986) and completed in 1956. At the time of its construction the 11-story, 2,740-unit Pruitt-Igoe, with its whole floor of communal facilities including laundries and meeting rooms, was widely heralded as ushering in a new age of public housing in the United States.

However, such hopes were dashed when the project—initially aimed at both black and white middle-income residents—rapidly became a poor black ghetto as white Americans increasingly migrated to the St. Louis suburbs. As in similar projects across the country, inhabitants felt divorced from the communal spaces of the project, which consequently became neglected and unsafe. Elevators were vandalized, corridors were defaced by graffiti, and the surrounding parkland became a depository for garbage. Crime was rife; arson was common. It was widely felt that "vertical slums" had replaced the old low-rise ones.

By 1969 even the secretary of the Housing and Urban Development Department conceded that "public housing built on the basis of sheer functionalism ... had the greatest vandalism and least interest among occupants in maintaining the building." Other critics complained that the projects had fragmented neighborhood identities and destroyed community pride. Some blamed Le Corbusier, others the low level of federal funding for the program, which had resulted in cramped housing units and poor maintenance; still others argued that the racism of the era had resulted in a metropolitan split between prosperous white suburbs and poor black city centers. When Pruitt-Igoe was finally demolished in 1972, it was widely seen as symbolic of the failure of the postwar federal housing program.

"Contemporary" housing

During the 1950s there was a concern not only with the quantity of housing but also with its quality. There was also widespread optimism about what might be achieved. After the difficult war years many Americans felt as if they were starting afresh as peace and prosperity enabled them to refocus their energies on the home and family life. For many, especially the returning veterans, it was the first time they had been able to buy their own home.

There was almost a national obsession with houses and home

The Pruitt-Igoe housing project in St. Louis, Missouri, was built in the 1950s and demolished in 1972. The majority of the residents detested living there.

MUTUAL HOUSING ASSOCIATIONS

One option open to American families in the 1950s was membership in a mutual housing association. In this cooperative venture families—perhaps as many as several hundred—would pool their resources to buy land that was then split into building lots. Architects were then invited to create a range of standardized house designs that could be quickly and cheaply constructed out of prefabricated components such as steel I-beams and concrete blocks.

The housing associations were often inspired by utopian or socialistic ideals: a desire to create a harmonious community removed from the stresses and tribulations of city life. A guiding spirit for many association members was the pioneering American architect Frank Lloyd Wright (1867–1959), who since the 1930s had been designing and building what he called "Usonian" settlements. These housing settlements featured low-cost, labor-saving homes for the middle classes. One of the most extensive realizations of Wright's Usonian ideas was constructed for a housing association in Pleasantville, New York, in the early 1950s.

The houses created under such plans were often very simple but "Contemporary" in style. For example, designs for the cooperative housing project at Brentwood, Los Angeles (completed in 1950), featured exposed concrete blocks in the houses' open-plan interiors.

improvements. Newspapers issued magazine supplements (such as the *Los Angeles Examiner's Pictorial Living*) that lavishly illustrated the best in contemporary home design, while home-improvement guides such as *Your Dream Home* (1950) by Hubbard Cobb and *Better Homes and Gardens Handyman's Book* (1951) regularly featured on the bestseller lists. Concern with the home went hand in hand with the reinvigorated consumerism of the period as people sought to fill their houses with the latest must-have appliances and up-to-date interior designs.

The optimism of the time also expressed itself in a new openness to modern developments in architecture and design. Before World War II few Americans had responded positively to the spare modernist housing designs by architects such as Frank Lloyd Wright (*see box*), Marcel Breuer (1902–1981), and Rudolf Schindler (1887–1953). All-white, cuboid designs such as Schindler's Buck House (1934) in Los Angeles were commissioned by a wealthy elite and were widely considered to be "clinical" and uncomfortable. Indeed, many people considered such houses to be more like factories than homes. By the late 1940s, however, attitudes to modernist housing design had undergone a profound change.

In 1945 George Nelson and Henry Wright published *Tomorrow's House: A Complete Guide for the Home Builder*. They declared their aim was "to disturb [readers] who keep their milk in the latest refrigerator, drive to business in the newest car, but persist in thinking that the Cape Cod cottage remains the snappiest idea in a home." Nelson and Wright argued that building "traditional" houses produced either "cheap imitation[s]" or "outrageously expensive fake[s]." If modern houses were to maintain their value, they warned, they needed to use the modern, functional styles and the latest technologies and materials. "Every architect," the authors declared, "[should] stiffen his backbone [and tell] the client 'You cannot walk backwards into the future.'"

While Nelson and Wright had been writing for a somewhat conservative readership, by the beginning of the following decade their ideas had found wide acceptance. Part of the reason for this change was, as mentioned above, the more optimistic, confident mood of the period. Another important factor, however, was that modernism itself had changed. The severe, rigorous "International style" of the European modernists had been tempered by a recognition that houses had to be more than "machines for living in" but instead comfortable, pleasurable, and relaxing places to be. This new, user-friendly kind of modernism became known as the "Contemporary" style.

The new style found its purest expression in the Case Study Houses commissioned by John Entenza, editor of the West Coast avant-garde magazine *Arts and Architecture*, and received widespread coverage in the media (*see box on p. 94*). The houses, usually featuring flat roofs and extensive use of glass and open-plan spaces, proved enormously influential on the housing of the time. While few developers were brave enough to produce such homes on a massive scale, most were willing to include concessions to some of their stylistic innovations, such as plate-glass "picture" windows, and the open-plan lounge and dining room, and above all the streamlined kitchen.

Inside the 1950s home

It was often inside the home that the 1950s "Contemporary" style was most in evidence. A visitor to even quite a modest house of the period would have been struck by the sense of space and light created in the open-plan area of the lower floor. This might include both the home's living and dining area (the "dinette") and frequently also the kitchen (*see p. 97*), although this was often made separate from the main living area through the use of a dividing

THE CASE STUDY HOUSES

The Case Study House program lasted from 1945 to 1966 and encompassed 36 projects for houses in and around Los Angeles; two-thirds of the projects were actually built. The motivation of the program's founder, John Entenza (1903–1984), was to put inspirational models of low-cost housing before the construction industry and the general public. Like many of his contemporaries, Entenza was deeply concerned by the nationwide housing shortage, but he was also worried that in the postwar rush to build homes, developers would produce substandard housing in outmoded traditionalist styles. For Entenza the "Contemporary" style was the best way to produce houses that were both economical and pleasurable and workable environments to live in. For this reason the completed houses also included furnishings, lighting, and fully equipped kitchens. The lifestyle of potential inhabitants was as much on show as the architecture itself.

The Case Study houses generated an enormous amount of publicity and excitement. Not only did Entenza publish photographs and plans of the homes in his magazine *Arts and Architecture*, but he also opened them up for viewings by the general public. In 1946–1947 some 368,000 visitors visited the first six houses to be completed. The mainstream press also brought the houses to national attention in features illustrated with glossy photographs.

Contributors to the program included some of the best-known architects and designers of the period, including Charles and Ray Eames (House no. 8; completed 1949), Craig Ellwood (House nos. 16, 17, and 18; completed 1953, 1955, and 1958 respectively), and Pierre Koenig (House nos. 21 and 22; completed 1958 and 1960 respectively). The houses were very varied, but all were concerned with creating the sense of light, spaciousness, and fluidity that was characteristic of the "Contemporary" style. Open-plan living, double-height rooms, Japanese-style interior partitions, and floor-to-ceiling sliding glass panels that brought the exterior garden "into" the interior were among the recurring features.

Innovative and experimental, too, was the use of materials and construction techniques. Ellwood's houses used steel frames, while Formica was often used for work surfaces and Naugahyde for upholstery. Many of the houses featured the state-of-the-art gadgetry popular in the 1950s: automated garage doors, hi-fi equipment, and multifunctional kitchen units, such as the combined stove/dishwasher/sink in Case Study House no. 21.

By the end of the 1950s, by which time living standards and consumer expectations had both risen dramatically, the program's initial concern with providing prototypes for low-cost housing had largely been jettisoned in favor of experimental design "statements." The Case Study Houses of this period tended to be extremely luxurious. Koenig's Case Study House no. 22 featured a swimming pool and was cantilevered out from a rocky outcrop of the Hollywood Hills overlooking Los Angeles. Nevertheless, the Case Study program proved remarkably influential on the housing of the period, providing the American public with inspirational "dream houses" to which all American homeowners could aspire in however small degree.

breakfast bar or two-way cupboard unit. Large glass windows let in plenty of light and allowed tranquil views onto the surrounding garden.

The rationale for the open planning of the "Contemporary" house was that owing to technological advances, interior walls no longer needed to be load-bearing and could therefore largely be dispensed with. Separate rooms serving different functions were simply an expensive waste of space. In the 1950s "Contemporary" house the open-plan living room was multi-functional and flexible. The housewife, for example, could cook dinner while keeping an eye on her children playing across on the other side of the room or could serve dinner to her family simply by passing the food across the cupboard divide or through a serving hatch. The open planning thus perfectly suited the more informal, family-oriented lifestyles that prevailed after the war.

Walls and floors

"Contemporary" decorations and fittings emphasized comfort and texture as well as functionality. Walls often featured a variety of coverings, from tongue-and-groove siding or large sheets of veneered plywood to exposed concrete or bricks. Some form of central heating was now quite common (*see box on p. 96*), so that carpets were no longer needed for insulation. Instead, floors surfaces were often wooden, perhaps wood block or parquet, although vinyl, rubber, or linoleum tiles were also popular. Such surfaces had the advantage of being easy to clean, an important consideration in the 1950s home, where middle-class households usually no longer had servants, and housewives had to take on the responsibility of cleaning and cooking themselves.

Even if people did not live in a house built during the 1950s, they could give a house a "Contemporary" feel through the use of furniture, lighting, and accessories. Furniture of the period, such as the wire or molded-plywood chairs designed by Charles Eames (1907–1978) and manufactured by Herman Miller, was often lightweight. This enabled it to be easily moved around the open-plan living/dining room both for the purposes of cleaning and to serve the different purposes required of furniture in a multi-functional space. Because such spaces had to be so functional, storage was crucial as a way of keeping the room free of clutter. Typical of the period were "storagewalls," a flexible grid of cupboards, drawers, and shelving that could be used to keep books and a radio as well to as to display ornaments or plants.

The bedrooms and bathroom were of course separated from the main living space. The upper-floor rooms were often reached by an open staircase. Quite often, however, homes were arranged over a single story, with the bedrooms housed in a separate "wing" that formed an L-shape with the main living block. Bathrooms were tiled and thus easy to clean, and bathroom suites (now often made out of synthetic materials such as fiberglass and plexiglass) were available in a wide range of colors. Showers were by now common in American homes.

The scientific household

The "Contemporary" household was designed with efficiency and user-friendliness in mind, and most new houses, such as those in the Levittowns, were sold complete with a full range of domestic appliances that promised to take the drudgery out of housework. One Levitttown advertisement lauded its houses' "automatic kitchen center" produced by General Electric and listed its benefits almost as if the housewife had no part to play at all: "[It] cooks food ... flushes away food waste ... washes dishes ... even cleans and dries clothes." The aim was to create—or at least create the illusion of—a scientific, self-servicing household that would liberate the housewife from her age-old chores.

Many of these products, from large-scale appliances such as electric ovens, refrigerators, and dishwashers to small devices such as toasters and blenders, had been available long before World War II, although often at a cost. During the late 1940s and 1950s, however, American companies such as Westinghouse, Sunbeam, Hoover, and General Electric led the way in producing affordable products that would have mass-market appeal. Many prewar "white" goods had been cumbersome and ugly. Now styling became at least as important as the technologies the products used. Pastel colors, chrome fittings, and curved, ergonomic shapes made what were relatively new technologies palatable to the general public. Small innovations, such as oven lights and timers, refined and extended the appliances' functionality.

Popular mass-market electrical kitchen appliances, such as this Sunbeam Mixmaster Junior electric mixer, were continuously restyled during the decade.

After the austerity of the war years, when much industrial production was geared toward the military, the 1950s consumer quickly developed a seemingly insatiable appetite for both domestic gadgetry and design. Companies brought out a succession of restyled models that often added little to those preceding them, but which sought to sustain the iconic image of the brand and to attract new custom, even among those who already owned the product. For instance, the popular Sunbeam Mixmaster, first introduced in 1930, went through a number of incarnations during the 1950s, featuring at various times "automotive" styling, pastel colors, and chrome. Even while advertisements promised product durability, 1950s consumers enthusiastically embraced the new "disposable" culture.

This picture shows a kitchen in a newly built house in Darien, Connecticut, in 1957. Open-plan kitchens replaced the more old-fashioned types that were normally hidden away.

HEATING HOMES

In 1940 just under two-thirds of Americans used coke, coal, or wood to heat their homes. Utility gas was used by some 11 percent of homes, while electricity was so rare that it was not included in Census statistics. During the postwar years gas-fired central heating systems soared in popularity, so that by 1960 almost half of households were using gas, while the share of coal, coke, and wood had dwindled to just over 16 percent. Many gas central heating systems still used the old-fashioned cast-iron radiators, but during the 1950s low "skirting" radiators were sometimes used or even set in grilled ducts in the floor in order to minimize their aesthetic effect. Despite the popularity of central heating, homeowners retained a nostalgia for the open hearth, and large "feature fireplaces" were built in homes throughout this period.

In the 1950s gas central heating systems took over from coke, coal, or wood fires as the most popular way of heating U.S. homes. Nevertheless, open hearths, such as this one, remained a central feature of many living rooms.

Many of the household electrical appliances of the decade have remained staples of the contemporary American household. A few, however, such as the automatic ironers, manufactured by the likes of Maytag and Conlon, and Westinghouse roasters (used as a subsidiary oven), proved to be short-lived fads. Microwave ovens, which were developed in the late 1940s, at first seemed doomed to go the same way. Initially both too large and too expensive for ordinary use, they became popular only in the 1960s, when tabletop versions were introduced.

Home improvements

Figures from the U.S. Bureau of Statistics showed that the housing boom of the late 1940s and 1950s had a hugely positive effect on the quantity of homes available to the majority of citizens. Overcrowding in housing—defined by the bureau as "units with more than one person per room"—fell from 20.2 percent in 1940 to 15.7 percent in 1950 and 11.5 percent in 1960.

There were also undoubted improvements in the quality of housing. Plumbing, for example, was one important area. In 1940 just over 45 percent of housing lacked "complete plumbing," defined as "hot and cold piped water, a bath-tub or shower, and a flush toilet." By 1950 that figure had fallen dramatically to just over 35 percent and by 1960 to just under 17 percent. Homes, moreover, simply became more comfortable places to be, as architects and industrial designers thought more carefully about the user-friendliness of their products, as general standards of living rose, and as the population turned its attention to the business of homemaking.

THE WONDER KITCHEN

"When a woman goes house-hunting, the place she usually heads for first is the kitchen," declared advertising copy for Levitt's surburban homes. During the 1950s the kitchen took center stage both in the homes of the period and in the aspirations of would-be homeowners. An up-to-date kitchen in the "Contemporary" style became a glamorous consumer icon in addition to being a symbol of prosperity and a leisured lifestyle.

During the 1930s kitchens had tended to be hidden away, secluded from the main living spaces of the typical family home. Stoves and storage units were often stand-alone units, and the whole kitchen was painted antiseptic white. Usually there were few electrical appliances. Cooking and washing were laborious and unsightly household chores, and in many middle-class homes much of this work was still done by a servant.

By the late 1940s and 1950s few households had domestic help, and for American women the kitchen became an important space—the "control center"—of the home. Accordingly, kitchens physically became part of the main domestic living space, so that the housewife could continue to play an integrated role in family life while still running the household affairs. Their new visibility also meant that kitchens had to be good to look at as well as pleasant places to be. White walls gave way to vibrant colors, and simulated-wood storage units became more like pieces of furniture.

Functionality, too, was crucial: American women wanted efficient, labor-saving kitchens that would enable them to spend as much time as possible away from them. The Levittown kitchens were thus fully fitted and streamlined, with sleek rows of cupboards, every electric appliance, and wipe-clean surfaces. Typical built-in gadgetry might include everything from a dishwasher and waste-disposal unit to a food-mixer. Everything was powered by electricity, which was considered much cleaner than the prewar gas.

An impressive, high-tech kitchen, such as this one in a luxury residence in Forest Hills, Long Island, was a vital part of the modern look of the time.

THE WESTINGHOUSE REFRIGERATOR

One of the most desirable domestic appliances of the 1950s, and subsequently a design icon of its age, was the Westinghouse refrigerator. Unlike most other household appliances, refrigerators actually got bigger in this period, and they took pride of place in the kitchen. A 1954 model, designed by Peter Muller-Munk Associates, for example, included a beverage drawer, tilting egg racks, fruit bins, and snack compartments as well as a 56-pound-freezer. The exteriors of Westinghouse refrigerators were "Contemporary" in style, featuring a molded-plastic casing in white or creamy yellow with a curved door and chrome handles.

Such refrigerators were glamorous as well as practical. In live television commercials the actress and pioneering presenter Betty Furness (1916–1994) was shown opening a Westinghouse to the tagline "You can be sure if it's Westinghouse," which became a national catchphrase. For contemporaries nothing perhaps seemed more representative of a culture of plenty and convenience than this chunky and capacious refrigerator design.

Actress Betty Furness films a Westinghouse commercial in 1952. Her catchphrase was "You can be sure if it's Westinghouse."

During the 1950s the American home, at least the American dream home found in advertisements and show houses, became the envy of the world. Both in the United States and overseas it became a symbol of the success and even righteousness of the American way of life and consequently came to occupy a central place in the communist–capitalist debate on the relative quality of life for peoples living under each system.

The "kitchen debate"

On July 24, 1959, Vice President Richard M. Nixon (1913–1994), during a visit to Moscow, showed the Soviet premier, Nikita Khrushchev (1894–1971), around an American trade and cultural exhibition. Very quickly a fierce debate broke out between the two politicians over the quality of life in their respective countries. Nixon claimed that in the United States "any steelworker could buy this house. They earn $3 an hour. This house costs about $100 a month to buy on a contract running 25 to 30 years." While Russians might be ahead of the Americans in space exploration, he suggested, in terms of everyday things such as televisions and washing machines, the opposite was the case. To all Nixon's arguments Khrushchev politely disagreed. American houses were not built to last, he said: "We build firmly. We build for our children and grandchildren."

The famous so-called "kitchen debate" shows the degree to which housing had become a central factor in the Cold War intellectual struggle between the two great political systems of the age. If capitalism could provide for the well-being of the mass of a country's citizens, what, critics asked, was the advantage of communism, which claimed that its main concern was the prosperity of the people.

Nixon's rosy picture of the state of American housing, however, concealed persistent problems. While private housing undoubtedly improved in terms of both quality and quantity during the 1950s, the same cannot be said for public housing, for all the idealistic ambitions of some authorities and architects in the postwar period. The subsequent failure of communal housing projects such as Pruitt-Igoe were emblematic of a broader failure of the federal authorities to provide adequate housing for the poor and especially for socially disadvantaged minorities. By the end of the decade there was an even greater polarization between the prosperous white suburbias and the underprivileged urban "ghettos" of the inner cities.

See Also:

Architecture • Automobile Culture • Black Americans • Design • Economy • Environment • Fuller, Buckminster • Nixon, Richard M. • Population • Poverty • Suburbs • Television

THE HOWDY DOODY SHOW

One of the first great successes of television, The Howdy Doody Show *was also one of the first programs to be aimed at children. It featured a puppet character with a cheerful freckled face and red hair, who became an enormous favorite of young viewers.*

The puppet that was to be the main character of *The Howdy Doody Show* throughout the 1950s first appeared on television in 1948. The previous year producers at NBC had decided that there was a need for a program for children to watch before dinner, after they had come in from playing. They discussed ideas for a program with Bob Smith (1917–1998), a talented entertainer who had starred in a children's radio show called *The Triple B Ranch*. Smith had developed a ranch hand character called Elmer, whose popular catchphrase was "howdy doody." When Smith brought brought his show to television in December 1947 as *Puppet Playhouse*, Elmer's name was changed to Howdy Doody, and Smith took the character name Buffalo Bob.

Development of Howdy Doody

The original Howdy Doody puppet was designed and made by Frank Paris. In 1948 Paris left the show with the puppet because of a disagreement over licensing rights. A new puppet was then built, complete with facial revisions. This was the model that became so recognizable: an all-American boy with a cheerful, freckled face and red hair, wearing boots and jeans.

The Howdy Doody Show helped establish television as a successful medium that could attract repeat viewers. It orginally went out as a one-hour show on Saturday afternoons, but its popularity soon prompted NBC to broadcast a half-hour show each weekday at 5:30 P.M. In 1948 and 1949 relatively few families had television sets, but those that did tuned in for suppertime viewing. Some families even went together to bars to watch because there were television sets there.

During the presidential election of 1948 the program launched a publicity campaign proposing Howdy Doody as president. Free campaign buttons were promised to anyone who would write in. The show's producers and NBC executives were astonished when, in response, they received some 60,000 letters, representing an estimated one-third of all television sets in America at that time. In 1949 *Puppet Playhouse* officially became known as *The Howdy Doody Show*.

Buffalo Bob, Howdy Doody, and Clarabell celebrate the 10th anniversary of *The Howdy Doody Show* in 1957. It was the first regular network series to be broadcast in color.

Since the program had such a loyal viewing public, it also became very popular with advertisers. It made big profits for products such as Kellogg's cereals, Ovaltine, Colgate, and Poll Parrot shoes. In a move that is familiar today but was innovative in 1950, the show eventually also made millions on merchandise, including comic books, lunchboxes, and bedroom décor that all featured Howdy Doody.

The other characters

As well as Buffalo Bob, *The Howdy Doody Show* had several other human characters. They included Clarabell the Clown, who only communicated by honking horns, Indian Princess Summerfall Winterspring, and Chief Thunderthud. There were also other puppets, including Dilly Dally, Phineas T. Bluster, the mayor of Doodyville (the town in which the program was set), and the Flub-A-Dub, who was an amalgamation of several animals. Another attraction was the live studio audience, known as the Peanut Gallery. Tickets for the audience were always in huge demand.

In 1956 *The Howdy Doody Show* was moved to Saturday mornings. It continued to be popular but eventually not enough to justify the mounting production costs. On September 24, 1960, it was taken off the air after 2,343 programs with the words "Goodbye kids," spoken by Clarabell—the first and last words the character ever said on the show.

See Also:

Advertising Industry • *Crockett, Davy* • *Mickey Mouse Club, The* • Television

IMJIN RIVER

The battle of the Imjin River at the height of the Korean War in 1951 was possibly the greatest individual action in the history of the British Army since World War II. Outnumbered ten to one by Chinese troops, the British 29th Brigade fought almost continuously for four days.

The U.S. Army 84th Engineer Battalion built the temporary Freedom Gate Bridge across the Imjin River in 1952, replacing the original structure destroyed by bombs.

The winter of 1950–1951 saw a dramatic reversal of fortunes for United Nations (UN) troops in Korea. Having advanced against North Korean forces right to the border with China, U.S.-led UN forces were then put into headlong retreat south by a massive Chinese invasion of more than 200,000 men in October 1950. The retreat was only stopped in late January 1951 when U.S. firepower and stretched Chinese supply lines pulled the Communist forces to a halt. UN and Chinese military units now faced each other from positions in the mountainous center of Korea.

The 6,000 men of the British 29th Brigade occupied positions just south of the Imjin River. The brigade consisted of the 1st Battalion Royal Northumberland Fusiliers, the 1st Battalion Gloucestershire Regiment (the "Glosters"), the 1st Battalion Royal Ulster Rifles, a small Belgian battalion, and some support elements from the 45th Regiment Royal Artillery, the 8th King's Royal Irish Hussars, and other units. The brigade was holding a 9-mile (14-km) section of front, its troops spread thinly in pockets.

Resistance and withdrawal

At 10:30 P.M. on April 21, 1951, 20,000 troops of the Chinese 63rd Army advanced across the shallow Imjin River to assault the 29th Brigade's positions. Despite mowing down huge numbers of Chinese soldiers, the British and Belgian troops could not stop the onslaught, and on April 23 Chinese forces managed to penetrate between 29th Brigade positions to attack from the rear. The Northumberland Fusiliers were forced to pull out, and the Chinese were able to occupy high ground from which they could fire down on the Allied soldiers. That evening the battle-scarred units of 29th Brigade tried to concentrate their positions together to make them more effective. The Glosters, however, remained stuck where they were and fought off 17 Chinese assaults during the night.

Despite heavy artillery support, the Glosters' fate looked sealed. They had virtually no ammunition, most men who were not dead had been wounded, and a relief effort on April 24 by tanks of the 8th Hussars ended in failure. Other units were also fighting desperately, and at one stage soldiers even resorted to throwing cans of food at the enemy, hoping to convince them the cans were hand grenades.

On April 25, having fought for 72 hours, the brigade was faced with a painful withdrawal under heavy fire. Troops of the Glosters, however, were unavoidably left behind. U.S. helicopters attempted to evacuate the Glosters' wounded but could not land because of heavy fire. Later that day the Glosters' commander, Lieutenant Colonel James Carne, gave the order for all surviving troops to attempt to break out. The Glosters suffered heavy casualties during the retreat, and half of the men were captured. Only 169 men of the 850 Glosters who began the action made it back to Allied lines.

The battle had cost 1,000 British casualties and was a crushing defeat. However, the courage of their resistance became a source of dark pride for the British people and produced a deep respect among Britain's allies.

See Also:

Armed Forces • China • Chosin Reservoir • Cold War • Inchon Landing • Korean War • Pusan Perimeter • Pyongyang • Seoul

IMMIGRATION

Legislators throughout the 1950s introduced a series of immigration laws that attempted to strike a balance between welcoming needed laborers and political refugees and preventing communists from infiltrating the country.

During the 1950s around 2.5 million people immigrated to the United States. Most were from Europe, whose countries were either still recovering from World War II (1939–1945) or coming under increasing Soviet domination. Significant numbers of immigrants also arrived from Latin America and Asia. Many more people wanted to move to the United States, but the federal quota system, which was first introduced in the 1920s, capped the annual numbers eligible for entry.

McCarran–Walter Act

In 1952 Senator Pat McCarran (1876–1954), a Democrat from Nevada, and Representative Francis Walter (1894–1963), a Democrat from Pennsylvania, sponsored a new immigration law: The Immigration and Nationality Act of 1952, also known as the McCarran–Walter Act, was in essence a piece of Cold War legislation that also recognized the newly independent former colonial countries in many parts of the world. The act permitted the exclusion or deportation of any alien who engaged or intended to engage in activities that were seen to threaten national security. This was a reiteration of one of McCarran's earlier pieces of legislation, the Internal Security Act of 1950 (the McCarran Act). That act—which was passed over the veto of President Harry S. Truman (1945–1953)—required communist organizations to register with the U.S. attorney general, who had the power to detain and deport communists in a national emergency.

The McCarran–Walter Act retained the national origin quota system established by the Immigration Act of 1924 but expanded it to all countries—excluding America's closest allies—and introduced a system of visa preferences. The act gave priority to immigrants with special skills and to relatives of people who were already living in the United States. More people from outside Western Europe were allowed in under the new legislation, but there were still tight controls on their numbers.

Policy toward Asians

From the 1920s onward American immigration policy had been specifically designed to restrict immigration from Southern and Eastern Europe while encouraging the arrival of Western Europeans. Furthermore, a series of explicitly racist laws effectively denied Asians the right of entry and naturalization. The provisions of the McCarran–Walter Act that lifted the bars to immigration and naturalization for Asians and Pacific Americans were written by a Republican congressman, Dr. Walter H. Judd (1898–1994), who had spent many years as a mission doctor in China. Judd's amendments

A group of Italian refugees, all tailors or seamstresses, pose at Idlewild Airport in 1956. They were flown to the United States by the Amalgamated Clothing Workers of America, which had assured them jobs.

INTERSTATE MIGRATION: MOVING FROM NORTH TO SOUTH

The postwar years were an era of internal migrations within the United States as the population became wealthier and increasingly mobile thanks to the widespread ownership of automobiles. When the workforce shifted away from traditional agricultural employment, many people began to move into cities to find work. City dwellers, in turn, sought the space and tranquillity of the new outlying suburbs. Many others, however, chose to migrate farther afield.

People began to move from the declining manufacturing centers of the so-called "Rustbelt" in the North and East, and headed for the "Sunbelt" of the Southwest. With the advent of new interstate highways in the 1950s transcontinental mobility was accessible to all, and people began to head where jobs could be found, showing a marked preference for sunny, less densely populated areas. Air-conditioning was a major factor in making the hot, humid states of the South more bearable. (In 1951 inexpensive window units were developed and were soon installed in thousands of homes.)

The 1950s were also the era when retirement communities began to emerge. Retirees were no longer tied to the places where they had lived and worked; they moved to the sunny climes of Florida, Arizona, Texas, and California, to communities that offered independent living and a variety of social and recreational opportunities.

Interstate migration was not welcomed by all, however. Some Mexican Americans in the Southwest were forced to compete for both white- and blue-collar jobs with the new migrants from the Rustbelt. The arrival of the Northeasterners also served to reinforce the status of Mexican Americans as second-class citizens.

replaced the blanket exclusion laws against the immigration of Asians with the territorial concept of the "Asia–Pacific Triangle." Immigration of people from within the triangle was capped annually at 2,000. A person of Chinese descent who was born in a European country was, nevertheless, counted as part of that quota. This rule applied solely to Asians.

Despite the discrimination implicit in the act, many Asians welcomed it. Beginning in the 1950s, many Chinese citizens from Formosa (now Taiwan) came to the United States to pursue graduate studies in American universities. If they could find employment after graduation, they were able to stay.

The ethnic bias of the McCarran–Walter Act was overwhelming: Around 70 percent of all immigration slots were allocated to people from the United Kingdom, Ireland, and Germany. However, some commentators claim that the act did not explicitly set out to be racist and retain the quota system on grounds of racial superiority; rather, it was a reflection of the sociological theories of the time relating to cultural assimilation. A 1950 report by the Senate Judiciary Committee explained why officials believed it was important to continue with national quotas: "Without giving credence to any theory of Nordic superiority, the subcommittee believes that the adoption of the national origins quota formula was a rational and logical method of numerically restricting immigration in such a manner as to best preserve the sociological and cultural balance of the United States."

Opposition to the act

Where there was opposition to the McCarran–Walter Act, it was scathing. The legislation, critics claimed, was restrictionist, and the continuation of the quota system was seen as inappropriate to the needs of U.S. foreign policy.

As with the 1950 Internal Security Act, President Truman was firmly opposed to the law. He vetoed the bill, but he was overruled by a vote of 278 to 113 in the House and 57 to 26 in the Senate. In his veto message he argued against "the absurdity, the cruelty of carrying over into this year of 1952 the isolationist limitations of our 1924 law." "We do not need to be protected against immigrants," he maintained, "on the contrary we want to stretch out a helping hand, to save those who have managed to flee into Western Europe, to succor those who are brave enough to escape from barbarism, to welcome and restore them against the day when their countries will, as we hope, be free again."

A vociferous Jewish lobby also opposed the legislation. They argued that the principles of democracy required ethnic diversity, and that the good will of many other countries depended on the willingness of the United States to accept their citizens as immigrants. Judge Simon H. Rifkind of the District Court of Appeals testified against the bill on behalf of Jewish organizations, stating that "The enactment [of the 1952 act] will gravely impair the national effort we are putting forth. For we are engaged in a war for the hearts and minds of men. The free nations of the world look to us for moral and spiritual reinforcement at a time when the faith which moves men is as important as the force they wield."

Refugee admissions

In total, fewer than half of the immigrants who entered the United States in the 1950s were admitted under the quota system. Many others arrived from the Western Hemisphere as nonquota immigrants, others as family members of existing residents, and others as refugees. The end of the

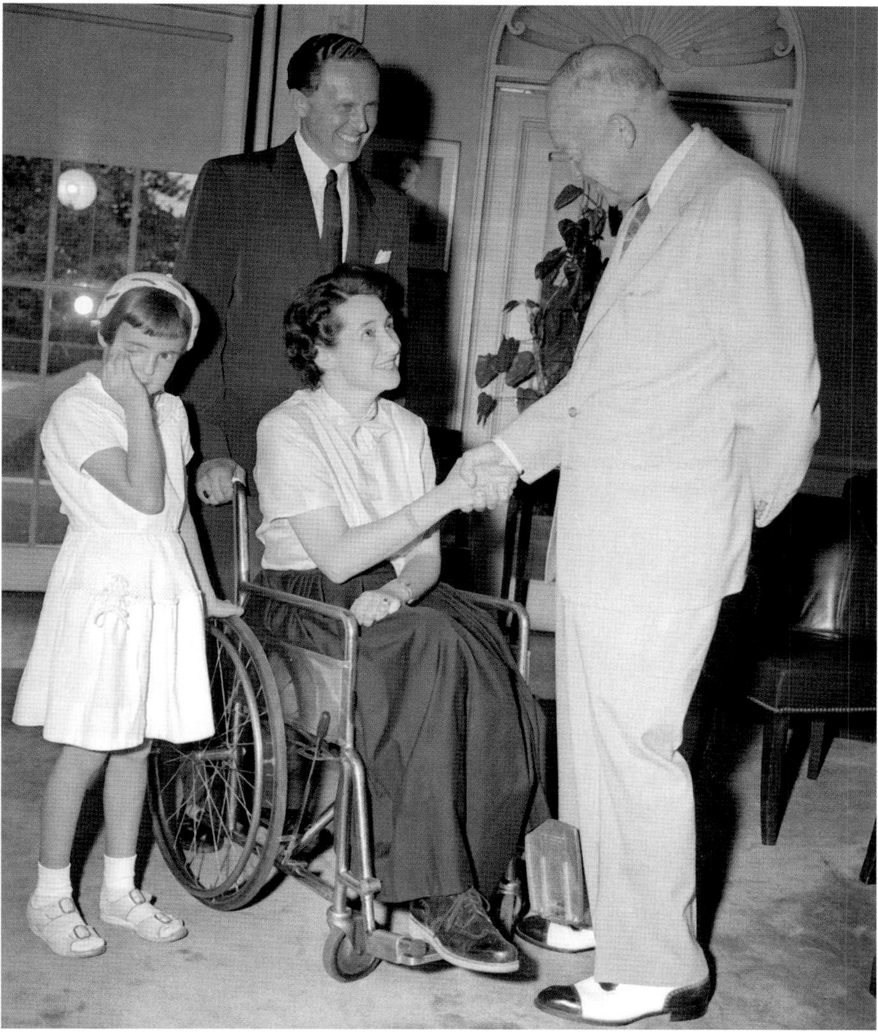

These Chinese immigrants are being questioned at Ellis Island in January 1951. They were suspected of being communists.

war in Europe left some 20–30 million people homeless. In the midst of this humanitarian crisis the United States created a series of exceptions to its strict immigration quotas. In 1945 the War Brides Act allowed the admission of the wives and children of members of the armed forces who had married foreign nationals. The Displaced Persons Act of 1948 authorized the admission of 205,000 Europeans uprooted by the war. The act was amended and extended in 1950.

In 1953 the Refugee Relief Act (RRA), amended further in 1954, approved the admission of 214,000 refugees from war-ravaged Europe and escapees from Communist-dominated countries. Thirty percent of the admissions under the act were from Italy, followed by immigrants from Germany, Yugoslavia, and Greece. The inclusion of refugees from Communist

President Eisenhower meets the Kapus family in 1954, the first Hungarian family to receive visas under the Refugee Relief Act. They had escaped Hungary by crawling across the border into Austria.

countries was a clear reflection of the atmosphere of the Cold War era. From 1953 to 1963 some 190,000 refugees came to America from behind the "Iron Curtain." In 1956, following the crushing of the Hungarian Uprising by Soviet troops, around 35,000 Hungarian refugees fled to the United States (*see box opposite*).

Korean immigrants

On the other side of the world Asia was embroiled in its own conflict between capitalism and communism, especially in Korea. In 1950 the Korean population in America stood at just 7,030. With the start of the Korean War (1950–1953) a wave of immigrants arrived. The two main groups were the wives of U.S. servicemen stationed in Korea and war orphans. After seeing a film about the plight of children orphaned in the conflict, Harry and Bertha Holt, from Oreswell, Oregon, decided to adopt eight Korean children. In 1956 they founded the Holt Adoption Program, which brought thousands of Korean orphans to the United States.

Since both the war brides and the orphans were dependents of U.S. citizens, their situations were significantly different from previous—and later—immigrants, who were able to retain a clearer cultural identity. The Korean wives of servicemen generally had low levels of education and occupational skills; they also experienced high levels of family conflict and divorce. They tended to be isolated from mainstream society as well as from Korean American communities. As for the war orphans, they were adopted primarily by white families of European descent who had little or no connection to Korean American communities. This meant that a whole generation grew up having no knowledge of its Korean cultural heritage.

Mexican Americans

Latin America gave rise to immigration problems on a far larger scale for the United States. During World War II, as more and more Americans went to fight in Europe and the Pacific, U.S. farms, particularly in the Southwest, grew desperately short of laborers. In response the U.S. and Mexican governments agreed on a guest-worker scheme in 1942 that allowed Mexicans to do contract work in the United States. The scheme was known as the Bracero Program (*bracero* is a loose translation of "arm man" or laborer).

Bracero workers were generally paid very low wages and often forced to work under conditions that most American agricultural laborers would have found intolerable. The program was popular with farmers, however, and lasted until 1964. By the time it ended, almost five million Mexicans had traveled north of the border, and hundreds of thousands stayed.

Operation Wetback

Meanwhile, illegal immigration was growing: More than 3.4 million illegal aliens were apprehended in the 1950s. In the late 1940s the United States began a campaign of large-scale deportation that lasted well into the 1950s.

One supreme effort to root out illegal immigration was known as Operation Wetback. In 1949 the U.S. Border Patrol seized nearly 280,000 illegal immigrants from Mexico. By 1953 the numbers had grown to over 865,000, and the government was forced to act. Operation Wetback was implemented in 1954 by the new commissioner of the Immigration and Naturalization Service (INS), General Joseph May Swing. It involved 750 INS and border patrol agents, who were stationed along the U.S.–Mexican border. Although the campaign was targeted at illegal immigrants, the authorities began to focus on Mexicans living legitimately in the United States. In the border region officials swept through Mexican barrios (Spanish-speaking areas of a town), targeting "Mexican-looking" citizens on the street and demanding identification. In 1954 agents discovered over one million illegal immigrants; however, many fled back over the border instead of

This picture shows Los Angeles policemen arresting a group of Mexicans who had tried to enter the country illegally in 1953. The men had spent two days hiding on a freight train without food or water.

HUNGARIAN CRISIS

When the Hungarian Uprising—a revolt against Soviet domination of the government during which Hungary attempted to seek a neutral status—was crushed by troops from the USSR in November 1956, some 200,000 people (2 percent of the population) fled the country. Many feared imprisonment and persecution as a result of a Soviet backlash and preferred to make the arduous journey across the Austrian border to Red Cross refugee camps. Within six months of the start of the exodus the UN High Commission for Refugees had found permanent asylum for them in 35 countries. Over $71 million was made available by America to meet the needs of the refugees.

The United States admitted 35,185 Hungarians as a result of the uprising. Some 6,130 were admitted under the Refugee Relief Act and the remainder as part of a humanitarian provision of the McCarran–Walter Act. More than 32,000 of the refugees were processed through the reception center at Camp Kilmer, New Jersey, a World War II transit camp reactivated for this purpose by the Army. The President's Committee for Hungarian Refugee Relief coordinated the activities of the numerous government and private agencies that assisted in the placement of the Hungarians in many communities throughout the nation. Most of the refugees were young, male, and well educated or skilled, and they soon settled in. By the end of 1957 more than 65 percent had found employment.

A Hungarian refugee family in 1957 enjoys a stroll along Main Street in their new home town of Patchogue, Long Island.

being arrested. The discriminatory practices of the INS angered many, and eventually Operation Wetback ceased.

Discrimination

Discrimination against both Mexicans working in the United States and Mexican American citizens was widespread in the 1950s. Civic organizations such as the League of United Latin American Citizens (LULAC) challenged discriminatory attitudes and the marginalized status of Mexican Americans. It was also during this period that the Chicano movement emerged, becoming part of the civil rights movement in the 1960s. The movement was born out of a general sense of disillusionment with the comparative poverty, low wages, and limited educational opportunities endured by Mexican Americans. This disillusionment was compounded by the fact that young Mexican American men who had served in the armed forces during World War II had suffered less prejudice. When the war was over and the servicemen returned home, they were faced with discriminatory practices such as exclusion from municipal swimming pools, barber shops, and at some eating establishments. As early as 1946 Mexican reformers in California were targeting segregation in schools, which, they argued, severely restricted the possibility of educational achievement. In 1947 the state's governor, Earl Warren, signed a school desegregation order into law.

Puerto Ricans

In contrast to the difficulties Mexicans had in crossing the border to the north, Puerto Ricans could move freely from their island to the mainland United States. Puerto Rico had been under American control since 1898, and U.S. citizenship was conferred on the island's people in 1917. During and after World War II labor shortages in the United States were critical, and economic conditions on the island were depressed. U.S. companies began to send agents to Puerto Rico to recruit workers as a cheap source of labor. The result was a marked increase in Puerto Rican immigration that continued long after the war. Average annual migration rose from 1,800 in 1930–1940, to 31,000 in 1946–1950, and to 45,000 in

PUERTO RICAN MUSICAL INFLUENCES

Musically, salsa has its roots firmly based in the Afro-Spanish traditions of Cuba, but its worldwide popularity should be attributed to the Puerto Ricans of New York City. Since the early 1800s Puerto Rico has borrowed musical styles from Cuba while preserving its own unique genres. These and other Puerto Rican influences are evident in the Latin music that emerged from New York in the forties and fifties, culminating in mambo and salsa.

When Puerto Ricans migrated to America, they often encountered a struggle for life in the ghettos. The only escape from the frustrations of their daily lives was through the traditional music of their homeland, the "plena" and the "bomba." Plena is a uniquely Puerto Rican style that deals with day-to-day events; it is often referred to as *el periodico cantado* ("the sung newspaper"). Popular artists used lyrics that told a story about the struggles experienced by an average Puerto Rican in New York. Others expressed feelings about their hopes for the future, their homesickness, and romance. Bomba is another uniquely Puerto Rican genre. It uses an aggressive Afro-Caribbean beat and is danced by a man and woman who take turns to show off their skills, competing with each other and with the music. Many New York artists used bomba to express their frustration with the conditions in which they were forced to live.

Some Puerto Rican immigrants, seen here in 1955; like many other New Yorkers, they enjoyed passing the time on the stoop outside their apartment building in East Harlem.

1951–1960. The peak year for Puerto Rican immigration was 1953, when more than 69,000 islanders moved to the mainland United States, mostly to New York City. By 1963 Puerto Ricans made up 9.3 percent of the total population of New York City, and it is estimated that over one million Puerto Ricans had left the island by that time.

Although New York City was the main destination for Puerto Ricans, a number settled in other urban areas such as Chicago, Boston, Philadelphia, Jersey City, and New Haven. From the outset they were paid little and forced to live in poverty-stricken ghettos in, for example, East Harlem (known as El Barrio) in New York City.

Cuban refugees

Cuban immigrants, on the other hand, generally enjoyed a more comfortable life. Until the late 1950s few Cubans immigrated to the United States despite the repressive regime of dictator Fulgencio Batista (1901–1973). In 1959 the revolutionary movement led by Fidel Castro (1926–) forced Batista and his cronies to flee.

At first Castro enjoyed the support of a wide range of Cubans because he promised to restore full democracy to the island. All that changed, however, as he revealed his plans for a communist economy. Between 1959 and 1962 around 200,000 middle- and upper-class Cubans fled the island and settled mostly in Miami, Florida, where they played an important part in developing the local economy.

See Also:

Asian Americans • Black Americans • Bracero Program • China • Cold War • Cuba • Foreign Policy • Germany • Japan • Korean War • Population • Puerto Rico • Segregation and Desegregation • U.S.–Mexican Relations

INCHON LANDING

Within days of North Korea's invasion of South Korea in 1950 General MacArthur, commander-in-chief of the UN forces, began formulating a plan to launch a major amphibious landing at Inchon. Although highly risky, the plan worked and turned the tide of the war.

On June 25, 1950, North Korea's Korean People's Army (KPA) crossed the 38th parallel and invaded South Korea. Within days the KPA had taken the South Korean capital, Seoul. South Korea was allied to the United States, which persuaded the United Nations (UN) to provide military assistance.

A little over two weeks after the war had started, U.S. General Douglas MacArthur (1880–1964) was appointed commander-in-chief of the UN forces in Korea. By that time, however, his main force, the U.S. Eighth Army, was penned in at the southeast corner of the Korean Peninsula, near the port city of Pusan.

Although the situation looked desperate for the UN forces, MacArthur believed that the North Korean forces were tiring and that their supply lines were overstretched. He thought that by severing its supply lines and recapturing Seoul, the UN forces could demoralize the KPA and bring a swift end to the war. To achieve this, he came up with a bold invasion plan that would include a large naval fleet and 70,000 troops. The target would have to be a place where the KPA would be caught off-guard. MacArthur chose Inchon, an ancient port city on the western side of Korea, only 25 miles (40km) from Seoul.

In late August 1950 MacArthur presented the invasion plan to his generals. At first the generals argued that the plan was far too risky, pointing out that the extreme tidal range, narrow channels, wide mud banks, and high seawalls at Inchon would leave the invasion force open to slaughter. MacArthur then rose to give a 45-minute speech. He explained that all the problems the generals had identified about Inchon were precisely why he believed it was the right place and plan of action: The North Koreans would never expect UN forces to invade there.

The military units shown here disembarking during the Inchon Landing were part of the largest invasion force since D-Day. The force included 70,000 soldiers, 260 ships, and hundreds of vehicles.

The invasion

A few days before the invasion a small reconnaissance group landed near Inchon. It assessed the strength of the KPA fortifications, surveyed the proposed UN landing sites, and noted the condition and extent of the tides and mud banks. Finally, it lit an abandoned lighthouse that would prove crucial for guiding the UN's 260 naval vessels to Inchon. For two days the air force bombarded the main KPA fortification near Inchon, destroying the heavy artillery there.

On September 15 the UN's Inchon invasion finally got under way. Landing at dawn, a battalion seized the KPA fortification without losing a single man. The remaining troops had to wait until late afternoon, when the tides were favorable, before attacking the rest of Inchon. Both the port and the city were firmly in UN hands by midnight. Two weeks later Seoul was handed back to the South Koreans. However, the war lasted almost another three years.

See Also:

Chosin Reservoir • Korean War • MacArthur, Douglas • Pusan Perimeter • Pyongyang • Seoul

INDUSTRY

During the 1950s the output and productivity of U.S. industry, which began the decade preeminent in the world economy, continued to grow. Yet America's share of the world's industrial production fell sharply as competitors, reviving after war, began a relentless rise.

For the first half of the 20th century the United States had pulled farther and farther ahead of the rest of the world in the volume and value of its industrial production. For most of that time the manufacturing output per capita of the United Kingdom, the world's first industrialized country, was only three-fourths that of the United States. For Europe as a whole the figure was three-fifths. But although at the end of World War II (1939–1945) the United States continued to lead the way, the trend began to move in the other direction in the 1950s as the rate of industrial growth around the world advanced at a rate never before seen. The global average growth rate increased from 2.2 percent each year on the eve of World War II to 4.1 percent in 1953 and a spectacular 5.3 percent in 1963. That leap forward in the industrialization of almost all countries was accompanied by a corresponding jump in the volume of world trade. In 1957—for the first time in history—trade in manufactured goods exceeded trade in raw materials and agricultural products.

The United States owed its industrial strength at midcentury to a number of factors, some of them provided by nature, some of them the fruits of American ingenuity. American corporations had increased industrial output faster than their international rivals partly because it was in the United States that the crucial innovations of product standardization and methods of mass production on the factory-floor assembly line had first been adopted. Those innovations meant that despite the highest wage rates in the world, American firms could keep costs down and compete successfully against foreign products

Men work on a Ford automobile on an assembly line in 1954. High productivity in U.S. manufacturing was gradually undercut as competitors invested in more modern plants.

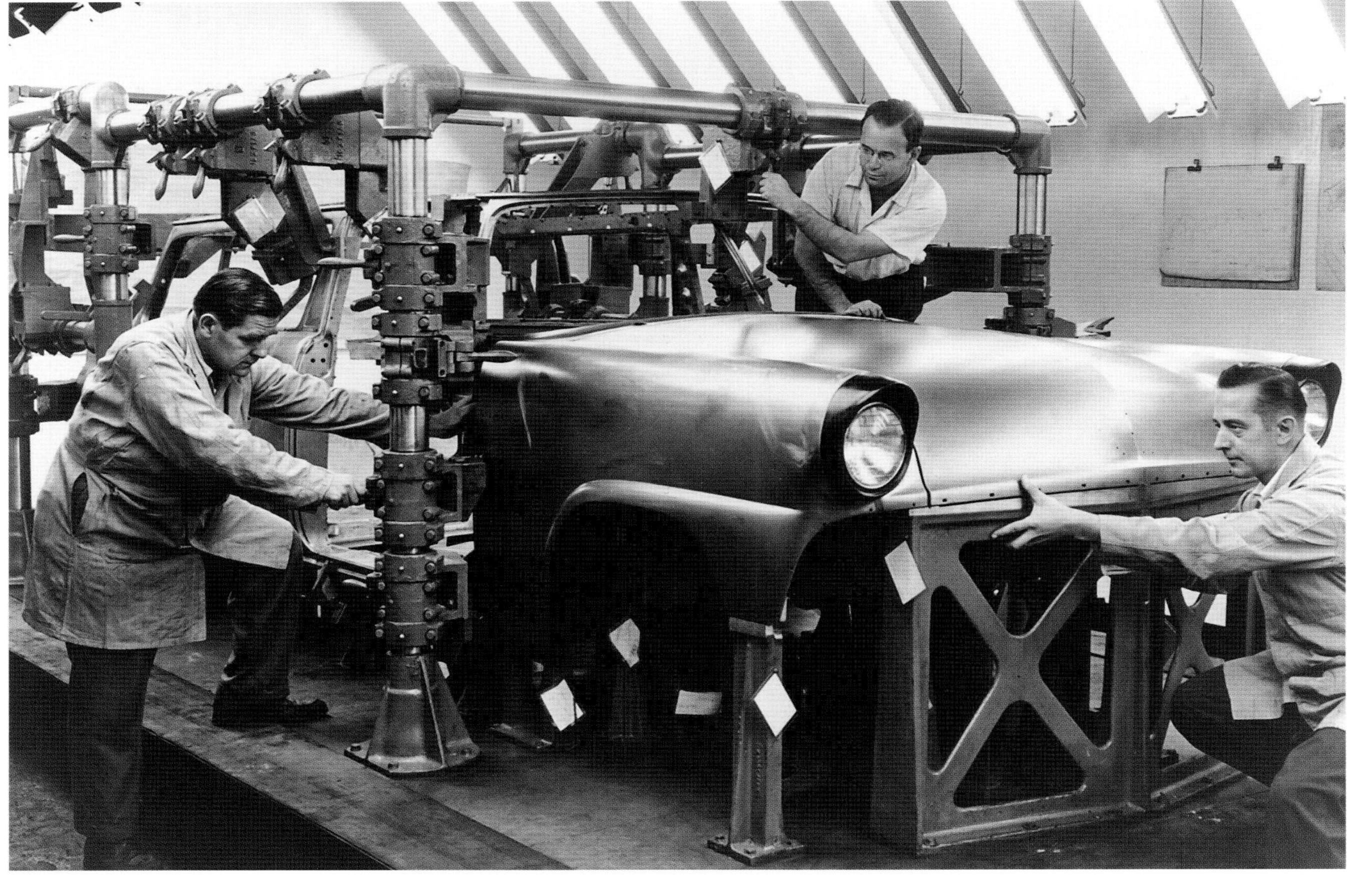

because productivity levels—the value of output each man-hour worked—were even higher. In the automobile industry, for example, the value of output each man-hour was three times that achieved in the United Kingdom and Germany.

Other background factors also contributed immensely to America's industrial dominance. Thanks to its geographical size the United States was blessed with abundant natural resources. Industry had benefited especially from the continuing availability of a cheap energy source in the form of petroleum. The production of crude oil increased thirtyfold between 1900 and 1950. The size of the American population—140 million in 1945—also meant that U.S. manufacturers could benefit from economies of scale in production for the huge domestic market without having to worry about exports. In addition, America's European industrial competitors had fought two exhausting wars on home soil, wars that had depleted their industrial capacity while at the same time giving a direct boost to the U.S. economy.

EMPLOYMENT IN INDUSTRY

The tables below, compiled by the U.S. Bureau of the Census, provide a breakdown of employment in the United States in the mid-1950s by type of industry and by type of occupation.

EMPLOYMENT BY TYPE OF INDUSTRY, 1956

Type of industry	*Number of workers*	*Percentage*
Total	64,979,000	100
Agriculture	6,585,000	10.1
Waged and salaried	1,692,000	2.6
Self-employed	3,570,000	5.5
Unpaid family workers	1,323,000	2.0
Nonagricultural	58,394,000	89.9
Waged and salaried	51,877,000	79.9
Self-employed	5,936,000	9.1
Unpaid family workers	581,000	0.9

MAJOR OCCUPATIONAL GROUPS, 1955

Occupational group	*Percentage of workforce*
Agriculture	
Farmers and farm managers	6.0
Farm laborers	4.5
Nonagricultural	
Professional technical	9.2
Company owners, managers	10.2
Craftsmen, foremen	13.2
Factory operatives	20.2
Other laborers	5.8
Clerical workers	13.3
Sales workers	6.3
Domestic workers	3.1
Service workers	8.2

Absolute growth, relative decline

America's economic supremacy in 1945, when its share of world industrial production was 50 percent, was therefore, in a sense, artificial. It reflected the temporary weakness of other nations, not only those of Western Europe, but also Japan. That high point proved to be unsustainable against the general expansion of manufacturing in the world, and by 1953 the share had fallen below 45 percent. It was not that Americans were producing less, simply that the rest of the world was producing more. Nor was it immediately apparent, amid the general prosperity of the U.S. economy in the 1950s, what was happening.

The sales of passenger automobiles in the United States, for example, rose from 6.7 million in 1950 to 7.9 million in 1955, the year in which General Motors (which sold about half of them) became the first American corporation to earn more than $1 billion—eight times the tax revenues of the state of New York. In 1960 the United States was still making more than half of the cars manufactured in the world, but that was down from nearly three-fourths only a decade earlier (the figure was even higher if cars made abroad by American subsidiary companies were included).

For General Motors, Ford, and Chrysler the 1950s were, in retrospect, a golden age of tail-finned, wrap-around-windowed gas-guzzlers. The number of cars coming off the assembly lines continued to increase after the 1960s, but by 1980 America's share of the world automobile market was to fall to 25 percent. The postwar automobile industry was gradually subjected to mounting competition from Europe and Japan. The age of European imports was announced by the arrival of the Volkswagen "Beetle" from Germany. For a time the car makers of Detroit (the center of automobile manufacturing in the United States) made no attempt to compete in the "compact car" market, believing that compacts were for foreign countries with overcrowded roads and high fuel costs. Not until 1959 did the big American corporations start to bring out compacts, and even then they were unable to stop the rise of the Beetle. The failure to foresee and keep pace with world trends in automobile manufacturing might suggest an entrepreneurial failure.

In 1955 Detroit was the seventh-largest city in the United States and the center of the automobile industry. Layoffs in the industry later caused severe hardship in the city.

America's ever more entrenched automobile culture, together with an ever rising volume of commercial road haulage, led to support in Congress for the grand interstate highway-building program announced by President Dwight D. Eisenhower (1953–1961) in 1956. The program gave a great boost to the automobile and construction industries. However, allied with the increase in air travel, the huge extension of freeways also hastened the decline of the railroads.

While car manufacturing suffered a relative international slippage, other older, established sectors of industry went into absolute decline. Employment in the textile industry fell by 50 percent over the space of a single decade. (One reason suggested was that people were marrying at a younger age than in previous generations, meaning that they stopped "dressing up" earlier and diverted their disposable incomes into spending on household goods and furniture.) Coal mining, too, continued to shrink irreversibly. In the 1950s oil displaced coal as the nation's primary energy source. The home-heating market for coal continued a downward spiral that had begun in the 1920s as homeowners turned to cleaner and cheaper oil heating. After World War II the railroads completed their conversion to diesel, and the age of the coal-fired steam engine vanished into history. Both the iron and steel industries also suffered. The Appalachian region lost 60 percent of its jobs in the 1950s.

Disappearing resources

The United States began in the 1950s to change from a "have" to a "have-not" country in its supply of natural resources. Between 1900 and 1950 production of bituminous coal had risen by 250 percent, copper by 300 percent, and iron ore by 350 percent. As nonrenewable domestic natural resources dwindled, manufacturers had to look beyond America's shores for raw materials. By the end of the 1950s the United States had become the world's largest importer of copper, lead, and zinc. Steel producers were driven to developing processes that used low-grade iron ores and to prospect for new deposits in difficult-to-access places such as Labrador.

Even more than the automobile industry, the steel industry exhibited symptoms of changing times in the 1950s as it was about to enter a period of serious and prolonged competitive crisis. From peak levels that accounted for nearly half of the world's output in 1947, American steel manufacturing plummeted to only 14 percent by 1980 and was overtaken by Japan as the world's leading producer. The warning signs were already present in the 1950s, when American wage costs were far higher than Japanese. The U.S. Steel Corporation was eager to point the finger of blame at the powerful United Steelworkers of America labor union for dulling its competitive edge, and there was something to that charge. Steelworkers received wages well above the average national industrial wage. U.S. Steel also blamed the federal government for laying heavy costs on American steel manufacturing in the shape of taxes, price controls, and regulatory burdens such as conservation and antipollution regulations, while steel companies in Europe and Japan benefited from government subsidy.

Economic historians have not found that argument to be convincing. Very quickly after the end of hostilities in 1945 the U.S. government dropped almost all wartime economic controls, including its elaborate system of production quotas and price controls, and it sold off the corporate assets it had acquired in order to give central direction to the war effort. More important—in most historians' view of the matter—were certain management failures. The largest American steel

(Right) Huge coils of steel are stacked near a 72-inch cold mill (so called for the width of steel sheeting it produced) in Lister Hill, Alabama, in 1959.

STEEL: THE TECHNOLOGICAL LAG

Until the mid-1950s the American steel industry had the world's biggest blast furnaces. Thereafter its overseas competitors surged ahead. Complacency at home and innovation abroad resulted in American producers lagging behind in the technology stakes.

Japan was the most threatening competitor. With its prewar industrial capacity destroyed during World War II (1939–1945), Japan was obliged to start from scratch. This gave it the opportunity to construct modern mills on clear sites and to experiment with new designs and implement new methods of production. It also built on a vast scale, installing furnaces that were as much as 50 percent larger than the biggest ones to be found in the United States. In Western Europe, too, the 1950s were a period of expansion and of siting new works at tidewater locations next to rich mineral resources.

The United States was slow to adopt foreign technology. Particularly costly was the unwillingness to abandon open-hearth processing and move over to what had become a clearly superior technology for processing low-grade iron, the oxygen converter. This process had been introduced in Austria in 1952. Two years later the technical director of the firm that had pioneered the new method visited the United States and explained to the American Institute of Mining Engineers that all mass steel production in the future would be by the oxygen process, and that many industries would benefit.

American observers were for the most part unconvinced. It was understandable that American firms were reluctant to change their methods: They were long-established and still profitable, and the cost of replacing them was high. Japan, having less of its industry tied up in old plant, was in a position to be innovative. But it was remarkable that even in the late 1950s the building of new open-hearth furnaces in the United States continued unabated. By 1960 still only 3.4 percent of American steel production was done with oxygen converters; in Japan the figure was 11.5 percent. Five years later the gap had grown wider: 17.4 percent compared to 55 percent. *Fortune* magazine commented that in the 1950s the American steel industry installed 40 million tons of melting capacity that was already "obsolete when it was built."

companies passed up a number of opportunities to stay abreast of their overseas competitors. Even in the 1960s, some years after most experts had concluded that old-style, open-hearth furnaces were outmoded, American steel corporations continued to build new ones instead of the basic oxygen furnaces that were much cheaper to run. British and Japanese manufacturers did not make that mistake. The American industry also appears to have taken longer than was necessary to invest in continuous casting mills rather than primary rolling mills. Continuous casting allows molten steel to be cast directly into the shape the customer wants, rather than the steel being shaped and rolled in a steel mill after it has first solidified in its mold (*see p. 111*).

The most recent historian of the U.S. Steel Corporation, Kenneth Warren, is scathing in his review of the company's management in the 1950s. Despite the increase in the national steel capacity by more than 50 percent between 1945 and 1960, the period heralded the decline of American steel on the world stage.

In Warren's view the main problem was one of "self-satisfaction and complacency" by the managers of the U.S. Steel Corporation, whom he likens to ostriches sticking their heads in the sand and ignoring the development of competition. The complex nature of the economic, geographical, and technological factors involved in the steady reduction in the U.S. share of the world steel market, Warren believes, allowed American steel managers to ignore their own responsibility for the decline, exhibiting an "overweening self-confidence" along with a constant tendency to underestimate their competitors abroad. By the end of the 1950s U.S. mills produced 26 percent of the world's steel—a smaller proportion, Warren notes, than at any time since the early 1870s. In the first 15 years after the end of the war this was a pattern repeated throughout the U.S. manufacturing industry.

Nowhere to go but down

American industry struggled to maintain its international lead in the 1950s because it started from so high a base, with much less room to improve its market share than its competitors and, compared to Japan, with more old, good-quality plant to protect. "A good open-hearth shop with half its economic life left can't be scrapped," said an accountant for the U.S. Steel Corporation. "You wait until you cross the economic line." But other considerations also played a part. An increasing proportion of the workforce moved from manufacturing and the extractive industries such as mining and oil drilling into the services sector. At the same time, U.S. investment in research and development (except for military purposes) shrank steadily by comparison with that of governments and private companies overseas.

The effects of those trends on productivity and employment levels were partially offset by eye-catching developments in high-tech industries such as computers, electronics, and aviation. IBM emerged as the world leader in the computer field. Transistors, developed in the years immediately following World War II, found more and more commercial applications, beginning with their use in hearing aids in 1957 (*see box opposite*). The manufacture of white goods (such as refrigerators and washing machines) and other household products, especially televisions, benefited from the consumer boom to which rising prosperity gave birth, as well as the rapidly expanding population of the time. So did the tobacco, soft drinks, food-processing, and airline travel industries. In general there was a shift away from the traditional heavy industries associated with the initial phases of industrialization toward light

COMPETITION FROM JAPAN

The 1950s were a high point for American industrial supremacy before overseas competition—both from old competitors reviving and new ones emerging—began to bite. This is illustrated by comparative figures for Japan and the United States on a range of cost and performance indicators in the steel industry.

The figures given are for Japan, expressed as a ratio to an American base figure of 1. So, for example, for every dollar that American steel manufacturers had to pay for iron ore in 1956, their Japanese counterparts had to pay $1.73. By 1976, however, Japanese manufacturers had to pay only a little more than half of the cost in the United States. In general, most Japanese costs decreased while productivity (the value produced for the company each hour worked) increased.

Costs	1956	1976
Iron ore	1.73	0.57
Coking coal	2.25	0.96
Fuel oil	0.98	1.03
Labor	0.12	0.43
Average costs	1.05	0.56
Productivity	0.41	1.17
Sale prices	1.20	0.73

TRANSISTORS AND SEMICONDUCTORS

Advances in electronics technology created three new postwar industries: electronic computers, computer software, and semiconductor components. Those innovations did not simply give rise to a host of new companies. They also revolutionized the workings of older industries such as telecommunications, banking, airlines, and railroads.

The electronics revolution had its roots in two key innovations, the computer and the transistor, both of which appeared in the 1940s. The transistor was developed at Bell Telephone Laboratories in 1947, but the first commercially successful product was marketed not by AT&T (of which Bell was a subdivision) but by Texas Instruments. Its silicon junction transistor, which allowed previously unknown levels of miniaturization, was rapidly taken up by the military for radar and missile applications.

The next major advance in semiconductor electronics was the integrated circuit. It was developed by Jack St. Clair Kilby of Texas Instruments in 1958. By incorporating all the necessary components onto a single piece of semiconductor material, it offered a solution to the unreliable performance of complicated electronic systems that used large numbers of separate transistors and in which one fault could cause the whole system to fail.

In 1955 the total worth of semiconductors produced in the United States, about two-fifths of them for the defense industry, was $40 million. In 1960, when defense was taking up nearly half of all semiconductors sold, their total value had risen more than tenfold to $542 million.

To show their size, three of Philco's subminiature M-1 transistors lie on the face of a dime in 1956.

industries such as chemicals, plastics, and pharmaceuticals.

Federal agencies and private companies fostered growth by encouraging people to spend money. Both the U.S. departments of Housing and of Veterans Affairs, for example, offered low-interest loans to facilitate suburban house-buying. Buying on the installment plan came into fashion, and the arrival of multiuse charge cards—the Diners Club card was the first on the scene in 1950—provided a spur to consumer spending. Over the decade private debt rose from $105 billion to $263 billion. One of the growth industries of the period was advertising. In 1950 the industry sold $5.7 billion worth of ads; by 1960 the figure had more than doubled to $11.9 billion.

Opening up the Southwest

The big regional winner from the new pattern of industrial development in the United States was the Southwest. The flow of investment, population, and jobs into the region had begun earlier—Houston, Texas, was known as "the city that never knew the Depression"—and World War II had also helped. Spending by the federal government during the war largely underwrote the expansion of oil refining and the petrochemicals industry, which supplied aviation fuel and petrochemicals for synthetic rubber and explosives. New refining processes greatly increased the production of high-octane aviation fuel, and America supplied 80 percent of that essential fuel used by the Allies during the war.

The production of petroleum rose from about 1.75 billion barrels in 1946 to 2.5 billion in 1950, and the demand for petroleum-based products such as plastics, synthetic rubber, and asphalt continued to rise during the 1950s. In the first years of the decade a dispute arose over who owned oil deposits lying offshore in the Gulf of Mexico and the Pacific. The quarrel temporarily hindered the development of the petroleum industry. The individual states nearest the deposits, such as Texas, Louisiana, and California, claimed ownership on the grounds that they were within the "tidelands" that fell inside state boundaries. The federal government argued that tidelands belonged to the whole nation. The dispute was resolved in 1953 by the

This picture shows an offshore drilling platform in the Gulf of Mexico, located on the tidal oil lands over which the states of Texas and Louisiana were given control in 1953.

Submerged Lands Act, which awarded them to the states, which were then free to lease offshore sites to oil companies.

The economy of Dallas–Fort Worth shifted away from agriculture to the high-paid petroleum and high-tech electronics industries. In addition, aircraft production stimulated the growth of Fort Worth and of Oklahoma City, which also moved from a wheat-based to an oil-led economy. From the mid-1950s a large aerospace and electronics industry also began to grow in southern California, to complement the hi-tech Silicon Valley of northern California. The economy of both regions was massively funded by military and space contracts from the federal government, as was the high-tech zone that grew up on Route 128 around Boston, Massachussetts.

The United States was by far the biggest consumer of energy in the world. American annual energy consumption per capita was 62.1 megawatt hours in 1952. The equivalent figure for the United Kingdom was 36.6, for France 18.9, and for the USSR 13.0—a rough-and-ready guide to the comparative industrial capacities of those countries. With few major hydroelectric sources remaining to be exploited once the development of the St. Lawrence Seaway project was completed in 1959, the search was on for new sources of energy. In the late 1950s the United States looked as if it would become dependent for its supply of electrical power on nuclear energy. The first large-scale commercial nuclear power reactor opened in 1957, and 14 more atomic plants were in the planning stage or early phases of construction. Together they would provide 10 percent more electric power than the American share of the St. Lawrence hydroelectric stations.

Research: the engine of progress

In the background of all the industrial activity of the postwar world were two underlying trends. One was an increased role for research and development (R&D); the other was for more and more automation. In 1945 Vannevar Bush (1890–1974), one of the most influential figures in the planning of 20th-century American science and the wartime director of the Office of Scientific Research and Development, published a report entitled *Science: The Endless Frontier* (1945). Commissioned by President Franklin D. Roosevelt (1933–1945), the report was one of the first to make the case for research as the root source of economic growth.

Bush called for the creation of a single federal agency, a national research foundation, to fund basic research in all areas, defense and non-defense, including medicine and health. He argued, somewhat controversially, that American industry had for too long relied on developing and applying scientific discoveries made in Europe. It was time for American universities to take the lead. Bush also wanted money for research to be given to universities without strings attached, so that scientists could work free of congressional oversight. In 1950 Congress did establish a National Science Foundation. Although it limited its appropriations to $15 million a year, and Cold War priorities were to doom Bush's broad vision, the foundation was a signal that the federal government was eager to provide national backing for scientific innovation in industry based on cutting-edge science, technological advances, and professional expertise.

Most federal money went into military research. By the end of the 1950s more than 90 percent of federal R&D spending was controlled by the Defense Department and the Atomic Energy Commission. That concentration of effort was given apparent justification by an investigation into the military capacities of the United States and the USSR. The committee undertaking the investigation, chaired by H. Rowan Gaither, Jr., the head of the Ford Foundation, issued its report in 1957. The Gaither report found, erroneously as it later turned out, that the Soviet Union had a substantial lead over the United States, giving rise to the phrase "the missile gap." Pressure on the White House as a result of the report led to a new wave of increased defense spending. By the beginning of the 1960s work to produce ICBMs (intercontinental ballistic missiles) was, according to one historian, involving 18,000 scientists and research technicians in universities and 70,000 working for industries awarded defense contracts across the United States.

Defense spending had important side effects that went far beyond purely military considerations. Industry in general benefited greatly from the money invested by the defense establishment in the improvement of semiconductors and computers. The close, almost symbiotic, relationship between industry and the military raised an important question, however:

DEFENSE INDUSTRY

The contribution of defense contracts to American industry in 1950s can be gauged by comparing the amount spent on defense in the United States against the much smaller amounts spent by other leading powers. American spending on defense averaged about 10 percent of the gross national product from 1954 (when the war in Korea was over) to 1960.

	USA (billions of dollars)	**USSR**	**UK**	**FRA**
1950	14.5	15.5	2.3	1.4
1951	33.3	20.1	3.2	2.1
1952	47.8	21.9	4.3	3.0
1953	49.6	25.5	4.5	3.4
1954	42.7	28.0	4.4	3.6
1955	40.5	29.5	4.3	2.9
1956	41.7	26.7	4.5	3.6
1957	44.5	27.6	4.3	3.6
1958	45.5	30.2	4.4	3.6
1959	46.6	34.4	4.4	3.6

Vannevar Bush was head of the Office of Scientific Research and Development. He believed that university-based research was crucial to economic growth.

THE MILITARY-INDUSTRIAL COMPLEX

Both at the beginning of his presidency and when he left the White House, President Dwight D. Eisenhower (1953–1961) warned the American people that a new specter had arisen out of the arms race with the Soviet Union: He called it "the military-industrial complex."

In April 1953, in a speech entitled "The Chance for Peace" and delivered before the American Society of Newspaper Editors, the new president warned of the "worst to be feared" and "the best to be expected" from an escalating arms race: "The worst is atomic war. The best would be this: a life of perpetual fear and tension; a burden of arms draining the wealth and the labor of all peoples.... Every gun that is made, every warship launched, every rocket fired, signifies, in the final sense, a theft from those who hunger and are not fed, those who are cold and are not clothed. This world in arms is not spending money alone. It is spending the sweat of its laborers, the genius of its scientists, the hopes of its children.... We pay for a single destroyer with new homes that could have housed more than eight thousand people.... This is not a way of life at all, in any true sense. Under the cloud of threatening war, it is humanity hanging from a cross of iron."

But Eisenhower was unable to stop the mushrooming growth of the arms industry. In his second term in office the secrecy required in the interests of national security prevented him from exposing the falsehood of the "missile gap" that had opened up, supposedly leaving the United States lagging behind the Soviet Union in nuclear weaponry. So Eisenhower left office still decrying, as he said in his farewell address of January 17, 1961, the new "conjunction of an immense military establishment and a large arms industry" and calling on the people of America to "guard against the acquisition of unwarranted influence ... by the military-industrial complex" with its "potential for the disastrous rise of misplaced power."

An inspector checks long belts of ammunition in the ammunition boxes of machine guns installed in the wing of a Curtiss fighter plane, Buffalo, New York, 1950.

H. Rowan Gaither, Jr., president of the Ford Foundation, is seen here in 1955. His report on military capacities was used to argue for continued expansion in military spending.

Was high expenditure on defense a response to real military requirements or to self-interested lobbying by corporations, labor unions, and institutions of higher education, which all did well out of it? The question worried President Eisenhower, who called on Americans to guard carefully against the rise of a "military-industrial complex" (*see opposite*).

A member of the Army Signal Engineering Laboratory tests a satellite designed to determine cloud cover over the Earth at the Atlantic Missile Test Range, Cape Canaveral.

Research and development became a prime requirement of nonmilitary industry and generated a demand within industry for scientifically qualified researchers and trained professional managers. During the 1950s universities and colleges vied with one another to attract students to their graduate courses in business management. By the end of the 1950s about 100 universities were following the lead of Harvard, Berkeley, and Stanford by offering a master of arts in business studies. At the same time, major industries such as AT&T, DuPont, General Motors, IBM, and RCA established their own research laboratories for both pure and applied research, and by paying high salaries lured scientists away from universities.

AT&T's Bell Telephone Laboratories, which in 1947 developed the germanium transistor, played a key role in making the United States the world leader in the telecommunications industry. The success of Bell Laboratories became the clinching argument in favor of corporate research as the foundation of industrial innovation and improved productivity, and therefore of profitability.

Automation and its effects

One of the fruits of corporate scientific activity was ever more sophisticated methods of production, which grew out of "process research." Their most visible and important effect was a greater reliance on machines and automatic processes and a decrease in the need for manual labor. The changes were summed up by the word "automation," a buzzword of the decade coined in 1948 by the Ford Motor Company to describe operations conducted by new "transfer machines" that mechanically placed body parts in line with machine tools that automatically drilled holes and fitted the pieces together. The Ford engine plant at Cleveland, Ohio, which opened in 1952, provided a continuous operation from the pouring of sand and the casting of molds to the flow of molten iron and and the emergence of fully cast engine blocks. The operation required few hands except those needed to check gauges and to manipulate cranes to lift the metals. Manual foundry work, once a back-breaking, grimy occupation, had largely given way to machines.

Continuous-flow, or automatic-handling, operations had actually been introduced in 1939 by Standard Oil, with new factories in which the raw material flowed through nonstop, 24-hour-a-day automatic processing stages to produce a never-ending stream of finished products. The plants were run by central control rooms, with mobile maintenance crews on hand to deal with breakdowns. Manual labor was reduced to operating control dials and skilled repair work. In addition to continuous-flow operations the term "automation" was generally understood to include three other labor-saving processes. The first was "automatic assembly" by machines. General Mills came up with a machine called Autofab that was able to assemble in one minute the number of electronic units that it had previously taken one worker a day to assemble. The second was self-correcting devices, which instructed machines by means of punched tapes. Such machines were able to oversee more than 1,000 different mixing formulas at a single concrete mixing plant. Third, there were data-processing systems. U.S. Steel introduced one of the first, a comprehensive system in which production schedules, shipping orders, financial transactions, and other activities were done by computers.

The effect of automation, of course, was to reduce the requirement for labor, especially repetitive, semiskilled labor. Output in the chemical industry rose by about 50 percent between 1947 and 1954. Over the same period the number of blue-collar (manual) workers employed in the industry increased by only 1.3 percent, while the number of people employed as managers, supervisors, or clerical and sales staff went up by 50 percent. The ratio of blue-collar workers to other staff narrowed from 3:1 in 1947 to 2:1

This advertisement for IBM electric typewriters dates from 1950. IBM was also a world leader in computers in the 1950s, but no one then saw them as a replacement for the typewriter.

THE "M-FORM" CORPORATION

The new face of American industry as it developed in the 1950s was a multidivisonal structure of corporate management that came to called the "M-form."

Before World War II (1939–1945) the giant companies were typically highly centralized in structure; they were unitary, or "U-form," organizations. Top-heavy U-form corporations suffered from two weaknesses. They were inefficient in dealing with a wide and diverse range of products, and they found it difficult to exercise control over operations spread over a broad geographical area.

Many of America's largest corporations—DuPont, General Motors, Sears, Standard Oil, and Westinghouse among them—saw in the decentralization of their management structure an answer to those difficulties. Instead of attempting to control all their operations from the center, they devolved responsibility to local managers who were on the spot. Regional—and later national—divisions of an M-form corporation were equipped with all the departments of the business: materials, engineering, manufacturing, marketing, and sales. Each such division was run as a quasi-independent, self-sufficient enterprise, although the central offices of the corporations continued to control capital investment, the appointment of divisional executives, and strategic decisions concerning diversification and expansion.

Concept of the Corporation, a best-selling book by Peter Drucker published in 1946, popularized the M-form as the ideal structure for a large corporation. The idea was taken up so avidly by management consultants that by the end of the 1950s it had become the standard form of corporate structure not only in the United States but also in the overseas operations of leading multinationals such as the Ford Motor Company and the rubber company B.F. Goodrich.

These women are working in a chicken cannery in 1950. By the end of the decade automation had greatly reduced the number of dull, repetitive jobs such as this.

in 1954. No longer dependent on a large labor force, corporations found a new freedom to locate factories away from large centers of population, bringing them in many cases closer to raw materials and fuels, thus making distribution easier and less expensive. For individual workers the loss of traditional jobs could be distressing. But automation took many men and women off mind-numbing work on the assembly line. By reducing the need for such jobs, automation also gave people impetus to train and study for jobs with greater skill levels, which also tended to be associated with higher productivity and higher pay, to the lasting economic benefit of the country as a whole.

See Also:

Advertising Industry • Agriculture • Arms Industry • Automobile Industry • Economy • Highway Network • Labor Relations • Leisure Industry • Retail Industry • Schools and Universities

INTERNATIONAL AID

After World War II the major task for U.S. foreign aid was to rebuild the infrastructures and economies of European and Asian nations shattered by conflict. By doing so, the United States also aimed to stem the spread of communism.

Giving aid to other countries in the form of grants, loans, equipment, technical advice, and training is something that the governments of all wealthy nations now do. This was not always the case, however. Before the 1940s most aid was given to support combatant nations in a war. During World War I (1914–1918), for example, the United States gave loans to its allies, while in World War II (1939–1945) it provided its allies with equipment and supplies in "lend–lease" arrangements, under which aid was given in return for something from which the United States would benefit, such as support for American troops stationed abroad. In practice, however, the United States often received very little in return.

The idea that international aid should be provided for purposes other than boosting a country's war effort first became widely accepted during World War II. In 1943 a total of 44 nations established the United Nations Relief and Rehabilitation Administration (UNRRA) to ensure that relief supplies (such as food, clothing, shelter, medicines, and fuel) and services run by trained personnel were provided to countries suffering from the destructive effects of the conflict. A further aim was to rebuild the economies of the affected countries. After the war UNRRA gave aid to the millions of refugees and displaced persons in Europe and Asia, providing them with camps and food while organizing their return to their home countries.

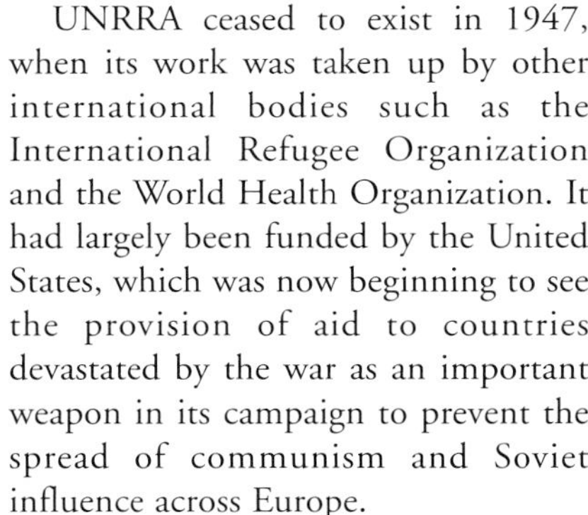

UNRRA ceased to exist in 1947, when its work was taken up by other international bodies such as the International Refugee Organization and the World Health Organization. It had largely been funded by the United States, which was now beginning to see the provision of aid to countries devastated by the war as an important weapon in its campaign to prevent the spread of communism and Soviet influence across Europe.

Aid to fight communism

In early 1947, when the British announced that they could no longer afford to provide economic and military assistance to the Greek and Turkish governments, President Harry S. Truman (1945–1953) felt that it was essential to intervene. The Greek government was embroiled in fighting Communist insurgency, while Turkey was being subjected to Soviet demands for a large chunk of its territory. In an address to Congress that became known as the Truman Doctrine the president stated that the United States was determined to oppose any further expansion of communist territory and so would provide economic and military aid to "free peoples who are resisting attempted subjugation" to bolster their defenses against internal and external communist forces. The aid achieved its desired effect in both Greece and Turkey.

The decision to provide aid to southeastern Europe was followed by the announcement of the European Recovery Program (ERP, or the

Jeeps are loaded on board the S.S. *Steel Apprentice* in Maryland in 1951. In the 1950s much aid was military equipment, destined for wars against communism.

THE MARSHALL PLAN

The U.S. Secretary of State George C. Marshall (1880–1959) first outlined his plan for reviving the economies of Europe in June 1947. At its core was the idea that if Europe received the funds to rebuild its economic infrastructure—in particular, its iron, steel, and power industries—there would be a major increase in industrial production and a corresponding expansion of European trade. However, it would take more than American funds to achieve this: Also essential were moves by the Europeans toward increased economic cooperation.

Immediately after the war the countries of Europe relied heavily on imports from the United States, but they did not have the money to pay for them. They also had no money to buy imports from other European countries. The Marshall Plan (or European Recovery Program, as it was officially named, and as Marshall himself preferred to call it) enabled the countries of Western Europe to continue importing goods from the United States and subsequently from each other. It also encouraged Americans to invest in European businesses.

At $13 billion the overall cost of the Marshall Plan as a percentage of U.S. national income was far higher than that of present-day American international aid programs. But it achieved its aim of stimulating Western Europe's economic recovery and ensuring that Europe would be a strong trading partner for the United States in the future. In 1953 Marshall accepted the Nobel Peace Prize on behalf of the American people, on whose money and efforts the program's success was founded.

A poster promotes the European Recovery Program (Marshall Plan). *Neues Leben für Europa* means "A new life for Europe."

Marshall Plan; *see box*), which provided some $13 billion in economic aid to the war-ravaged countries of Europe between 1948 and 1952. The plan was hugely successful in helping achieve the economic reconstruction of Western Europe. However, it was only partially successful in preventing the spread of communism across the continent because the states of Eastern Europe refused the aid that was offered or were prevented from accepting it by the Soviet Union.

During the 1950s the Cold War intensified between the United States and its allies on the one hand and the Eastern Bloc led by the Soviet Union on the other. Both sides regarded the supply of economic and military aid to other countries as a way of gaining support. This aid was, however, rarely provided without strings attached. Frequently, for example, the receiving country—often a developing nation—was obliged to buy goods or services from the donor country at prices that might not be the lowest available in the world. The receiving country might also be obliged to provide something in return, such as land for the construction of military bases by the donor nation. One of the largest recipients of this type of U.S. aid was South Korea, following the end of the war against Communist North Korea in 1953. Israel and Japan were also major recipients.

International organizations

It was not only individual countries that supplied aid in the 1950s. In 1945 the International Bank for Reconstruction and Development (usually known as the World Bank) was established by the United Nations with the purpose of making loans to governments or to private businesses backed by a government guarantee for specific projects. During the 1950s most of its loans were used to finance the construction of roads, ports, airports, inland waterways and pipelines, and the generation and distribution of electricity. In 1959 the Inter-American Development Bank, the first of a number of regional development banks, was set up to make loans to the countries of Latin America.

By the end of the 20th century it had become apparent that international aid alone cannot guarantee the economic development of the countries to which it is given. However, in the late 1940s and 1950s it played an important part in helping countries recover from the devastating effects of World War II and create the necessary conditions for their economic growth and prosperity.

See Also:

Cold War • Economy • Foreign Policy • France • Germany

WANDA JACKSON 1937–

Widely acclaimed in the late 1950s as the "First Lady of Rockabilly," Wanda Jackson wrote and recorded some of the wildest songs to be performed by a female rock-'n'-roll star before returning to the country music with which she had started her singing career.

With the emergence of rock 'n' roll in the mid-1950s a young female performer appeared whose wild energy, daring lyrics, and unashamed sexuality rivaled that of any male singer. For most of her career Wanda Jackson was a country singer. However, for a few brief years she was the incredibly raunchy first female star of rock 'n' roll.

Born October 20, 1937, in Maud, Oklahoma, Wanda Jean Jackson learned to sing in a church gospel choir. At the age of 12 she won a local radio talent contest and was awarded her own daily 15-minute show. The country singer Hank Thompson heard the show and asked her to tour with his band. Her first record, a duet with a member of the Thompson band, Billy Gray, was "You Can't Have My Love." Released by Decca Records in 1954, it reached Number 8 in the country charts.

First experiments in rock 'n' roll

After graduating from high school in 1955, Jackson toured the South with a group of country singers that included Elvis Presley (1935–1977). He convinced her to try rockabilly, the early version of rock 'n' roll. Capitol Records signed Jackson in 1956 and released "I Gotta Know," a mixture of raunchy rock with a whining country refrain that made the country Top 20. Her first Capitol album, released in 1958, included the famous "Let's Have a Party," which had previously been recorded by Presley.

Jackson, in a tight sheath dress, stilleto heels, and plenty of lipstick, was every bit as sexy and rebellious as Presley. (The Grand Ole Opry in Nashville forbade her to appear on its stage unless she covered her shoulders.) Her rasping, untamed voice pounded out lyrics in numbers such as "Cool Love" and "Hot Dog! That Made Him Mad." On occasions she could verge on the outrageous. "Fujiyama Mama" included highly controversial lyrics about the atomic bombs dropped in 1945 on Nagasaki and Hiroshima. Yet the song was a big hit in Japan, where Jackson toured to sell-out crowds.

In 1958, when this picture was taken, Wanda Jackson made her first rockabilly album. It included some dynamic songs but was not a commercial success.

Abroad Jackson was acclaimed as the "First Lady of Rockabilly." At home she was too shocking for many people, and by the end of the 1950s, with sales falling, her future as a rock singer appeared dim. However, in 1960 a disc jockey in Des Moines, Iowa, started playing "Let's Have a Party," and it suddenly looked as if Jackson's rock career might revive. Capitol rereleased the song with "Cool Love," and it made the pop Top 40 in the United States and Britain. On the back of that success Capitol brought out an album of Jackson's rock singles, *Rockin' with Wanda* (1960). It was not, however, a big seller, and by 1963 Jackson had abandoned rock 'n' roll and returned to country music for good.

See Also:
Country Music • *Grand Ole Opry* • Popular Music • Presley, Elvis • Recording Industry • Rock 'n' Roll • Teenage Culture

JAPAN

As the 1950s began, Japan was still under U.S. military occupation. The U.S. government's priority of stopping the spread of communism led it to reverse its earlier aim of a neutral Japan, and the U.S. military presence continued to be controversial for the rest of the decade.

Japan, a country that had never before experienced occupation by a foreign power, was from the end of World War II in August 1945 until April 1952 placed under the military rule of the United States. At the head of affairs was General Douglas MacArthur (1880–1964), Supreme Commander, Allied Powers, or SCAP, which also became the commonly used term for the U.S. administration of Japan. MacArthur's mission was to democratize Japanese government and liberalize its economy and society, while keeping the country permanently disarmed. Benevolent government from a country that had suffered the shock of attack at Pearl Harbor in 1941 and endured savage combat in the Pacific came as a pleasant surprise to the Japanese people, themselves traumatized by the dropping of atomic bombs on Hiroshima and Nagasaki. Against the odds, most Japanese people, exhausted by the war effort, accepted the occupation in good spirit.

Rebuilding civil society

MacArthur's initial task was to bring Japanese war criminals to justice and to remove from positions of responsibility those who were tainted by their involvement in Japanese aggression since the 1930s. About 200,000 officials lost their jobs in the purge, and an international tribunal sentenced to death seven men who had been political leaders during the war. Numerous extreme nationalist societies were closed down. Trials held throughout Japan and the regions it had formerly occupied ended in the execution of nearly 1,000 more officials and army personnel convicted of grossly cruel treatment of prisoners of war and of civilians under Japanese occupation.

From the outset MacArthur balanced retribution with a program of comprehensive reform aimed at transforming a traditionally inward-looking, semifeudal society into a modern democracy. Thousands of political prisoners were released from jail, and the opening up of the political system to a modified form of representative government and the extension of rights to women and other minorities were accompanied by a

President Harry S. Truman talks with General Douglas MacArthur in 1950. Truman appointed MacArthur as Supreme Commander, Allied Powers in Japan in 1945.

THE EMPEROR BROUGHT DOWN TO EARTH

The new constitution of 1946 placed the sovereignty of Japan in the hands of the people. Accordingly, in a historic radio broadcast on New Year's Day Emperor Hirohito (1901–1989) overturned centuries of tradition and renounced his divine status. "The ties between us and our people," he told the Japanese nation, "do not depend upon mere legends and myths. They are not predicated on the false conception that the emperor is divine." The imperial family had come down from the clouds.

Japan was henceforth to be, like the United Kingdom, a constitutional monarchy. The emperor's household staff was reduced from 8,000 to 1,000. His role in politics and government became merely symbolic. Hirohito took to walking among his people in ordinary civilian clothes, rather than military uniform or elaborate traditional costume. After so little direct contact with the world he was prone to making embarrassing remarks. While visiting the ruins of Hiroshima, he remarked that "there seems to have been considerable damage here." Yet he held his place in the affections of the people and, against advice from many quarters, refused to abdicate the throne in favor of his son. Abdication would have been a selfless act and an implicit admission of his and his nation's responsibility for war. Unlike the situation in Germany, Hirohito's continued presence perhaps encouraged the refusal of countless Japanese, in and out of government, to admit defeat or to reassess the dark years in which Japan had fallen into the hands of militarists and waged war in the Pacific on behalf of Nazism and fascism.

Hirohito, emperor of Japan, is seen here in the 1940s wearing imperial regalia and the headdress of a Shinto priest.

broadening of opportunity in education. On the economic front MacArthur endeavored to introduce a free-market economy by breaking the massive power of the handful of huge corporations, known as the *zaibatsu*, that monopolized Japanese industry and commerce. Labor unionism was allowed to flourish, and the legal rights of workers, including the right to strike, were greatly enhanced. Land was expropriated from the great landowners and redistributed to create a new class of independent small farmers.

Demilitarization proceeded swiftly. Weapons arsenals and ammunition depots were destroyed. Tanks, guns, aircraft, and antiaircraft devices were reduced to rubble, and naval ships were either scuttled or distributed among the victorious Allies. Atomic-energy equipment and all nuclear-related materials were seized, and a ban was placed on all industrial activity geared to armaments production. The Japanese army, navy, and air force were all disbanded, and the new post-1945 constitution outlawed the maintenance of armed forces in Japan and barred the Japanese government from going to war. Japan was to be the Asian equivalent of neutral Switzerland.

Rebuilding an economy

Alongside MacArthur's economic reforms, and somewhat at odds with them, went the efforts of the U.S. government to curb the economic power of Japan in order to prevent a revival of its imperialist aggression in East Asia. In 1945 President Harry S. Truman (1945–1953) had appointed Edwin Pauley, an oil magnate and Democratic Party fundraiser, to oversee the industrial recovery of Germany and Japan. Pauley drew up plans to redress the uneven balance between Japan—the industrial giant of Asia—and its neighbors. At the center of the plan was a proposal to transfer iron and steel factories from Japan to Manchuria. Doing so would build up China's industrial capacity as a counterweight to Japanese industrial dominance.

The advance of the Chinese Communists changed thinking in Washington. By 1949, when Mao Zedong (1893–1976) came to power in China and the U.S.-backed Nationalists under Chiang Kai-shek (1887–1975) were forced into exile on the island of Formosa (Taiwan), the balance of power in Asia had shifted. China, with its huge population and industrial and military potential now on the side of international communism, became the foe. Japan was to be transformed from enemy and occupied nation into a vital U.S. ally and strategic partner. No longer a military threat, Japan (on whose prosperity many countries in Southeast

Asia were dependent) was to be a showcase of the capitalist, democratic alternative to Chinese communism.

As a result, the war reparations payments to various Allied countries that MacArthur had imposed on Japan were ended. So, too, was the assault on the *zaibatsu* monopolies. Hundreds of "purged" individuals were allowed back into business and public life. There was a crackdown on strikes, while labor union membership, which had soared from under 1,000 in 1945 to about 6.5 million in 1949, began a process of steady decline that continued throughout the 1950s.

U.S. Army officers confer with an interpreter at a Japanese construction site in about 1950. The U.S. administration directed much of the rebuilding work in postwar Japan.

A rearmed Japan?

Above all, the rearmament of Japan came onto the agenda. As early as 1948 U.S. Defense Secretary James Forrestal had instructed the department of the army in Tokyo to begin limited rearmament, and after the outbreak of war in Korea in the summer of 1950 it was decided to establish a 150,000-strong Japanese army. There were two snags, however: the constitutional ban on armed forces and the risk of provoking a hostile reaction from the Soviet Union. So the new army was called a "national police force." An American military report stated that even though such a force was intended for domestic use only, "an augmented Civilian Police force would be the vehicle for possible organization of Japanese armed forces at a later date." MacArthur objected vehemently, pointing out the convulsions that rearmament would cause in Australia, New Zealand, and the Philippines.

Rearmament was given a boost by the peace treaty negotiated with Japan (formally ending World War II) in the spring of 1951. By placing John Foster Dulles, the leading Republican spokesman on foreign affairs, in charge of the negotiations, Truman ensured bipartisan support in Congress for the treaty, which was signed in San Francisco in September by 49 nations, although not by the Soviet Union and its satellite states in Eastern Europe, nor by China. Soviet anger was principally directed against the article that recognized Japan's "right of individual or collective self-defense." The United States pledged itself to come to Japan's

defense in the event of attack, and a separate security treaty concluded between Japan and the United States allowed for American troops to be stationed in Japan. In order to reassure Australia, New Zealand, and the Philippines, mutual defense agreements were made between those countries and the United States to provide for their security against Japanese aggression.

The San Francisco peace treaty liquidated the empire that Japan had gradually accumulated during the previous half-century. American control of the Ryukyu Islands was confirmed, and Japan recognized the independence of Korea and renounced all claims to Formosa, southern Sakhalin, and the Pescadores and northern Kuril Islands.

Trade tensions

The United Kingdom had pressed for the treaty to include restrictions on Japanese trade and economic growth, but the British lost the argument. The Japanese government was thus free to develop its overseas trade as it saw fit. At the beginning of 1953 trade with Communist China began. It remained small in scale, however, and an effort to increase it in 1958 foundered on the question of official recognition of the Communist government. The West still recognized the Nationalist government-in-exile on Formosa as the legitimate government of China. Japan was eager not to offend the United States by adopting a different position, nor to imperil its brisk trade with Formosa. As a result, a Sino-Japanese trade agreement of 1958 never came into force, and China severed all commercial and cultural contact with Japan.

The U.S. Senate ratified the peace treaty in March 1952, and American occupation came to an end in April. It came amid a rising tide of anti-Americanism, marked by violent May Day riots against the continued presence of American troops in postoccupation Japan and the subordination of Japanese foreign policy to the U.S. State Department. Pacifist sentiment was strong in Japan, and the rearmament program was deeply resented in many quarters. The statement by Vice President Richard M. Nixon (1913–1994), on a visit to Tokyo in 1953, that the "no war" clause in the constitution had been a mistake, fanned anti-American flames. The "Bikini incident" of 1954 provoked the most dramatic outbreak of anti-Americanism (*see box opposite*), but it did not deflect the Japanese government from its essentially conservative, pro-American course.

Further anti-American sentiment

In 1959 Asanuma Inejiro, a leading member of the Japanese Socialist Party, paid a visit to Peking (Beijing) during which he declared that the United States was the "common enemy" of Japan and China. A year later Japan negotiated a revision of the 1951 security treaty with the United States. The new agreement, which was to last for 10 years, did little more than renew the right of the United States to have military bases on Japanese soil in return for pledging to defend Japan against aggression. Perhaps because of fears of the Soviet Union's nuclear capacity anti-American demonstrations reached new heights. Opposition members kidnapped the speaker of the Japanese parliament in an effort to stop the treaty from being passed. Millions of Japanese petitioned for elections to get rid of the government, and students

Vice President Richard M. Nixon visits Tokyo in November 1953. The occupation and the Korean War had ended, but military cooperation remained a source of tension.

THE BIKINI INCIDENT

In March 1954 the United States tested a hydrogen bomb at Bikini Atoll in the Pacific, and the resulting fallout showered a small Japanese fishing boat with radioactive ash. The members of the fishing party came down with radiation sickness, but their tuna catch was examined and found to be infected only after half of it had been sold at market. To a people who ate as much fish as the Japanese, the news caused panic, and to this was added anger at the silence from the White House. The Eisenhower administration was not willing to make an apology or even to send expressions of sympathy to the hospitalized victims until a report formally assigned responsibility to the Americans. Adding to the ill-feeling was the reported remark of the head of the U.S. Atomic Energy Commission that the Japanese vessel had perhaps strayed into the danger zone around the test in order to spy on it—a charge that later proved to be unfounded.

A wave of anti-Americanism swept over Japan, challenging the pro-American position of the Japanese government. In his history of Japan Richard Storry pointed out that "it has never been appreciated in the West that this affair caused resentment in Japan at least equal to that occasioned by the atomic attacks on Hiroshima and Nagasaki." After all, these attacks occurred in the context of a long and bitter struggle. However, the testing of the hydrogen bomb at Bikini Atoll took place at a time of peace. Moreover, the nation responsible was one that claimed to be both a friend and ally of Japan.

Strikers (wearing white helmets) attempt to get past police and into their factory to eject strikebreakers in Tokyo, 1959. Labor unrest grew as the *zaibatsu* reasserted their power.

surrounded the parliament building. Street protests went on for weeks and drifted into violence and terrorism. Asanuma was stabbed to death in 1960 at a public meeting by a member of a far-right society. President Dwight D. Eisenhower (1953–1961) was forced to cancel a state visit during which he had been due to sign the new security treaty.

An uneasy stability

The 1950s ended with Japanese–American relations at a low ebb. A blow had been delivered to Japanese democracy by the massive police presence needed to quell opposition to the American alliance. Japan had settled into a period of virtual one-party rule by the right-of-center Liberal Democratic Party (which was to govern Japan for decades to come) in league with the *zaibatsu*. Japanese democracy was not a sham, but nor was it a vigorous medium for the airing of competing opinions. The labor movement was impotent, and the impetus behind many of General MacArthur's reforms had long since faded away. Officials in the State Department and the Defense Department could, however, look back with some measure of gratification on the United States' part in raising Japan from its knees in 1945 to a position of strength in the world and strategic importance on the side of the West in the Cold War.

See Also:

Armed Forces • China • Cold War • Foreign Policy • Formosa/Taiwan • H-bomb Tests • International Aid • Korean War • MacArthur, Douglas

JAZZ

During the 1950s jazz acquired a respectability and status it had not enjoyed before. Both of the two major schools of jazz, those of the East Coast and the West Coast, were recognized as making an important contribution to American culture.

The aftermath of World War II (1939–1945) was a time of political and cultural upheaval. Many art forms underwent periods of change, and jazz was no exception. In the prewar era the dominant form of the music was swing. Typically played by big bands such as those led by Duke Ellington, Louis Armstrong, and Benny Goodman, swing was an upbeat and easily accessible form of dance music. In the forties and early fifties, however, a radical new form of jazz emerged, one that was characterized by frenzied tempos, advanced harmonies, and virtuoso improvisations. It became known as bebop.

The bebop revolution

Bebop was a focused attempt by black musicians to move jazz away from the simple harmonies and basic rhythms that were currently dominating popular music. When bebop emerged in the early 1940s, it was the first significant departure from the swing sound. Bebop was typically played by small groups of musicians, usually between four and six in number. In contrast to swing, bebop placed more importance on solo musicians than ensemble playing. The music was characterized by complex melodies and chord progressions, and a new prominence was given to the rhythm section. The musicians experimented with discordant sounds and irregular phrasing, creating music that was a self-conscious art form. For the first time it was imperative for the audience to listen intently to the music, especially the improvised solos. Another contrast to the music of the big bands was that bebop was not suitable for dancing. At times this unconventional music placed great demands on its audience. Even many established jazz musicians, including the great Louis Armstrong (1901–-1971), condemned the new music as noisy and virtually unlistenable.

Bebop was very much an East Coast phenomenon. It evolved and flourished among the black musicians of New York City. The development of bebop is attributed in large part to the unique talents of saxophonist Charlie Parker (1920–1955) and trumpet player Dizzy Gillespie (1917–1993). Parker, born in Kansas City, Missouri, was self-taught. As a professional musician, playing with Jay McShann and Earl Hines, he gravitated to New York and the legendary jazz club Minton's Playhouse

Art Blakey performs at the Club Saint Germain, Paris, in 1958. As leader of the Jazz Messengers, Blakey was at the forefront of the hard bop movement.

JOHN COLTRANE

The tenor saxophonist John Coltrane (1926–1967) was a revolutionary musician whose work was widely imitated. Coltrane played in a U.S. Navy band before joining trumpeter Dizzy Gillespie in 1949. However, Coltrane really rose to prominence when he became part of the Miles Davis Quintet in 1955. There his flowing style and expansive tone provided an exciting counterpoint to Davis's more inward-looking trumpet. After a six-month interlude with Thelonious Monk's quartet in 1957 Coltrane recorded his own *Blue Train* album. He returned to work with Davis later in the year, appearing on the landmark album *Kind of Blue* in 1959.

Coltrane then formed his own group with pianist McCoy Tyner, drummer Elvin Jones, and (from 1961) bassist Jimmy Garrison. The band made its debut at New York's Jazz Gallery in May 1960. In the early 1950s Coltrane's career had been disrupted by an addiction to drugs and alcohol. Toward the end of the decade, however, he overcame these problems. This personal victory, and the profound religious experience associated with it, was eventually celebrated in the 1964 album *A Love Supreme,* which sold around a quarter of a million copies. Coltrane turned to increasingly radical musical styles in the mid-1960s, and these controversial experiments attracted large audiences. His unflagging support of young musicians and his obsessive quest for a musical ideal meant that he became a cult figure. He died from cancer in 1967.

This portrait of John Coltrane dates to 1960, by which time the saxophonist had conquered his heroin addiction.

in Harlem, which was regarded as the shrine of modern jazz. There he met Gillespie and other innovative musicians such as the pianist Thelonious Monk (1917–1982). Parker, with his technical ability and harmonic genius, was a jazz pioneer. In the late forties and early fifties he performed and recorded with a number of ensembles, producing revolutionary music that was marked by the saxophonist's wild and unpredictable solos. Even during his most creative period, however, Parker was plagued by heroin addiction and alcoholism. Eventually they took their toll, and he died in 1955 at age 35.

Dizzy Gillespie, who first played with Parker at Minton's in the early 1940s, is generally credited with the invention of the term "bebop," although the word probably originated from the scat vocals that were an improvised accompaniment to the new music. Like Parker, Gillespie was a musical revolutionary, and the breakneck speed and unpredictability of his trumpet playing ensured that he stood out from his contemporaries. Gillespie was also a great showman and a dedicated teacher who nurtured the talents of a number of fellow musicians. The 1950s saw Gillespie exploring the bebop style with both small ensembles and big bands, and in 1956 the U.S. government sent him on tour abroad as a cultural ambassador.

From bebop to hard bop

Bop broke away from jazz conventions, experimenting with new harmonies, rhythms, and tempos. In the 1950s musicians began to explore the rhythmic element still further. The drums had already developed from their traditional role as a background instrument that simply laid down a heavy beat; now they rose to new prominence, becoming a frontline instrument in their own right. The piano was treated more as a source of percussion, and rhythmic exchanges between drums and piano became common. The drums underpinned the raw and hard-driving music that became known as hard bop. Like bop, hard bop was an East Coast phenomenon, focused on New York City, although there were important exponents in the jazz communities of Philadelphia, Indianapolis, and Detroit. Hard bop musicians began to create original compositions, breaking away from the bebop convention of

BLUE NOTE

The story of the Blue Note label began in 1925 in Berlin, Germany, when Alfred Lion (Blue Note's eventual founder) happened on a jazz concert by American pianist Sam Woodyard and experienced a musical epiphany. By 1938 Lion had relocated to New York, where, overwhelmed by the wealth of jazz talent on display, he became determined that the music should be recorded. Within a few weeks he had arranged finance, rented a studio, and was recording the work of two virtuoso boogie-woogie pianists, Albert Ammons and Meade "Lux" Lewis. Blue Note records was born. In 1941 Lion was joined by Francis Wolff, who became the label's business manager, leaving Lion free to concentrate on overseeing recording sessions. Lion and Wolff were at jazz's cutting edge, recording representatives of all the latest musical styles. The list of artists who were signed to Blue Note reads like a litany of the all-time jazz greats: Among others, Miles Davis, John Coltrane, Thelonious Monk, Horace Silver, and Art Blakey all recorded for the label. Lion's appetite for new music was enthusiastic and wide-ranging. Unlike other labels, Blue Note paid for rehearsal time prior to a recording session, and the investment yielded handsome returns. Artists felt familiar with the material they were recording and were therefore more confident about improvising during sessions.

However, it was not only the sound that was distinctive. Francis Wolff was responsible for creating the Blue Note look, which was defined by his raw photographs of recording sessions, with close-cropped portraits of the musicians involved. These photographs often found their way onto album covers, many of which were the work of designer Reid Miles, who began working for Blue Note in 1956 and designed some 500 covers in his 15-year career. His minimalist style is instantly recognizable.

Blue Note went through a fallow period in the seventies and early eighties but was reborn in 1985 when Capitol Records acquired rights to the label and began to sign up new jazz artists and release classic albums on CD.

taking pop tunes as a starting point for improvisation. Some of the classic hard bop songs include Clifford Brown's "Joy Spring," Cannonball Adderley's "Work Song," and Benny Golson's "Blues March."

In the early 1950s the leading exponents of the developing hard bop style were trumpeter Clifford Brown, tenor saxophonist Sonny Rollins, and the bands led by drummer Art Blakey. Clifford Brown was born in 1930 and died in 1956 in a car accident. In his brief life he became a jazz legend, playing with Charlie Parker and fellow trumpeters Miles Davis (1926–1991) and Fats Navarro (1923–1950), whose style was a major influence. In 1954 Brown formed the Brown-Roach quintet, together with saxophonist Harold Land and drummer Max Roach. In 1955 the tenor sax player Sonny Rollins (1930–) replaced Land as a member of the group. In a professional career that was shorter

Trumpeter Dizzy Gillespie, shown here, was one of the most important figures in fifties jazz, largely responsible for the development of the style known as bebop.

than five years, Brown gained many admirers for his flowing improvisations and flawless technique. He was also a role model for other musicians in an era when jazz was all too frequently coupled with the excesses of drug addiction and alcoholism. Brown was clean-living and drug-free, and much admired by Rollins, who said: "Clifford was a profound influence on my personal life. He showed me that it was possible to live a good, clean life and still be a good jazz musician."

Rollins continued to record with Max Roach after Brown's death in 1956, before leading his own ensembles. One of Rollins's most acclaimed recordings with Roach was *Saxophone Colossus* (1956), which featured the calypso "St. Thomas." Rollins's parents were immigrants from the Virgin Islands, and Rollins was not afraid to use Caribbean rhythms in his work. Such experiments were typical of the innovative approach that Rollins brought to the art form.

In the early 1950s drummer Art Blakey (1919–1990) performed with both Rollins and Brown, as well as legendary trumpeter Miles Davis. However, the closest musical relationship he developed was with the pianist Horace Silver (1928–). In 1955 Blakey and Silver formed a cooperative group named the Jazz Messengers. Silver left the following year, but Blakey carried on, playing with a succession of talented, young upcoming musicians. The Jazz Messengers were the archetypal hard bop group of the late 1950s, playing a driving, aggressive extension of bop. Silver, along with bassist Charles Mingus and organist Jimmy Smith, was inspired by gospel music and was known for giving hard bop music a soulful edge.

On the street

Both bebop and hard bop developed in New York. By the 1950s the city had been a hotbed of jazz for a considerable period of time. In the 1920s and 1930s Harlem had been the epicenter of the jazz world. Its nightclub scene acted as an exotic magnet for wealthy whites, who were eager to experience the raw excitement of Harlem for themselves. However, by the mid-1940s the neighborhood had become increasingly rundown and dangerous for interlopers, and New York's jazz heart had moved to 52nd Street, between Fifth and Seventh Avenues, two blocks of modest brownstones that housed an array of jazz clubs including the Spotlite, the Yacht Club, Jimmy Ryan's, the Onyx, and the Three Deuces. During the heyday of these venues musicians moved freely between the clubs, sitting in on one another's gigs, creating a uniquely vibrant jazz community.

The postwar years saw the relative decline of the 52nd Street neighborhood as jazz clubs were gradually taken over by sleazy strip-joints. Some clubs still thrived, however. The most famous was the legendary Birdland (named for Charlie "Bird" Parker), which opened in late 1949, with a bill that included its namesake, Lester Young, Max Kaminsky, and Lennie Tristano. Located on Broadway between 52nd and 53rd Streets, the club boasted lifesize photographs of contemporary jazzmen such as Dizzy Gillespie, Tristano, and of course Bird himself that loomed dramatically against jet-black walls. Exotic live birds perched in cages behind the bar, although many eventually suffocated in their cages from the smoky atmosphere. The master of ceremonies was Pee Wee Marquette, who only stood 3 feet 9 inches (114cm) tall. Dressed in a zoot suit and snazzy tie, he smoked huge cigars and was famous for his mispronounced introductions. Legendary Birdland performers included Bud Powell and Max Roach. The club survived into the mid-1960s.

The Birdland jazz club was one of the most fashionable venues in New York City during the 1950s. It was named for trumpeter Charlie "Bird" Parker.

A handful of midtown clubs fought the trend and survived through the 1950s: The Embers, Basin Street East, and a relocated Jimmy Ryan's. In the 1960s, however, the center of the jazz scene moved downtown to Greenwich Village and became well established in a number of internationally famous clubs such as the Jazz Gallery, the Five Spot, and the Village Gate. The most famous of the Greenwich Village clubs was the Village Vanguard, which opened in the early 1930s.

Birth of the Cool

While the frantic sounds of hard bop were being heard in clubs in New York, a lighter, more laidback style was evolving on the West Coast. Developed mainly by white musicians, it combined the rhythms and harmonies of bebop with the more melodic and accessible feel of earlier music to produce an aura of emotionally detached "coolness."

For all its associations with the West Coast, the origins of this style of jazz lay in the work of a New York-based musician—Miles Davis. Davis left Charlie Parker's group in 1948 and, together with other New York musicians, began to create a new sound that was marked by lush orchestration. In order to put his ideas into practice, Davis formed a nonet (nine-piece band) that featured a number of instruments that were not normally associated with jazz, such as the French horn and tuba. Davis's ensemble made a series of experimental recordings that were eventually collected and released under the title *Birth of the Cool.*

One of the key personnel in Davis's group was saxophonist Gerry Mulligan (1927–1996). After working with Davis, Mulligan moved to Los Angeles, where he formed a quartet with the trumpeter Chet Baker (*see box opposite*). The two musicians soon became dominant figures in the West Coast jazz scene and were the first artists to record for the Pacific Jazz label. The unique sound of their group owed much to the fact that they did not use a pianist or a guitarist. Mulligan and Baker became known for their distinctively clean, laidback sound. As their popularity grew, Los Angeles became a major jazz center. Clubs such as the Lighthouse on Hermosa Beach and the Haig in Los Angeles thrived. Among the prominent jazz musicians who settled on the West Coast during this time were trumpeter Shorty Rogers, saxophonists Art Pepper and Bud Shank, drummer Shelly Manne, and clarinetist Jimmy Giuffre.

Another key aspect of cool jazz was the prominent role played by arrangers. Among the most important were Miles Davis's collaborator Gil Evans, Tadd Dameron, Claude Thornhill and Mulligan himself, who was as talented an arranger as he was a saxophonist. Such arrangers focused on creating instrumental colors and spacious, slower-moving harmonies. Dissonance also played some part in the music, but in a softened, muted way.

Cool jazz was often influenced by classical music. For example, the California pianist Dave Brubeck (1920–) studied composition at Mills College, Oakland, under French composer Darius Milhaud. Brubeck formed his own quartet in 1951 and integrated odd meters and classical forms into his compositions. One of his most famous pieces was "Blue Rondo à la Turk," which reworked Mozart's "Turkish Rondo." "Blue Rondo" appeared on Brubeck's 1959 album *Time Out,* which also featured his most famous piece, "Take Five," written in the unconventional time signature of 5/4. Brubeck's intellectual take on the genre, together with his habit of playing concerts on university campuses, ensured that he developed a white, middle-class following.

Latin Influence

Another development that occurred in jazz during the 1950s was the absorption of influences from Latin America. In the early 1950s a group of

Brazilian guitarist João Gilberto, pictured here in the 1970s, was partially responsible for the creation of the bossa nova sound, which combined jazz with Latin elements.

CHET BAKER

One of the leading jazz trumpeters of the 1950s, Chet Baker (1929–1988) has become an icon, famous as much for his good looks and self-destructive drug dependency as for his musicianship. Baker was born in Oklahoma. He started to play trumpet while still in his teens as a member of the 298th Army Band. After his discharge from the Army in 1952 Baker moved to Los Angeles, where he participated in some historic Pacific Jazz recording sessions at the Haig Club with a group led by Gerry Mulligan. This group was to evolve into the famous pianoless Gerry Mulligan Quartet. Baker played a plangent, melancholy trumpet and also contributed occasional vocals in a fragile tenor voice that, for many, remained an acquired taste. In 1953 the Chet Baker Quartet was established when Mulligan temporarily retired from music. The handsome and charismatic Baker came to be seen as an epitome of cool. However, he was locked in a spiral of self-destructive heroin addiction. In the late fifties and early sixties he pursued a nomadic lifestyle. Baker spent much of this time touring Europe, and these tours were punctuated with arrests, hospitalizations. attempts at rehabilitation, and retreats into dependency. In March 1964 he was deported back to the United States from Germany. His 1960s recordings, made for Pacific Jazz and Verve, were disappointing. Baker's life hit a further low in 1966, when he lost some teeth in a violent mugging in San Francisco, probably the result of a botched drug deal.

Against the odds, however, Baker gradually controlled his drug addiction through the use of methadone and in 1974 began to record again. His work at last started to show more range and authority, which he combined with a heartfelt lyricism. In May 1988, however, Baker's career was cut short when he fell out of his hotel room window in Amsterdam, probably a drug-related accident.

Chet Baker poses with his wife Liliane before a concert in London in 1955. Baker spent much of the late 1950s touring Europe.

Brazilian musicians living in the Copacabana area of Rio de Janeiro were exposed to jazz records from the West Coast. They included Luiz Bonfa, Antônio Carlos Jobim, and João Gilberto. Gilberto (1931–) was a self-taught guitarist who had moved to Rio de Janeiro in 1950 and experienced moderate success singing with the chorus group Garotos da Lua. During the 1950s Gilberto developed a style of music that became known as bossa nova (or "new beat"). Bossa nova combined the syncopated rhythms of samba with harmonies that were reminiscent of West Coast jazz. Bossa nova became well known through the album *Chega de Saudade* and song of the same name, performed by Gilberto and composed by Antônio Carlos Jobim and Vinícius de Moraes. Released in 1959, the album became an instant success. Besides a number of Jobim compositions the album featured older sambas and popular songs from the 1930s influenced by the works of Pixinguinha, a legendary musician who spearheaded the development of modern Brazilian music.

In 1962 the guitarist Charlie Byrd, who had toured Brazil and become immersed in its music, recorded *Jazz Samba* with saxophonist Stan Getz. It was to become an immediate success, and a host of jazz musicians, including the saxophonists Coleman Hawkins and Sonny Rollins, began to make bossa nova recordings. By the mid-1960s a number of bossa nova compositions, including perhaps the most famous, Jobim's "The Girl from Ipanema," had become standards in the jazz repertoire.

Jazz divas

Although several mainstream female vocalists such as Ella Fitzgerald enjoyed considerable success in the 1950s, the world of innovative jazz was largely male-dominated. Nevertheless, a number of female vocalists emerged who experimented with the human voice, pushing it to its limits. One such performer was Sarah Vaughan, who was born to a musical family in New Jersey in 1924. In the 1940s she began to perform with many of the pioneers of

JAZZ ON A SUMMER'S DAY

One wintry night in 1953 a socialite from Newport, Rhode Island, named Elaine Lorillard complained to George Wein, a pianist, impresario, and jazz enthusiast, that the summer scene was "terribly boring" and suggested that some jazz might liven things up. At the time Newport was a genteel summer resort for wealthy East Coasters, who were not seen as a typical jazz audience. After Lorillard's husband, tobacco heir Louis Lorillard, provided a $20,000 donation, Wein seized the opportunity to create the first American jazz festival. The festival opened on July 17, 1954, at the Newport Tennis Casino, with a stellar lineup that included Billie Holiday, Oscar Peterson, Dizzy Gillespie, Count Basie, Louis Armstrong, Stan Getz, and Dave Brubeck. The festival immediately attracted media attention because it broke new ground, introducing an essentially urban art form to the well-manicured lawns of the staid and wealthy.

Newport's influence was soon felt beyond the United States. Starting in 1955, the Voice of America began taping festival concerts for broadcast, and jazz festivals began to spring up throughout Europe. As Wein remarked, "Jazz musicians needed a festival. By bringing many groups together we could draw many kinds of jazz fans. It became a great source of public relations for the music." At the second Newport festival, in 1955, Miles Davis played alongside a modernist lineup that included Thelonious Monk, Gerry Mulligan, and Zoot Sims. Davis's magical solo on "Round Midnight" was the highlight of the weekend, bringing the Newport audience to its feet. Jazz had arrived in Rhode Island.

Pianist and bandleader Dave Brubeck performs at the Newport Jazz Festival in 1958. By this point the festival was established as a major event in the jazz calendar.

the bebop style, including trumpeters Dizzy Gillespie and Fats Navarro, saxophonists Dexter Gordon and Sonny Stitt, bassist Oscar Pettiford, and drummer Art Blakey. Vaughan developed an ear for the intricate harmonies and melodies of bebop. She signed with the Musicraft label in 1945, recording songs such as "Lover Man" and "East of the Sun and West of the Moon." By this point Vaughan's radical experiments with melody and vocal timbre had gained her the respect of her contemporaries.

In 1954 Vaughan joined Mercury Records. The contract that she signed with the label allowed her to pursue two contrasting careers. The singer's more mainstream material appeared on the Mercury Label, while her more experimental jazz work was issued on a sister label, EmArcy. Among other artists, she collaborated with Clifford Brown and Cannonball Adderley. Vaughan continued to record until the 1980s, when her health began to worsen. She died in 1990.

Betty Carter

Perhaps the most experimental female jazz vocalist of the late 20th century was Betty Carter, whose adventurous scat singing pushed the limits of the human voice as an instrument. Carter was born in Michigan in 1930 and studied the piano at the Detroit Conservatory of Music. As a teenager she sat in with a number of prominent bebop musicans such as Charlie Parker when they performed in Detroit. Carter moved to New York at the age of 21, and the 1950s saw her performing at the famed Apollo Theater in Harlem, singing with Dizzy Gillespie and Max Roach.

Carter made her first recordings in 1955 with the pianist Ray Bryant. However, the album got little recognition. With her idiosyncratic interpretations of classic tunes Carter was popular among hardcore jazz fans, but critical and popular acclaim eluded her until she toured with Ray Charles in the late 1950s. Their joint album, released in 1961, was greeted with both critical and popular acclaim. Her remarkable career spanned 50 years, and she remained active in the 1990s, performing for President Bill Clinton at the White House in 1994. She died of cancer four years later.

Singer Sarah Vaughan prepares to make a recording in a New York studio in 1955. Vaughan collaborated with a number of prominent bebop musicians.

The way ahead

By the early 1960s, despite a decade of experimentation and innovation, jazz was beginning to slip out of the mainstream of commercial music. The arrival of rock 'n' roll in the mid-1950s had lured many potential teenage fans away from the genre. Competition now came from the developing Motown sound and the so-called British invasion spearheaded by bands such as the Beatles and the Rolling Stones. In the face of such challenges jazz musicians began more and more to turn to avant-garde experimentation or to "fusion" music, which combined jazz with the increasingly popular genres of rock, soul, and funk.

See Also:

Armstrong, Louis • Davis, Miles • Holiday, Billie • Parker, Charlie • Popular Music

LYNDON BAINES JOHNSON 1908–1973

Although best known for his vision of a "Great Society," his civil rights programs, and for the escalation of the Vietnam War during his presidency, Lyndon Baines Johnson spent the 1950s becoming one of the most effective and powerful leaders the Senate has ever known.

Lyndon Baines Johnson was born on August 27, 1908, and grew up in the Hill Country of central Texas in a home whose political and economic fortunes varied wildly during his childhood. His father, Sam Johnson, was a man of great ambition: He was a member of the Texas legislature and also speculated in risky investments. A combination of bad luck and poor planning cost Sam Johnson his political career and all his family's money. Young Lyndon would respond to the humbling of his father by becoming perhaps the most ambitious, talented, and ruthless politician in American history.

Lyndon Baines Johnson was 20th-century America's consummate politician. His unerring instinct for power bore fruit in both the Congress and the White House.

Early career

From an early age Johnson's great gift was to be able to recognize how to gain power in any situation. The means to power would vary according to the situation: At Southwest Texas State Teachers College he quickly realized that campus elections could easily be stolen since there was so little supervision of them. Johnson also learned that a combination of flattery and hard work was irresistible to college administrators and professors. He became an assistant to the president of his college and acquired connections and influence of which few undergraduate students could dream.

As an aide to Democratic Representative Richard Kleberg in the early 1930s Johnson virtually created the modern notion of a congressional staffer. He used this influence to gain the attention of President Franklin D. Roosevelt (1933–1945), who made Johnson the Texas state director of the National Youth Administration, a major jobs program of the New Deal. Through maniacal hard work and a shady network of supporters Johnson won election to the U.S. House from Texas in 1937, shortly before his 30th birthday. Since his mentor Roosevelt enjoyed a large majority in Congress, Johnson fashioned himself as a loyal supporter of the New Deal. The young Johnson met frequently with Roosevelt in the White House, and he parlayed the impression of a close relationship with the president into votes for many of his local projects, including rural electrification and flood control in his poor Hill Country home district.

Foothold in the Senate

After a narrow loss in a special U.S. Senate election in 1941 Johnson ran again for a seat in 1948. He won the Democratic nomination by 87 votes (out of almost one million cast) thanks to a ballot box stuffed with Johnson votes that were "discovered" after the initial vote count indicated that he had lost. The size of Johnson's victory, and the blatant corruption behind it, earned him the ironic nickname "Landslide Lyndon." His electoral machinations were only part of Johnson's approach to politics. He also built a multimillion-dollar fortune through his control of radio and later TV stations in Austin, Texas. These properties were always kept officially in his wife's name, but behind the scenes Johnson used his political influence to gain more advertising revenue for his growing communications empire.

Johnson's boisterous demeanor seemed to make him a poor fit for the Senate, whose members prized elegant speeches and respect for seniority. As usual, however, Johnson proved a master at accumulating power. He gave very few speeches. Instead, he dedicated his energies to cultivating personal relationships with fellow senators. While in the House, Johnson had built

THE LEADERSHIP TACTICS OF LYNDON JOHNSON

Johnson's great talent was to be able to recognize how to gain power in any situation. The means that were appropriate would vary according to the situation and ranged from stolen elections and the accumulation of wealth to the cultivation of friendships.

Sometimes the situation would call for flattery of an older, more powerful person. On other occasions it would call for earnest, heartfelt praise of an overworked subordinate. And sometimes the situation would call for bullying and physical intimidation, which Johnson, at 6 feet 3 inches (190cm) tall, could dish out ably. Depending on what image he needed to project, Johnson could make others see an idealistic New Dealer, a conservative Texas rancher, or a most unlikely champion of civil rights.

As the Senate majority leader Johnson developed an encyclopedic knowledge of the needs (and the weaknesses) of his fellow senators. When he needed one more vote, he knew what to offer to a key swing voter or what to threaten him with. If he needed to stall for extra time to get another vote, Johnson knew how to keep the Senate from voting. One favorite tactic was to send Hubert Humphrey out to give an impromptu speech to delay the vote: The brilliant and long-winded Minnesotan could be counted on to speak for a while about almost anything. If a vote needed to happen right away, on the other hand, Johnson could make that happen too. Time and again on any number of issues Johnson engineered exactly the outcome he wanted. He made the Senate work like a machine. That had never happened before the mid-1950s and has rarely happened since.

As president Johnson continued to use his personal knowledge of politicians in Congress—a knowledge probably unmatched by any other modern president—to ensure passage of the landmark but controversial civil rights and social assistance bills that defined his vision of a "Great Society."

a close friendship with senior Texas Representative Sam Rayburn (1882–1961), who would ultimately become speaker of the House.

Johnson tried the same tactic in the Senate, this time by reaching out to Senator Richard Russell (1897–1971) of Georgia, the leader of the bloc of conservative southern senators. Johnson ingratiated himself to Russell by doing whatever seemed necessary: Among other tactics, he feigned an interest in baseball in order to have an excuse to accompany Russell to Washington Senators games. Johnson came to be perceived as Russell's likely successor as the leader of the southern states in the Senate, and Russell used his own great influence to further Johnson's rise.

At the same time that he was building a base of power among conservative southerners, Johnson was also building a friendship with the idealistic young liberal Hubert Humphrey (1911–1978) of Minnesota,

Johnson is welcomed back to Washington after winning the leadership of the Texas delegation to the Democratic National Convention, May 1956. Sam Rayburn stands on his right.

also first elected to the Senate in 1948. While Johnson was convincing Russell that he was the natural successor as a defender of the South and segregation, he was also persuading Humphrey that he was a liberal at heart and a figure who could bring the northern liberals and southern conservatives together. Which was the true Johnson? Commentators argue that he was both and neither. Johnson would assume whatever image, and pursue whatever line of argument, that would best advance him in the particular situation. "One on one," a colleague attested, "Lyndon Johnson is the best salesman who ever lived."

Johnson as president in 1966 poses with his wife "Lady Bird" Johnson. Lady Bird used her family inheritance to fund her husband's first congressional campaign.

Walking the tightrope

Johnson used his connections with the Democratic Party's two rival camps of southern conservatives and northern liberals to win positions in the party's leadership in the Senate. After only two years in office he became the chief whip (assistant party leader). When the Republicans won control of the Senate in 1952, the Democrats made the 44-year-old Johnson their leader. After the Democrats retook the Senate in 1954, Johnson became the youngest majority leader in the upper house's history. At the end of his first term in office he had become the leader of an institution that prized seniority and patience above all. It was an astonishing rise.

At that time, however, the majority leader position in the Senate did not have the prestige or power that it has today. In fact, it was Johnson who remade the job into its modern role as the main leadership force in the Senate. As Democratic leader Johnson slowly stripped power and control away from the committee chairmen. He centralized control of the calendar in his own office, thus gaining the power to decide when proposals would be voted on by the full Senate. He also subtly challenged the system of seniority, in which power and the choicest committee assignments were given to senators who had served the longest. The relatively young Johnson worked behind the scenes to reduce the reliance on seniority and to concentrate authority on his own office instead. He transformed the position of majority leader from an almost powerless figurehead into something close to a counterpart to the influential speaker of the House, the job held by his old friend and mentor, Sam Rayburn.

A sign of things to come

Perhaps Johnson's single greatest accomplishment as majority leader was the passage of the Civil Rights Act of 1957. The legislation itself was modest: It provided some protection for African Americans in the South who were trying to exercise their right to vote but did nothing to challenge the deep inequalities of segregation that went far beyond the denial of voting rights. However, Congress had not passed civil rights legislation since the 1870s. For 80 years conservative senators from the South, all of them white men, had been a consistent barrier to any progress on civil rights.

Johnson used his credibility with his fellow southerners, especially Russell, to win acceptance of the need to pass at least a token package of civil rights reforms. In large part Johnson and Russell were motivated by a desire to establish Johnson as a contender for president in 1960. Russell had tried and failed to win the Democratic presidential nomination in 1952, and Johnson himself failed in his pursuit of the nomination in 1956. The passage of a civil rights bill might soften the resistance to Johnson should he try for the presidency again. To his liberal allies Johnson made the case that the passage of even a weak civil rights bill in 1957 would open the door to much more significant civil rights legislation in the future.

Both arguments turned out to be true. Johnson was elected as John F. Kennedy's vice president in 1960 and ascended to the presidency in 1963 on Kennedy's assassination. Then, as president, Johnson won the passage of the truly epochal civil rights legislation of the 1960s. The relentless ambition and raw political talent that Johnson displayed in the Senate were a feature of his presidency as well.

See Also:

Civil Rights • Democratic Party • Politics and Government • Segregation and Desegregation

ESTES KEFAUVER 1903–1963

Estes Kefauver was a southern Democratic senator whose televised hearings into organized crime in the early 1950s made him a national figure. A campaigner for civil rights, he ran as the running mate of Adlai Stevenson in the 1956 presidential election.

Carey Estes Kefauver was born on a farm in Tennessee on July 26, 1903. He practiced as a lawyer before being elected to the U.S. House of Representatives as a Democrat in 1939. He was serving his fifth term when he won the election to the U.S. Senate from Tennessee in 1948. It was an upset victory that was secured despite the efforts of the corrupt political machine of E.H. "Boss" Crump, who had long ruled Memphis.

Kefauver immediately made his mark on the Senate. He was one of only two senators from the South who refused to join the Southern Caucus, a group committed to using the filibuster to defeat civil rights legislation. In May 1950, with only a year of experience in the Senate, he was made the chairman of a five-member special committee created to investigate organized crime. Over a period of 15 months what came to be known as the "Kefauver Committee" toured the nation, holding hearings in 14 cities and publicly questioning some 800 witnesses. The committee gradually attracted the interest of the news media, especially the new medium of television. The hearings in New Orleans and Detroit in 1950 were broadcast on local television.

When the Kefauver Committee arrived in New York City in 1951, the hearings were broadcast live nationwide in what was then unprecedented TV coverage. With relatively few homes yet having TV sets, crowds packed bars and electronics stores to watch the hearings, which featured Mafia boss Frank Costello. The total viewing audience was estimated at 30 million people. As *Life* magazine put it, "Never before had the attention of the nation been riveted so completely on a single matter."

In 1956 Estes Kefauver became Democratic candidate for the vice presidency despite not being popular with his fellow southerners because of his support for civil rights.

Ambitions to be president

The hearings made Kefauver an instant celebrity. Sensing an opportunity, he broke the informal party rules and expectations of loyalty to challenge for the Democratic nomination for president in 1952. He defeated President Harry S. Truman (1945–1953) in the New Hampshire primary before Truman himself decided to leave the race. At the 1952 Democratic National Convention Kefauver was the early front-runner among the delegates, but a late surge of support for Illinois Governor Adlai Stevenson (1900–1965) left him a distant second.

Kefauver sought the presidential nomination again in 1956. He defeated Stevenson in the Minnesota caucus and then went head-to-head against him in the first-ever televised debates prior to the Florida primary. Stevenson rallied to beat Kefauver in Florida and then California, forcing Kefauver to drop out of the race.

At the 1956 convention Stevenson took the unusual step of allowing the delegates to choose his running mate, and Kefauver immediately declared his candidacy for vice president. However, Stevenson had been informed by Senate Majority Leader Lyndon Baines Johnson and House Speaker Sam Rayburn that the ambitious Kefauver was unpopular in Congress. He preferred the young senator from Massachusetts, John F. Kennedy. The contest between Kefauver and Kennedy came down to the last few votes, but Kefauver prevailed. The Stevenson–Kefauver ticket was then overwhelmingly defeated by President Dwight D. Eisenhower (1953–1961) in November.

Kefauver continued to serve in the Senate until his death in August 1963. As chairman of the Senate Subcommittee on Antitrust and Monopoly he earned a reputation as a defender of the public interest and champion of consumer protection.

See Also:

Civil Rights • Democratic Party • Election of 1952 • Election of 1956 • Law and Order • Politics and Government • Stevenson, Adlai

JACK KEROUAC 1922–1969

The novelist Jack Kerouac was one of the foremost members of the literary movement known as the Beat generation. His most famous work was the 1957 semiautobiographical novel On the Road, *which chronicled his numerous journeys across America.*

Jack Kerouac was born Jean-Louis Lebris de Kerouac in Lowell, Massachusetts, on March 12, 1922. His French-Canadian parents spoke a dialect called *joual*, and Kerouac himself spoke no English until he was six years old. Life was hard for Kerouac's parents. His father was a printer who took up gambling after being forced out of business by financial difficulties, while his mother worked in a succession of factories.

Kerouac possessed a great talent for football, and in 1940 he began a football scholarship at Columbia University in New York City. However, after a major disagreement with the coach he returned to Lowell, where, soon after the United States' entry into World War II in 1941, he landed a job as a sports reporter. While in college, Kerouac had written many poems and short stories, and he now spent the afternoons writing his first extended piece of prose, an autobiographical work that he never completed.

In March 1942 Kerouac left Lowell for Washington, D.C, where he drifted from one job to another before moving to Boston and joining the Merchant Marine. After a difficult journey to Nova Scotia and Greenland—which he later described in his book *Vanity of Duluoz*—he returned briefly to Columbia before signing up for the Navy in 1943. Kerouac's dislike of receiving orders soon became apparent, and he was discharged, officially on psychiatric grounds. He then made a trip to England as an ordinary seaman before returning to New York and his sometime girlfriend Edie Parker, whom he married in 1944.

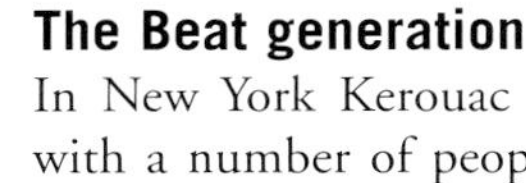

The Beat generation

In New York Kerouac became friends with a number of people who were to have a huge influence on his life, among them Neal Cassady (1926–1968) and the writers Allen Ginsberg (1926–1997) and William S. Burroughs (1914–1997). Kerouac, Ginsberg, and Burroughs formed the core of what became known as the Beat generation, a literary movement that favored spontaneous, freeflowing prose and championed unconventional lifestyles. In 1945 Kerouac divorced his wife and began work on his first novel, *The Town and the City*, which was to receive a lukewarm response when it was published in 1950.

In the late 1940s and early 1950s Kerouac lived in New York in winter and spent the summers traveling round the country, driving or hitchhiking

This photograph of Jack Kerouac dates to 1958, by which time the publication of *On the Road* had made him a major literary star.

ON THE ROAD

Jack Kerouac's most famous novel, *On the Road*, is now recognized as a modern classic, although it met with a very mixed reception when it was published in 1957. Its central character is Dean Moriarty—a thinly disguised Neal Cassady—who travels backward and forward between the East and West coasts accompanied by the book's narrator, Sal Paradise, the fictional name for Kerouac. Dean is the living epitome of the Beat generation, totally rejecting any form of conventional lifestyle. Instead, he is always on the move, constantly in search of new experiences and experimenting with drugs, sex, and mysticism.

Kerouac had made a few attempts at writing a book about his travels before sitting down in April 1951 to produce the first complete draft of *On the Road*. Wanting the book to be a spontaneous outpouring of thoughts, he produced 175,000 words in the form of a single paragraph in just three weeks. According to literary folklore, Kerouac typed at a rate of 100 words a minute. He used a continuous roll of paper so as not to be interrupted by putting sheets of paper into his typewriter. By June the manuscript was in book form, but Kerouac could not find a publisher for it until he eventually agreed to make some major revisions in 1956. The book was finally published in September 1957, and with the help of a good review in *The New York Times* it quickly became a bestseller. Later reviews were less kind, but by 1959 *On the Road* had sold 20,000 hardcover and 500,000 paperback copies. Kerouac was by then regarded as the leading representative of the Beat generation, while *On the Road* was seen as its major text.

This sign marks a street in San Francisco that was named for the author of *On The Road*. Kerouac spent a large amount of time in the city, which had a thriving literary scene.

between New York, San Francisco, and Mexico City. He was often accompanied on these travels by Cassady. Kerouac described these journeys in *On the Road*, the first draft of which was finished in 1951 (*see box*). The same year he separated from his second wife, Joan Haverty, after a marriage of only a few months during which she became pregnant with a daughter.

Kerouac could not immediately find a publisher for *On the Road*. But this did not deter him from continuing to write, and over the next few years he produced a number of manuscripts—including early versions of the novels *Visions of Cody*, *Dr. Sax*, and *The Subterraneans*—between traveling and visiting his friends in various parts of the country. In 1955 he journeyed to Mexico to meditate after becoming interested in Buddhism, but at heart he remained a devout Catholic.

On the Road was finally published in 1957. It received a mixed reception from critics but became a popular success. Kerouac soon came to be seen as a personification of the carefree and hedonistic Beat spirit, although he himself did not feel particularly comfortable with the role or with his newfound fame. In response Kerouac left New York, where he was treated as a celebrity, and went to Florida to stay with his mother, Gabrielle, to whom he remained very close. He would sporadically return to spend time with her for the rest of his life.

Descent into alcoholism

In reply to a request from his publisher to produce a more accessible work, Kerouac quickly wrote *The Dharma Bums*, which was published in 1958. Kerouac's old manuscripts now began to be published, and along with his Beat friends he performed poetry and prose readings in clubs, often to jazz accompaniment. However, after *The Dharma Bums* Kerouac did not write another book for four years. He became increasingly unhappy about the attention he was receiving. A lifelong heavy drinker, Kerouac now became an alcoholic.

In 1961 Kerouac moved to California, where he wrote his final, semiautobiographical novel, *Big Sur*, named for a remote stretch of the California coast. There were to be several more moves, always in the company of his mother, Gabrielle. In 1966 Kerouac married his childhood friend Stella Sampas, and the couple and Gabrielle moved to St. Petersburg in Florida. By now Kerouac's health was deteriorating rapidly, largely as the result of his alcoholism. He died from liver failure on October 20, 1969.

See Also:

Beat Movement • Burroughs, William • Ginsberg, Allen • Literature

KIM IL SUNG 1912–1994

As the leader of the Democratic People's Republic of Korea (North Korea) from 1948 until his death, Kim Il Sung led his country into the Korean War before establishing a Communist and militaristic regime that became renowned for its repressive policies.

Born Kim Song Ju on April 15, 1912, in Mangyongdae, near Pyongyang, Kim soon became a passionate nationalist who was resolved to free his country from Japanese rule, which had begun in 1910. In 1920 he and his family fled to China, where he joined Chinese guerrillas fighting the Japanese. After the guerrillas were routed by the Japanese in 1941 during World War II (1939–1945), Kim fled to the Soviet Union and later led a unit of Korean troops as a major in the Soviet Red Army.

Kim Il Sung is pictured in 1950, soon after launching a war to reunify Korea. By mid-1953 the border between north and south was back almost where it had been at the start.

The Korean War

Following the surrender of Japan in 1945, Korea was divided along the 38th parallel into the Soviet-occupied north and the U.S.-supported south. In the north in 1948 the Soviet Union established a Communist regime under Kim's leadership, believing that he would be both effective and controllable. Kim, however, was determined to reunite North and South Korea as soon as possible. On June 25, 1950, he launched an offensive. The North Korean troops made rapid progress and nearly gained control of the entire peninsula. However, a U.S.-led counteroffensive involving an audacious landing at Inchon in South Korea turned the tide of the war and pushed North Korean forces almost back to the border with China. The Chinese then launched a successful attack in support of North Korea. But by July 1953, when a formal truce was signed, they had been driven back north of the 38th parallel.

The "Great Leader"

Kim's attempt to reunite Korea had failed, and in three years of savage fighting huge areas had been devastated and around three million Korean lives had been lost. Over half of these losses were in the north, where Kim began the job of reconstruction by tightening his grip on the Korean Workers' Party, the government, and society in general. His principal opponent, Foreign Minister Pak Hon-yong, was arrested, put on trial, and executed in 1955, and other opponents were removed from the party. At the same time, numerous statues of Kim were erected, and people were forcefully instilled with the belief that he was the "Great Leader" who would eventually achieve reunification and provide all Koreans with a glorious future.

Kim believed that North Korea should rebuild its economy through the development of heavy industry by the state. Furthermore, it should be self-reliant and achieve industrial growth through its own efforts. Initially this policy was very successful, and the country maintained industrial growth of around 25 percent each year between 1954 and 1964. By the 1970s, however, the rate of growth had dropped considerably.

Meanwhile, Kim had created one of the most isolated and repressive regimes in the world, in which the leading figures were his old comrades in the Korean Workers' Party and members of his family. In 1972 he gave up the post of premier, but he kept his position as chairman of the party and became the country's president. In 1980 he appointed his son Kim Jong Il (1941–) to high posts in the party and army, effectively designating him as successor. When Kim died in July 1994, Kim Jong Il succeeded him with the title "Dear Leader."

See Also:

China • Cold War • Korean War • Soviet Union • United Nations

MARTIN LUTHER KING, JR. 1929–1968

Martin Luther King, Jr., a black Baptist pastor, emerged in the mid-1950s as the most charismatic leader of the U.S. civil rights movement. Basing all his actions on the principle of nonviolent resistance, he led the movement until his assassination in 1968.

Martin Luther King, Jr., was born on January 15, 1929, in Atlanta, Georgia. He was the son of a Baptist pastor, and at age 15 he entered Atlanta's Morehouse College, an all-black, all-male school, where he studied sociology and eventually decided to follow his father into the ministry.

In 1948 King was awarded a scholarship to the Crozer Theological Seminary in Chester, Pennsylvania, where he experienced integrated education for the first time and became the first African American to be elected president of the student body. On graduating in 1951, he went to Boston University to study for a doctoral thesis in systematic theology. While in Boston, King met Coretta Scott (1927–), who was studying to be a singer. The couple married in 1953 and went on to have four children. In 1954 King decided to take up the pastorship of Dexter Avenue Baptist Church in Montgomery, Alabama. He had been in Montgomery for just over a year when he became actively involved in the city's civil rights movement.

An outstanding orator, Martin Luther King, Jr., presented civil rights as a moral issue, appealing to his hearers' noblest instincts as he challenged them to live up to their ideals.

Direct action in Montgomery

On December 1, 1955, a black woman named Rosa Parks was arrested after refusing to give up her seat on a bus to a white passenger. Black leaders responded with a decision to organize a bus boycott, and on December 5 they formed the Montgomery Improvement Association, with King as president. That day King made his first political speech, displaying the eloquence for which he was to become famous. Drawing on the teachings of Indian nationalist Mohandas Gandhi (1869–1948), he condemned violence while asserting the need for black people to take action in support of their rights.

KING AND THE FBI

In February 1957 the South Christian Leadership Conference (SCLC), of which King was leader, called on President Dwight D. Eisenhower (1953–1961) to hold a conference at the White House to discuss civil rights. If he failed to do so, the SCLC would organize a Prayer Pilgrimage in Washington, D.C., to increase general awareness of the wrongs being suffered by black people.

Among those who drafted the SCLC request, which Eisenhower turned down, was a white civil liberties activist called Stanley Levison. A socialist, Levison had given financial support to the Communist Party during the Senate hearings led by Joseph McCarthy, and he was to become a close friend of King. This connection, coupled with King's growing prominence in the civil rights movement, came to the attention of J. Edgar Hoover (1895–1972), director of the FBI. Hoover was a fervent opponent of both communism and black activism, and so gave the order for King be placed under surveillance.

King was not a communist, but he believed that black and white workers had much in common. For Hoover this was enough to merit a long-term operation whose findings were regularly reported to the president. The reports not only gave evidence of King's alleged communism but also details of his personal life, and in the 1960s they put pressure on President John F. Kennedy (1961–1963) not to concede to King's demands on civil rights. However, Kennedy resisted this pressure and continued with his attempt to get a civil rights bill passed by Congress.

Martin Luther King, Jr., center, leads a 1965 civil rights march from Selma to Montgomery. Twice turned back by troops, the protestors reached their goal at the third attempt.

The boycott continued, with King being subjected to much harassment. In January 1956 he was arrested—the first of 30 times over the following 12 years—and imprisoned. A few days later a bomb exploded outside his home. However, King refused to be intimidated, and in December 1956 Montgomery's first desegregated buses appeared.

The boycott had received much attention in the media, and King was now an international figure. In early 1957 he became president of the newly formed Southern Christian Leadership Conference (SCLC), which aimed to coordinate the civil rights campaign in the South through the black churches. King began to undertake numerous fundraising activities and public-speaking engagements, and launched a "Crusade for Citizenship" in an attempt get more black voters registered before the 1960 presidential elections. In 1960 he moved back to Atlanta to become copastor of his father's church.

Success in the 1960s

King was at the height of his influence on the civil rights movement in the years 1960–1965, when his tactics of active nonviolence, such as sit-ins and marches, often met with great success. However, there were also occasions when the tactics failed, as in Albany, Georgia, where in 1961–1962 local black activists fought a campaign to secure total desegregation. King joined the campaign and was arrested several times, but he was out-maneuvered by the authorities and finally left the town without having secured desegregation.

In May 1963 a campaign in the highly segregated city of Birmingham, Alabama, attracted worldwide attention when the police turned high-pressure water hoses and dogs on protestors—many of them children—and arrested more than 2,000. In the following 10 weeks there were demonstrations in 186 American cities, and on August 28, 1963, around 250,000 demonstrators gathered in Washington, D.C., to hear King make the most eloquent speech of his career. It included the famous words "I have a dream" and expressed his faith that one day all boys and girls, no matter the color of their skin, would grow up to be brothers and sisters.

In the summer of 1964 King was invited to Washington to witness President Lyndon Baines Johnson's (1963–1969) signing of the Civil Rights Act, whose contents included the banning of racial discrimination in employment, voting, and use of public facilities. Later that year King was awarded the Nobel Peace Prize.

The final years

There had been signs in Birmingham that not all blacks supported King's policy of nonviolence. From 1965 this became increasingly apparent as young black radicals from the ghettos of the northern cities as well as from the South accused King of being too cautious in his approach and argued that violence should be met with violence. King continued, however, to campaign in cities throughout the country and was in Memphis, Tennessee, to support a strike by sanitation workers when he was killed by a bullet fired by James Earl Ray on April 4, 1968. President Johnson declared a national day of mourning on April 7 for a man who, as a speaker and figurehead for the civil rights movement, had achieved so much.

See Also:

Black Americans • *Brown v. Board of Education* • Civil Rights • Montgomery Bus Boycott • Segregation and Desegregation

ALFRED KINSEY 1894–1956

Dr. Alfred Kinsey published two ground-breaking reports on human sexual behavior in 1948 and 1953. Kinsey wanted his research to show that human sexuality was not all the same but immensely varied. In so doing, he created a furor that hastened his death in 1956.

Alfred Charles Kinsey was born on June 23, 1894, in Hoboken, New Jersey. Kinsey was a sickly child, confined to home by rheumatic and typhoid fever. At an early age he resolved to study biology, but his domineering father refused and forced him to study engineering instead. After a poor sophomore year, however, Kinsey plucked up the courage to tell his father he was switching to biology. He graduated magna cum laude from Bowdoin College, Maine, in 1916.

Kinsey studied for his doctorate at the Bussey Institute of Harvard University. Awarded a fellowship in 1919, he traveled across the United States collecting gall wasps, his chosen field of study. In 1920 he started teaching zoology at Indiana University. Through the twenties and thirties he continued to research gall wasps and wrote a high school book, *An Introduction to Biology*, that sold half a million copies.

Dr. Alfred Kinsey, seen here in 1953, was the first researcher to attempt a scientific and statistical approach to documenting human sexual behavior.

From wasps to humans

Kinsey's life changed in 1937 when he became involved in a college student dispute. Students were demanding a course on sex education. Kinsey volunteered to teach it and was appalled by his students' lack of knowledge. He attributed their ignorance to the sexually repressive laws and attitudes of the country. His course, which was presented as preparation for married life, featured his work on gall wasps as well as the mechanics of sexual intercourse. It was hugely popular, and enrollment reached 400 by 1940.

Kinsey took his teaching a step further and decided, using his scientific training, to investigate his perception that human sexuality was far more diverse than contemporary opinion allowed. He designed a questionnaire for his students to answer anonymously so that he could learn about their sexual habits. Soon he resolved to expand the study beyond the campus, by conducting interviews in Chicago.

When local ministers complained that Kinsey was teaching material that should be left to them, the president of the university issued Kinsey with an ultimatum to stop either the course or the interviews. To the president's shock, Kinsey resigned from the marriage course. He then threw himself into his research. In 1941, funded by the Committee for Research in Problems of Sex (CRPS, which received its funding from the Rockefeller Foundation), and Indiana University, Kinsey interviewed African Americans in Gary, Indiana, and prison inmates.

CONTINUING CONTROVERSY

Early biographies of Kinsey noted that he was a devoted family man who spent all his time in dispassionate research. However, a biography, *Alfred C. Kinsey: A Public/Private Life*, published in 1997 by the historian James H. Jones, stirred up controversy.

Jones interviewed many of Kinsey's associates. He learned that Kinsey was motivated not only by scientific discovery but also by a desire to challenge the attitudes to sex that were ingrained in American society in the 1950s and sometimes the legal statutes derived from them, such as the criminalization of homosexuality.

Jones argued that while Kinsey cultivated the image of a collector of data and a statistician, he was determined to challenge the guilt and repression that he believed surrounded human sexuality in those days.

From the start researchers were concerned that the people Kinsey interviewed were unrepresentative of the whole population. Kinsey said that a truly random sample was impossible in sex research because many groups, such as religious conservatives, refused to participate. The American Statistical Association agreed that Kinsey's sample was as good as it could be in the circumstances.

Dr. Alfred Kinsey (seated) is seen with his family at Bloomington, Indiana, in 1953, at the time of the publication of *Sexual Behavior in the Human Female*.

Applauded and attacked

Over the next few years his funding increased, and Kinsey created the Institute for Sex Research (now the Kinsey Institute), affiliated with Indiana University. In 1948 he published *Sexual Behavior in the Human Male*. Based on 5,300 case studies, the book was an overnight publishing sensation. It sold 200,000 hardback copies in two months. Kinsey's main point was that men have always had strong sexual urges and that unless those urges were harmful to others, it was pointless for society to repress them. A backlash started almost immediately, with religious leaders particularly outraged.

Kinsey used the book's royalties to expand the institute. He wanted enough researchers to conduct 100,000 interviews. In 1953 he published a companion to his earlier book, *Sexual Behavior in the Human Female*. In August that year, when Kinsey was on the cover of *Time* magazine, *U.S. News* claimed he was the most recognized man in the country after the president. However, the Rockefeller Foundation, troubled by questions over the representativeness of Kinsey's interview sample, withdrew its funding before the book was published.

In *Human Female* Kinsey published data that he interpreted as supporting the idea that sex before marriage led to a more fulfilling sex life in marriage for women. His data also showed that 26 percent of the married women interviewed had been unfaithful.

Just as before, Kinsey's critics were quick to condemn both the doctor and his book, with some claiming it was part of a communist plot to undermine American morals. In 1954 a congressional committee summoned Kinsey to appear before it, although its members stopped short of denouncing him as a communist. Kinsey, already weakened by heart trouble, redoubled his efforts to secure new funding and to produce a volume on homosexuality. He continued interviewing, despite his poor health, and conducted his last interview on May 24, 1956. He died of a heart attack on August 25 the same year in Bloomington, Indiana.

Kinsey died before the sexual revolution of the 1960s. While his work cannot be said to have brought about a change in sexual attitudes, his books created a climate in which sex could be seriously discussed in society for the first time. He remains a controversial figure today (*see box*).

See Also:

Beauvoir, Simone de • Birth Control • Cold War • Health and Healthcare • Homophile Groups • Women's Movement

KOREAN WAR

Initially a conflict between Communist North Korea and its pro-Western neighbor to the south, the Korean War soon came to involve two of the world's most powerful countries—China and the United States. It was thus one of the major events of the Cold War.

The Korean War of 1950–1953 has been described as "the forgotten war." The conflict is overshadowed by both World War II (1939–1945), which ended only five years beforehand, and the Vietnam War of the late sixties and early seventies. However, the Korean War was a major event in recent history. It was the first military clash of the Cold War and cost millions of lives.

Superficially, Korea seemed an unlikely battleground. Set at the extreme edge of East Asia, it was a largely undeveloped nation with scant natural resources and an unforgiving landscape: The 600-mile-long (965km) peninsula is almost entirely covered in mountain chains. Moreover, Korea's turbulent political life made it an unattractive prospect for foreign investment. The country became a Japanese protectorate in 1905 and was formally annexed in 1910. The Japanese had imposed a harsh rule over Korea until the Allied victory in the Pacific in 1945.

At the Cairo Conference of 1943 the United States, Britain, and China had agreed that independence should be restored to Korea in due course. In the immediate postwar period Korea gained a new strategic importance. China, Korea's neighbor to the north, became a battleground between the Soviet-backed Communist revolutionaries of Mao Zedong and the U.S-sponsored Nationalists led by Chiang Kai-shek. When Mao's Communists took control of China in 1949, the victory presented a problem for President Harry S. Truman (1945–1953). From 1947 U.S. foreign policy became dominated by the principles of the so-called Truman Doctrine, which emphasized the overriding importance of containing communism. Mao's rise to power led opponents of Truman's government to question whether this policy was working. Korea was now at the center of the world's political stage.

Origins of the conflict

The United States' involvement in Korea dated back to the end of World War II. In August 1945 the U.S. State-War-Navy Coordinating Committee proposed to the Soviet Union that Korea be divided at the 38th parallel of latitude. The United States would accept the Japanese surrender south of the line, while the Soviets would accept it in the north. Soviet leader Joseph Stalin agreed to the proposal without much consideration—Europe was the major focus of his energies—and the U.S. Army XXIV Corps was moved into the south as an occupation force. The corps's commander, Lieutenant General John R. Hodge, became the effective political leader of this portion of the country, a role for which he had few skills and little support.

At the end of World War II the Korean Peninsula was divided for administrative purposes at the 38th parallel. The advance of North Korean troops across the boundary in June 1950 precipitated the Korean War.

NORTH AND SOUTH KOREAN FORCES

There were huge differences in the quality and quantity of military forces available to North and South Korea in June 1950. The RoK Army comprised some 95,000 troops arranged into eight divisions. Four of these divisions were not effectively combat ready, and the remaining four were poorly armed and short of ammunition: Initially, the RoK Army had enough ammunition to last for only six days of fighting. The RoK Army received all its military supplies from America, but the United States refrained from providing the Koreans with any tanks, heavy artillery, or combat aircraft. What weapons or vehicles the RoK troops did have were frequently outdated or worn out (around 33 percent of the RoK Army's vehicles needed critical repairs). Compounding equipment problems, the RoK Army was corrupt, demotivated, and very poorly trained.

By contrast, North Korea's Korean People's Army (KPA) had 135,000 well-trained and highly motivated soldiers arranged in 10 divisions, of which eight were at full strength. Many of its soldiers were combat veterans with experience of fighting in the Soviet Union and China during World War II. The KPA's armored brigade had 150 Soviet T-34 tanks—still one of the best tanks in the world at the time—and the North Korean air force had some 200 Yak-9 fighter and Il-10 bomber aircraft. Furthermore, the KPA possessed the heavy artillery, including 122mm howitzers, that the RoK forces lacked—a total of 1,693 guns in all. The disparity in military strength between North and South Korea would become painfully obvious during the first weeks of the conflict.

An RoK soldier stands on guard duty. The RoK Army was less well equipped than its North Korean counterpart.

While a Communist government established itself in the north of the country, the United States presided over a long period of poor administration in the south. U.S. forces initially retained the services of huge numbers of Japanese troops and civil servants. This move provoked such hostility from the Korean population that the United States was forced to send almost 700,000 Japanese home by the end of 1945. Nevertheless, administrators retained many former collaborators in the security forces and inexplicably excluded anyone who had been a prisoner of the Japanese from holding public office.

Fearful that left-wing factions would succeed in drawing the south toward communism, the U.S. government engineered the appointment of pro-Western exile Syngman Rhee (1875–1965) as a leading figure in the new Korean Democratic Party (KDP) and the South Korean Interim Government. The KDP was a grouping of conservative politicians; the Americans filtered out undesirable socialist and Communist elements. There now began a fruitless attempt to make a unified Korea through the newly created United Nations (UN). The UN voted in November 1947 to establish a Temporary Commission on Korea that would oversee the process of unification and the subsequent elections to establish a government. The authority of the commission was instantly rejected by the Soviet Union. Under UN auspices elections for a South Korean government alone were held on May 10, 1948. The result was that Rhee was elected president of the Republic of Korea (RoK) and head of a 200-man assembly. In September an official government was also established in North Korea. The region would now be known as the Democratic People's Republic of Korea (DPRK), while its leader would be Kim Il Sung (1912–1994).

The problem with this arrangement was that both North and South Korea claimed jurisdiction over the Korean Peninsula as a whole. In September 1947 the USSR had proposed that both Soviet and U.S. forces withdraw from Korea entirely, leaving the country to forge its own future. However, by that time Rhee had already alienated most of his country through a mixture of violent intimidation and economic mismanagement. The United States, therefore, rejected the Soviet proposal since it recognized that the South Korean people themselves might move in favor of a communist government.

By the end of 1948 both North and South Korea had sovereign governments, so the UN General Assembly called for U.S. and Soviet forces to pull out of Korea. Both parties complied, the Soviets withdrawing their troops by the end of December, and the United States following suit by mid-1949.

The outbreak of war

Under Rhee's presidency South Korea plunged into chaos. His regime was marked by ruthless suppression of his political opponents. Rhee's police made 89,710 arrests between September 1948 and April 1949 alone. Having taken a majority of seats in the Korean elections in 1948, Rhee's right-wing parties took only 49 out of 200 seats in general elections in 1950. South Korea was slipping into economic and political collapse, but with the Soviets withdrawn from North Korea, the United States showed little concern. The North Korean government, however, smelled blood.

Initial skirmishes between the two countries occurred in 1949, when North and South Korean forces engaged in some localized fighting on the 38th parallel. During one incident in May 1949 RoK troops pushed 2.5 miles (4km) into North Korean territory. Sensing a potential military clash, the United States supplied arms to South Korea, but most of them were outdated or worn-out. The equipment did not include the heavy weaponry needed to counter the far more impressive forces of the Korean People's Army (KPA; *see box opposite*). There is some evidence to suggest that around December 1949 Stalin had been involved in debate about a North Korean invasion of the South. Details of the decision-making behind the invasion are lost to history, but what is certain is that massed KPA forces rolled across the border on the morning of Sunday June 25, 1950.

The invasion began at 4 A.M., the North Koreans first pounding RoK troops on the 38th parallel with a massive artillery bombardment. Although the North Korean government claims to this day that it was first attacked by the South, and that the invasion was simply a defensive action, there seems little doubt that the North Korean move was an act of unprovoked aggression that took the South Koreans by surprise. KPA units then crossed the border with four main spearheads, each one led by armored units. The bulk of the forces pushed toward Seoul (the South Korean capital) and down the Pukhan River, with another major force driving down the eastern coastline through the Taebaek Mountains.

KPA tactics were basic but effective. The North Korean T-34 tanks would cut straight through an enemy position—something they were able to do easily because of the South's complete lack of effective antitank weapons—and take up positions in the enemy's rear. KPA infantry would then swarm around both flanks of the position to surround and destroy it.

Faced with such tactics, the South Korean forces crumpled. The ill-equipped and badly led RoK troops were either killed or sent into terrified retreat. Southern towns and cities fell quickly; the KPA 6th Division took the town of Ongin within the first day. On June 26 the RoK 1st Division—one of the RoK Army's most formidable divisions under the competent commander Major General Paek—was put into retreat from its positions on

Commander-in-Chief of UN forces General Douglas MacArthur (seated center) observes the shelling of the Korean port of Inchon from the deck of the U.S.S. *Mt. McKinley* in 1950.

the Imjin River after the defeat of the 7th Division holding its right flank. On June 28 KPA troops began the takeover of Seoul itself, while other units cut deeper and deeper into the south of the country. It looked as if nothing could stop the Communist onslaught.

Enter the United States

The United States was completely unprepared for the war in Korea. In the aftermath of World War II it had massively downgraded its armed forces. At the time of the North Korean invasion total U.S. service personnel numbered about 1.4 million: There had been 12.5 million at the end of World War II. In the same period spending on the armed forces had dropped from $82 billion to $13 billion. In Asia the nearest U.S. military unit capable of responding to the Korean situation was the occupation force in Japan, although the troops there had grown accustomed to easy living and were far from ready for combat.

However, the U.S. government quickly decided to commit military resources to Korea. The Truman administration was still smarting over the "loss" of China to the Communists in 1949, a disaster for America after it had spent more than $3 billion between 1941 and 1945 supporting Chiang's Nationalists fight against the Communists. Public opinion at home also, in general, favored a decisive response to the spread of communism.

The overall commander of U.S. forces in East Asia was General Douglas MacArthur (1880–1964), a powerful and controversial figure who had been in command of the Southwest Pacific Theater in World War II. MacArthur was instructed to strip whatever weapons and equipment he could from occupation forces in Japan and send them to Korea. The U.S. Seventh Fleet was moved into Korean waters, and U.S. aircraft began to make combat sorties against Communist forces. More significantly, on June 30 the U.S.

Ethiopian troops, part of the UN contingent, undergo training in Korea. Although the United States supplied the bulk of the UN forces, many other countries were involved.

MEETING ON WAKE ISLAND

On October 15, 1950, President Harry S. Truman had a meeting with General Douglas MacArthur on Wake Island in the Pacific. It was the first time the two men had met in person, and the occasion highlighted the hostility of MacArthur toward the president. MacArthur saw the meeting as a public relations stunt intended to boost the president's popularity. The trip certainly provided Truman with excellent photo opportunities and connected him with the military success U.S. forces had experienced to this point (the Chinese had yet to enter the war). MacArthur was, by contrast, hugely inconvenienced—he had to fly a round trip of 4,000 miles (6,440km)—and little of consequence was discussed.

An interesting moment in the meeting came when MacArthur greeted the president. MacArthur did not salute Truman as he should have (the president is the commander-in-chief of the U.S. armed forces) but instead shook the president's hand as an equal. He also rejected Truman's request that they share lunch together and quickly took the plane back to his headquarters in Tokyo. Although Truman hailed the meeting as the most "satisfactory conference since I've been president," the encounter clearly showed that MacArthur felt his status was equal to that of the president. It thus prefigured the later conflict between Truman and MacArthur that would lead to the general being relieved of his command.

Senate approved a military assistance bill that committed the United States to putting actual combat troops in South Korea to stop the Communists. Although this move was described by Truman as a "police action"—a phrase that would later haunt him given the future scale of the conflict—it was in effect a step into war.

Other countries would soon also become involved in the conflict. On June 25 the UN, at U.S. bidding, called for a halt to the invasion. The Soviet Union was boycotting the UN at that time because of the organization's refusal to admit Communist China as a member. Two days later the UN passed a resolution asking member states to make direct military contributions to the developing war. Although the U.S. contingent would dwarf all other allied nations in Korea, the war quickly became a truly international conflict. Forces from the United Kingdom made up the next most sizable non-Korean contingent, but Australia, Belgium, Canada, Colombia, Ethiopia, France, Greece, Luxembourg, the Netherlands, New Zealand, the Philippines, South Africa, Thailand and Turkey also sent troops, making the UN force one of the most mixed in history. MacArthur, however, would be in total control of all UN forces in the theater; he was appointed commander-in-chief of the United Nations Command on July 10.

U.S. weaknesses

As was the case in Vietnam some 15 years later, the American forces were hampered by their own overconfidence. Crude racial attitudes led both the U.S. government and its soldiers to underestimate the tenacity and talents of the KPA. Moreover, the U.S. Army was chronically short of vehicles, weapons, and ammunition. The troops also lacked suitable clothing: The Korean climate is characterized by extremes of heat and cold, particularly the latter in the mountainous regions. The men who made up the U.S. forces were either old hands softened from Japanese occupation duties or conscripts with very little training. The U.S. government extended the conscription program, but such was the rush to get men to Korea that some new conscripts simply stepped onto a transport ship in America, received some basic weapons training while under sail, and then were taken straight into action once they stepped off the ship in Korea.

In the first two months of their involvement the performance of the U.S. troops was consequently little better than that of the RoK. Task Force Smith, the name given to the 1st Battalion, 21st Regiment (1/21st) of the 24th Infantry Division, was the first U.S. combat unit sent into action. The unit was commanded by Lieutenant Colonel Charles Smith. It met the advancing Communist forces near Osan on July 5. The youth of the soldiers led one officer to comment to Smith: "They look like a bunch of boy scouts out there." Shortly after daybreak the 1/21st was in defensive positions when a massive force of T-34 tanks and swarms of infantry attacked. The Americans attempted a desperate defense with totally inadequate weapons. In one incident a soldier fired 22 bazooka rockets at the KPA armor, but all the rockets simply bounced off the T-34s' armored hulls. The 1/21st was soon put into flight southward.

Further U.S. defeats

The next major combat unit to face the North Korean onslaught was the 24th U.S. Infantry Division, followed by the 25th Division and the 1st Cavalry Division. U.S. forces in South Korea were placed under the command of Lieutenant General Walton H. Walker and designated as the Eighth United States Army in Korea (EUSAK). The three divisions fared little better than Task Force Smith. Major General William Dean's 24th Infantry took up positions at Ansong and Pyongtaek on July 5, short of ammunition and with no effective communications. Within hours of the Communists touching their front lines, the U.S. soldiers were retreating, along with thousands of

CHINESE ENDURANCE

Compared to a typical U.S. infantryman, the Chinese soldier of 1950 traveled light, carrying only basic weaponry and food rations. He was usually armed with a bolt-action rifle such as the Type 88 Hanyang or a similar weapon captured from the Japanese during the 1930s or World War II. He would carry about 80 rounds of ammunition and four or five hand grenades, plus some additional ammunition for unit machine guns and mortars. For survival the soldier would carry a small pack of rice, tea, salt, and occasionally meat. Such a package would provide five days of rations; additional food would be found from foraging and plunder. The People's Liberation Army (PLA) was not a mechanized force (meaning it did not travel in vehicles), so most larger supplies were carried by porters, who could transport around 100 pounds (45kg) of supplies each. The porters transported supplies in baskets suspended on a pole carried across the shoulders.

Both porters and soldiers could walk astonishing distances day after day. In the early days of Chinese involvement in the war U.S. commanders were shocked at the sheer speed of the Chinese advance. The lack of mechanized vehicles actually allowed the Chinese to move more quickly because they did not have complex logistical arrangements to hold them back. Furthermore, the poverty prevalent in China meant that its soldiers could survive hardships that U.S. troops struggled to endure.

desperate South Korean civilians and RoK soldiers. By July 22 the 24th had lost nearly one-third of its men.

A similar fate befell the 25th Division and the 1st Cavalry. The KPA took advantage of the confusion by sending a division through undefended sectors beneath Taejon in the west of the country, which then hooked around toward the port of Pusan on the east coast. The Eighth Army was now in danger of being cut off, so it retreated across the Naktong River to take up last-stand defensive positions around Pusan. The Pusan Perimeter had to be held, otherwise the whole of South Korea would fall.

Desperate defense

Based on the experience of the past two months, it looked as if the Pusan defense would fail despite the United Nations pouring in troops of all nationalities. For six weeks fatigue-shattered men desperately fought off attack after attack from the North Koreans. The fighting was intense and included a large tank battle near Taegu between KPA T-34s and U.S. Pershing tanks. Slowly, however, the tide began to turn. The U.S. Air Force had complete air superiority, and KPA tanks and infantry suffered constant rocket, bomb, and napalm attacks. In late July the infantry was given a new 3.5in bazooka antitank weapon that was capable of punching through the T-34's main armor. On the first day of use, July 20 near Taejon, the new bazookas destroyed 10 T-34s. Combined with huge volumes of artillery and machine-gun fire, such weapons were starting to take a devastating toll on the North Koreans. On August 31 the North Koreans made a last-ditch attempt to break the perimeter. It failed and ended the KPA hopes for a quick victory.

The holding of the Pusan Perimeter was soon to be the least of the KPA's problems. In mid-August MacArthur, against the advice of almost every military authority around him, devised and authorized a plan to open a second

U.S. marines use scaling ladders to storm ashore during the amphibious attack at Inchon. The brainchild of General Douglas MacArthur, the assault was a huge success.

front in the Korean War. Known as Operation Chromite, the plan involved a high-risk landing of the 1st Marine Division and the 7th U.S. Infantry Division (known together as X Corps) at the port of Inchon hundreds of miles northwest of Pusan on the western South Korean coastline near Seoul. MacArthur intended to put a powerful force ashore at Inchon, push out and take Seoul, and then wait for U.S. forces at Pusan to drive up to meet them and expel the Communists from the South.

Desperate Korean civilians scramble to escape from the port of Hungnam in December 1950 in the face of the southward advance of Chinese forces.

Despite incredible complexities, the Inchon landing successfully took place on September 15 after a blistering naval and aerial bombardment, and the U.S. X Corps captured Seoul on September 27. By this time the KPA was in a desperate retreat northward, pushed by the advancing Eighth Army from Pusan. Shortly after the fall of Seoul X Corps and the Eighth Army met up near the 38th parallel.

MacArthur, however, was not satisfied with simply pushing the North Korean troops back beyond the original border. Persuading the U.S. administration that the Communist North itself should be invaded and occupied, MacArthur sent the UN forces across the 38th parallel on October 9. The invasion of North Korea had its risks. Some people feared that China would become involved in the conflict once it felt threatened by U.S. and UN forces closing up to its border. However, most in the West believed that the Chinese would not be foolish enough to risk a war with the U.S. superpower.

China enters the war

American assumptions proved to be wrong, however. The Chinese were highly alarmed by the U.S. counteroffensive, especially when the North Korean capital Pyongyang fell to U.S. troops on October 19. The U.S. advance up North Korea then separated into two—X Corps under Major General Edward M. Almond advanced

up the eastern side of the country, while Walker's Eighth Army took the western route. Crucially for subsequent developments, X Corps and the Eighth Army were separated by the mountainous ridge that ran up the length of the Korean Peninsula. This meant that the two contingents would be unable to help one another if things went wrong.

By the time RoK troops reached the Yalu River on China's border around October 25, the Chinese had deployed around 200,000 troops in the area. UN forces were technologically superior to the Chinese People's Liberation Army (PLA); but most Chinese troops were combat veterans, and they required a fraction of the logistical support that U.S. troops needed to fight. A PLA division needed only 40 tons (36 tonnes) of supplies each day. By contrast, a U.S. Army division, with a heavier reliance on motorized transport, needed 600 tons (544 tonnes) of supplies (*see box on p. 152*). The Chinese had fewer support weapons such as artillery but could deploy very quickly.

The Chinese invasion

Despite the huge buildup of Chinese forces on the border, U.S. and Allied intelligence services failed to provide any forewarning of a Chinese attack. One serious problem was that UN airplanes were forbidden from crossing the Yalu River. However, by October 25 British, U.S., and RoK troops were reporting engagements with what appeared to be Chinese troops (the Chinese soldiers wore distinctive quilted uniforms), with the RoK II Corps and U.S. 1st Cavalry suffering some heavy casualties. These actions were interpreted as being nothing more than a limited show of force by China, not the beginnings of a full-scale invasion. However, the combat steadily intensified as the Chinese slipped 130,000 troops of the Thirteenth Army Group across the border, the Ninth Army Group joining them in late November. Thus began the second disastrous retreat of UN forces down the length of Korea.

The collapse of UN forces in Korea in the winter of 1950–1951 is one of the most embarrassing episodes in American military history. Despite having complete air and naval superiority, better equipment, and heavier firepower than the Chinese, the U.S. forces were routed. American veterans have described a phenomenon they called "bug out fever"; just the hint that Chinese troops were in the area seemed to make even large units abandon their positions in fear and flee south. The Korean winter had also arrived with a vengeance, with temperatures of -4°F (-20°C). Great numbers of UN troops fell to frostbite and hypothermia (*see box opposite*). Vehicles and weapons froze solid, making mobility and fighting a huge labor. The Chinese forces suffered under even worse handicaps and had frightful cold-related losses. However, their motivation, combat experience, and formidable discipline ensured that they dominated the U.S. troops.

United Nations forces recross the 38th parallel during the withdrawal from the North Korean capital Pyongyang in late 1950.

WINTER IN KOREA

During the Korean winters casualties caused by the weather far outstripped those caused by the fighting. Here a British soldier, Alberic Stacpoole, who served in Korea between 1952 and 1953 with the 1st Battalion Duke of Wellington's Regiment, describes what it was like in the freezing conditions:

> It was really terribly terribly cold. I remember being out on patrol and we went to ground for just twenty minutes and in that time we froze to the ground, and our machine guns, light machine guns and our moving parts of our automatic weapons all froze. You had to keep sliding them (the moving parts) quietly for your own circulation of your body, but also to keep your weapons circulated, otherwise they simply froze stiff. As you tried to get up off the ground all your clothes would be sticking to the ground with a kind of white dry ice because it was twenty degrees below zero or something. It could be terribly cold. We had space heaters, which were in the living hootchies and things, which were essentially a large open space like a huge saucepan, one of those pressure cookers, into which one dripped naked petrol. That burned away inside and got these things glowing and it just burned straight petrol at a drip speed. They were fine in a way if they worked and they didn't always work. Some of them went up in flames.
> (Source: Imperial War Museum, London)

A U.S. soldier uses a poncho to protect himself from the cold during the U.S. retreat southward in January 1951.

By January 1951 U.S. forces had been thrust back across the 38th parallel, with Seoul falling once again to the Communists on January 4. The success of the Chinese offensive meant that the U.S. forces lost almost all of the territory that they had gained in their 1950 advances north of the parallel. Soldiers were no longer sure what they were fighting for, especially because the U.S. government now began to talk of an armistice and the restoration of the border between North and South Korea at the 38th parallel as the best option for ending the conflict. Moreover, American soldiers witnessed every day how brutal, corrupt, and dictatorial Rhee's regime really was. Rhee's police and soldiers executed and tortured their own people at will, and the president treated American requests for restraint with contempt.

The Chosin Reservoir

Postwar reviews of the U.S. military during the China offensive highlighted poor leadership, overreliance on vehicles, inadequate training in defensive tactics, and the poor quality of many conscripts as the main reasons for the U.S. collapse. There were, however, units that showed extreme bravery and professionalism. The U.S. 1st Marine Division, the U.S. 7th Infantry Division, and the British 41 Independent Commando Royal Marines distinguished themselves by making an epic fighting retreat from the frozen Chosin Reservoir in North Korea down to Hungnam. Almost every inch of the retreat was made under the fire of around 200,000 Chinese troops of the Ninth Army Group. Out of 20,000 U.S. and British troops who were established around the Chosin Reservoir on November 26, 1950 (the date when the battle began) some 15,000 would be dead or wounded by the time units reached Hungnam around mid-December. They had, however, inflicted an estimated 40,000 casualties on the Chinese. A similar sacrifice was made on the Imjin River by the British 29th Brigade, which fought against two divisions of Chinese troops and lost more than 1,000 soldiers plus 808 missing, many of whom were taken prisoner. Despite such examples of bravery, the Chinese

A Korean girl carries her infant brother across a battlefield in June 1951. In the background stands a stalled M-26 tank.

winter offensive almost crushed the U.S. Army in Korea. The tide was about to turn, however.

Restoration and stalemate

The Chinese territorial gains had come at a considerable cost. By the end of January 1951 China's forces had been decimated by a combination of U.S. firepower and the cold, and their supply lines were stretched to snapping point. China's problems were exacerbated by a change that occurred within the command structure of the U.S. forces. On December 23, 1950, the Eighth Army's commander, Lieutenant General Walton Walker, was killed in a vehicle accident. His replacement was Lieutenant General Matthew B. Ridgway (1895–1993), a distinguished and highly capable veteran of World War II.

Ridgway's appointment proved to be a catalyst for change. He worked tirelessly to provide U.S. troops with proper food, clothing, and weaponry. He dismissed poor leaders and enforced discipline among the troops. With a reinvigorated army Ridgway stopped the Chinese advance in early February 1951. He then managed to put the Chinese into retreat, pushing them back to positions around the 38th parallel by late April.

In the same month Ridgway was unexpectedly promoted. Since the beginning of the Chinese offensive MacArthur had increasingly set himself at odds with the U.S. government. Although the official policy of the Truman administration was that the conflict should be confined to the Korean Peninsula, MacArthur believed that U.S. forces should attack China directly, even if such a move led to an all-out confrontation between communism and the West and the use of atomic weapons. When MacArthur made his feelings public, it proved to be a step too far for Truman and the Joint Chiefs of Staff. On April 11 MacArthur was dismissed from his office, and Ridgway took command of all U.S. forces in Asia. Although many U.S. soldiers and civilians regretted the fall of MacArthur, who was by now an American legend, they were not sorry to see Ridgway's appointment. Many believed that the end of the war was now in sight.

In July 1951 representatives of the UN coalition met with Chinese and North Korean representatives at Kaesong to discuss a possible armistice. In fact, the Chinese used the six weeks of talks as a breathing space to create heavy defensive positions around the 38th parallel and prepare for further offensives. As talks collapsed, bloody fighting began again. Between August and October U.S. and Chinese forces battled for possession of territory around the Hwachon Reservoir, with fighting concentrated on two particular hills that came to be known as Heartbreak Ridge and Bloody Ridge. On October 19 the U.S. 2nd Division finally took the positions and made a 19-mile (31-km) advance above the 38th parallel. By this point the Chinese had lost thousands more men, and negotiations began again on October 25 at Panmunjom. Again the Chinese used the time to create defensive positions. When the talks collapsed on December 27, the U.S. and Chinese forces found themselves locked in a stalemate, facing each other from massive fortification systems.

While the land forces were entrenched around the 38th parallel, the air war intensified. The battle pitched U.S. F-86 Sabres against Soviet-built MiG-15 jet fighters, which were largely flown by Chinese pilots. The F-86 Sabre was roughly equivalent to the MiG in terms of performance. U.S. pilots, however, were far better trained, and this disparity was reflected in the amount of losses suffered by the respective sides: 379 MiGs were shot down by U.S. pilots, while the U.S. forces lost only 78 Sabres.

Closing the war

The election of a new U.S. president, Dwight D. Eisenhower, in November 1952 marked the beginning of the end of the war. As part of his election campaign Eisenhower had promised to bring the conflict to a swift conclusion. In the preceding year U.S. and

U.S. warplanes return to the aircraft carrier the U.S.S. *Boxer* after a combat mission over North Korea in September 1951. The United States enjoyed clear air superiority.

Communist forces had barely moved at all from their stalemate positions around the 38th parallel. The war was having a devastating effect on the Chinese economy; and when the Soviet leader Joseph Stalin died in March 1953, the Chinese felt even more uncertain about the prospect of future success (much of China's weaponry was supplied by the Soviet Union). As further negotiations began, Eisenhower hinted at a dark possibility—the use of atomic weapons against Peking (now Beijing) and North Korean targets if the Chinese did not negotiate a peace agreement.

The battle for Pork Chop Hill

Fighting still continued intermittently since each side wanted to grab additional territory and use victories to give it the advantage in the armistice talks. On April 16, 1953, for example, two Chinese divisions attacked a site known to the Americans as Pork Chop Hill (on account of its shape). The hill was occupied by 96 men of the U.S. 7th Division. The battle for Pork Chop Hill eventually became legendary in U.S. military history. Swamped by the Chinese, the U.S. positions withered until at one stage only 55 men were occupying small parts of the hill, the Chinese having taken the rest. The Americans sent in a battalion of troops to recapture the ground, but it would take another brutal day of close-quarter combat and artillery duels (U.S. artillerymen fired 77,000 shells in one day alone) before the Chinese finally withdrew on April 18. The Chinese renewed their attack on Pork Chop Hill on July 6, using about a division of troops against five U.S. battalions. After four days of bitter fighting the Americans finally decided to withdraw troops from the hill. By this time negotiations were nearing a conclusion, and the geographically insignificant area was no longer deemed worth the human cost.

Representatives of the U.S. and North Korean armies sign maps showing the demarcation zone between North and South Korea during the Panmunjom cease-fire talks in 1951.

The negotiations at Panmunjom dragged on for another two weeks. Finally, on July 27, 1953, a treaty was signed with an agreement for a cease-fire and an exchange of prisoners of war. It was signed by Kim Il Sung, General Mark Clark (who had replaced Ridgway as commander of all UN troops in Korea in May 1952), and Peng Dehuai, head of the Chinese forces. South Korean President Syngman Rhee, however, was not present. He did not want the war to end and at one stage actually released large numbers of Communist prisoners in the hope of jeopardizing U.S. plans. Such actions infuriated Western leaders, with many calling for Rhee to be replaced.

KOREA AND THE ATOMIC BOMB

The Korean War teetered on the edge of becoming an atomic conflict. Declassified documents have shown that many senior figures in the U.S. military believed that atomic bombs should have been used against Communist military and industrial targets, especially during the Chinese winter offensive of 1950–1951, when the United States was at a loss as to how to stop the Communists. From mid-November 1950 the U.S. Army Plans and Operations Division, along with the Joint Strategic Survey Committee, made recommendations that atomic weapons should be made ready for use in Korea. By this time nine B-29 bombers equipped with atomic weapons were already stationed on the island of Guam in the Pacific.

On November 30 President Truman increased tension over the issue of the atomic bomb when he stated at a press conference that "There has always been active consideration of its use." Some senators pointed to how effective atomic weapons had been in ending the war in the Pacific in 1945, an argument that was endorsed by General MacArthur. Not everyone was so comfortable with the idea of the use of the bomb, however. The British Joint Chiefs of Staff argued that atomic bombs "must in our view be kept in reserve for use in the proper place in the event of a major war with Russia."

The possibility of using the atomic bomb heightened under the presidency of Eisenhower, who looked for ways of gaining a dominant position at the negotiating table during talks with North Korea and China. In the spring of 1953 reports of U.S. willingness to use tactical nuclear weapons were filtered out to the Communists. Whether the threats were a bluff or not, they certainly encouraged the Communists to reach a negotiated cease-fire.

A repatriated U.S. prisoner of war embraces members of his family after returning home from Korea in September 1953.

The armistice saw the border between North and South Korea reestablished roughly along the 38th parallel. A Military Demarcation Line was created, with a "demilitarized zone" (DMZ) extending 1.2 miles (2km) on either side of this line. The purpose of the demilitarized zone was to keep the North and South Korean military forces separated to reduce the risk of conflict occurring again.

The war ended with many observers asking whether it had been worth fighting at all. The Korean Peninsula was devastated, with over five million civilians left homeless and a million killed. The true death toll will never be known. Figures for military casualties vary greatly. However, it is generally agreed that RoK forces lost around 415,000 men, while the KPA suffered around 500,000 fatalities. According to Western estimates, about one million Chinese soldiers died. The U.S. death toll was around 37,000. About 100,000 U.S. soldiers were wounded.

The conflict ended with neither side having much to show for the huge losses incurred. The boundary between North and South Korea lay in almost exactly the same position that it had been before the war began. And while the U.S. forces had prevented a Communist takeover of South Korea, the country's inhabitants now lived under an autocratic regime far removed from the democratic ideal envisioned by U.S. politicians.

See Also:

Asian Americans • China • Chosin Reservoir • Cold War • Eisenhower, Dwight D. • Foreign Policy • Imjin River • Immigration • Inchon Landing • Kim Il Sung • MacArthur, Douglas • Pusan Perimeter • Pyongyang • Seoul • Truman, Harry S. • United Nations

LABOR RELATIONS

The labor unions became less radical and less powerful in the 1950s as a result of new labor legislation, a growth in white-collar employment, and increased cooperation between management and unions. The most disruptive labor dispute was the steel strike of 1959.

The United States emerged from World War II (1939–1945) with its massive industrial infrastructure unscathed, its resources of manpower plentiful, and its confidence in the future unshaken. The labor movement, too, looked forward with high hopes. During the Great Depression of the 1930s and the war years union activists had succeeded in organizing workers in the core industries of the economy. New Deal legislation introduced by President Franklin D. Roosevelt (1933–1945) had given workers legally sanctioned union rights, including the right to strike and the right to collective bargaining with employers. In addition, the war itself had stimulated an expansion in manufacturing and a great increase in union membership in the dominant heavy industries, including coal, iron, steel, the railroads, and building construction.

Postwar era

In 1945, therefore, organized labor found itself with greater power and influence than ever before. Through an alliance with the Democratic Party union leaders had come to play an important part in politics and government. With the coming of peace the American labor movement, like its European brethren, looked forward to a more equal distribution of wealth and an increased participation in industrial decision-making. However, the future for organized labor turned out to be less bright than anticipated.

The foundation of postwar labor relations was the Labor–Management Relations Act of 1947, which was enacted by a Republican Congress over the veto of President Harry S. Truman (1945–1953). The act is also known as the Taft–Hartley Act, named for its sponsors Senator Robert Taft and Representative Fred Hartley. Strictly, it

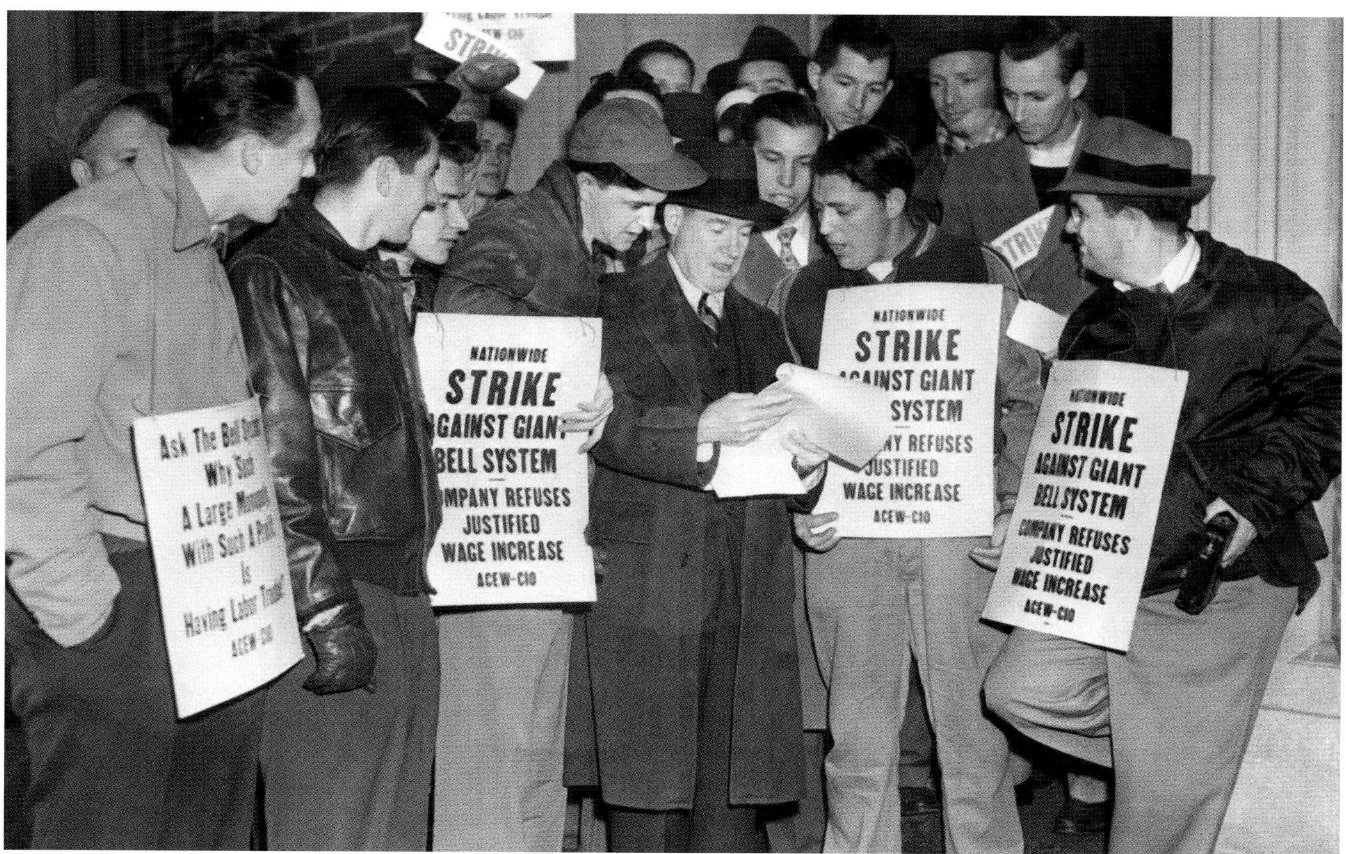

An injunction sought by the Bell Telephone Company is read out to strikers from the Communications Workers of America picketing exchanges in Philadelphia in November 1950.

CHANGES IN CLASS STRUCTURE

The table below gives a breakdown of the industrial workforce (excluding agriculture and mining) by occupation in 1947 and in 1956. It shows the rapid growth of white-collar compared to blue-collar job opportunities. Many contemporary analysts believed that the decline of blue-collar occupations made labor unions more willing to cooperate with industrial management.

	1947 (1,000s)	1956 (1,000s)	Percentage change
White-collar occupations			
Managerial	5,795	6,552	12.1
Professional and technical	3,795	6,096	60.6
Clerical	7,200	8,838	22.8
Sales	3,395	4,111	21.1
TOTAL	20,185	25,597	26.8
Blue-collar occupations			
Craftsmen	7,754	8,693	12.1
Operatives	12,274	12,816	4.4
Laborers	3,526	3,670	4.1
TOTAL	23,554	25,179	6.9

was an amendment to the National Labor Relations Act (Wagner Act) of 1935, which had given workers the legal right to organize themselves into unions for the purpose of collective bargaining with employers, as well as the right to strike and to picket in support of a strike. The Wagner Act had also established the National Labor Relations Board to oversee disputes between workers and management. The Taft–Hartley Act, however, sought to remedy what Republicans believed were union abuses allowed under the Wagner Act. It narrowed the definition of unfair labor practices, thereby permitting employers to adopt certain practices previously deemed to be unfair. Employers were given a free hand to fire and blacklist union agitators, for instance, and to use spies to report on union meetings.

End of the "closed shop"

Most important of all was the provision banning the "closed shop." A closed shop was a workplace in which a union had the power to compel all employees to become union members. Outlawing the closed shop meant that non-unionists were able to work for a company alongside union members. To the unions this represented a threat to their power of collective bargaining and strike action as a means of winning concessions from management. To the employers it represented a guarantee of individual freedom of choice.

The Taft–Hartley Act had other provisions that labor leaders disliked. Employers were allowed to require union officials to swear under oath that they were not communists. Unions were made legally liable for any acts of violence committed by their members, and the federal government was authorized to impose an 80-day injunction if it considered that a strike posed a threat to national health or safety. That power was frequently invoked by the government in the 1950s.

Representatives of the United Steelworkers, U.S. Steel, and Republic Steel leave the White House after a session of talks in 1952. There were further steel strikes in 1956 and 1959.

The provisions of the Taft–Hartley Act helped foster divisions in the labor movement between communists and noncommunists and favored management by taking away the element of surprise from big industrial strikes (unions had to give 60 days' advance notice of any strike). Critics denounced the act as a "slave labor bill," although it preserved the legal right of workers to organize and to bargain collectively, and it also upheld, within new restrictions, the right to strike.

What the act helped achieve was to confine the labor movement to the workplace and to the industrial sector. It was the foundation on which the postwar compromise between labor and capital was built. That compromise meant that in return for legal bargaining rights and the right to strike for such things as higher wages, better working conditions, and shorter working hours, unions acknowledged that it was the sphere of industrial owners and managers to organize production, set prices, and make all the decisions about how an industry was run. The compromise also had a political dimension. The union leaders, flattered to be wooed by business and to be called the "new men of power," ceased to be the radical spokesmen they had been a generation before.

The white-collar sector

In addition to changes in the law there were also developments in the American economy that had a considerable effect on the growth and power of labor unions. In the late 1940s and 1950s the growth sectors of the economy were in white-collar jobs and the service industries; those were sectors that were resistant to union organization. Government statistics for 1956 revealed that for the first time ever there were more white-collar workers in nonagricultural employment than blue-collar workers (*see box opposite*). That shift was associated with new levels of investment in research and development, with jobs for highly skilled professionals, and with automation, which turned unskilled, manual jobs into semiskilled ones. As more and more workers moved into salaried jobs, their view of themselves and their place in society began to change. Some workers started to consider themselves "middle class" and distanced themselves from the radicalism of old New Deal labor and the idea that class divisions could be impediments to personal advancement.

The rise in the numbers of white-collar workers—including large numbers of women who worked on a part-time basis—meant that the unions lost much of their power. White-collar workers were traditionally reluctant to join unions (*see box on p. 166*) and often worked for small companies that

Pickets parade in front of the Chevrolet plant in Baltimore, Maryland, in October 1952. As many as 3,000 workers went on strike at two General Motors plants.

TRUMAN AND "BIG LABOR"

When, amid the turbulent industrial unrest of the late 1940s, President Harry S. Truman, a Democrat with a record of support for blue-collar workers, reacted angrily against strikes in the coal and railroads industries, the portents for the labor movement were not good. He accused the railroad workers of wanting to "tie up this whole country," questioned the patriotism of union leaders, and threatened to bring in legislation empowering the government to draft strikers into the military. Truman disliked John L. Lewis (1880–1969), the head of the United Mine Workers, who boasted of holding the fate of American society in his hands: "I can squeeze, twist, and pull," he once said, "until we get the inevitable victory." Truman regarded Lewis as little better than a racketeer.

Truman went to court to get an order prohibiting a proposed strike by the miners in 1946. When the miners nevertheless walked out, Lewis was cited for contempt of court. He was personally fined $10,000, and his union was forced to pay a staggering $3.5 million by a judge who described the miners' strike as "an evil, demoniac, monstrous thing that means hunger and cold and unemployment and disorganization of the social fabric." That was language associated with the big-business opponents of what they called "Big Labor." For a Democratic president nurtured in the New Deal to harmonize his attitude with those voices was an ill omen for the future of the labor movement.

This cartoon from 1952 shows United Mine Workers President John L. Lewis as a volcano erupting with "new demands in coal industry."

had no links with unions. Therefore white-collar workers remained largely unorganized, while blue-collar workers made up nearly three-fourths of the country's union membership.

Further changes in the economy also contributed to the erosion of union power in the 1950s. For example, employment opportunities shifted to the petroleum and electronics industries in the South and Southwest, regions of the country that had never been fertile breeding grounds for organized labor.

In addition, critics point out that during the decade the labor movement as a whole became defensive, narrowing its conception of unionism's role in politics and society and encouraging compromise between management and labor. Previously unions had sought to have a say in the way that industry was organized and, more widely, to exercise influence over the general management of the American economy. Now, however, large obstacles stood in the way of a more ambitious labor program. It was difficult for labor to behave as a national movement for social progress beyond the workplace when, as at the end of the 1950s, only about 16 million workers, or one-fourth of the total workforce of 65 million, were organized in unions. That represented a decline in union membership not in actual numbers but as a proportion of the workforce—a drop of 4 percent since 1945. Union membership failed to keep pace with the growth in population in part because of the new labor legislation. For example, a controversial clause in the Taft–Hartley Act gave state legislatures the right to pass "right-to-work" laws protecting employment opportunities for workers who chose not to join a union.

AFL–CIO

One of the most important developments of the decade was the merger of two key labor organizations. In 1955 the American Federation of Labor (AFL) merged with the Congress of Industrial Organizations (CIO) to form the AFL–CIO. The AFL had traditionally represented skilled workers in craft-based industries, while the CIO had represented workers in mass-production industries. The AFL had historically adhered to a somewhat cautious, conservative view of the role of labor unions, preferring to restrict its activities to negotiations with employers and steering clear of direct participation in party politics.

That left open the question, however, of how great a say labor unions should have in the day-to-day running of companies' affairs. And that was the issue in the years between 1945 and 1960 that was settled largely in favor of the owners and managers of industry.

Amid the generally good times of the 1950s workers were more interested in getting what they could out of the capitalist system than in attempting to change the political and economic climate of the United States. Those who recommended a more aggressive form of labor unionism were branded as socialists or communists. But following the diligent efforts of the AFL and the CIO to expel communists from their ranks, there were few of them left by the early 1950s. In 1949 the CIO, which had been the more militant of the two organizations, expelled 11 communist-led unions, with a total membership of 900,000. This was a blunt way of dealing with the problem since no one believed that the majority of individual members of those unions were communists. It was an assault on union democracy to stop members from electing the leaders they wanted, but it removed the "trouble-makers," paving the way for the AFL–CIO merger and for a more cooperative approach with management.

UAW strike

The pattern for cooperation between management and workers was set by the settlement in 1948 of a long strike at General Motors by workers in the powerful United Auto Workers (UAW) union. The workers had walked out when the management refused to consent to their demand for a 30 percent wage hike. However, the strike became a far wider contest than a mere wage demand. Led from 1946 by the fiery Walter Reuther (1907–1970), a radical activist on the left wing of the labor movement, the UAW had historically spoken out in favor of a strong voice for labor in the management of large corporations. The strikers at General Motors claimed that a wage increase was justifiable because the company could award it to them without having to increase the cost of its cars to consumers. When the company denied the truth of that claim, the UAW challenged it to let union officials see the details of the company's financial position.

That challenge was resisted by management. General Motors was dismayed when an independent committee appointed by the federal government to investigate the dispute gave its opinion that the ability of a company to pay higher wages was a legitimate consideration in any settlement of a dispute. Management walked out of negotiations in protest, leading to a 113-day strike during the

Adlai Stevenson, two-time Democratic nominee for the U.S. presidency, addresses the American Federation of Labor during an election campaign.

winter of 1945–1946 and, with all General Motors plants shut down, losses to the company of tens of millions of dollars.

Escalator clauses

In the end the UAW capitulated, but the workers won a substantial victory of their own. The settlement included a provision that future contracts would include an "escalator clause," which tied increases in wages and benefits to rises in the cost of living and improved productivity. The workers also gained more control over the day-to-day organization of work on the shopfloor. However, the UAW abandoned its quest to have a say in such matters as the distribution of profits to shareholders, investment, and price policy—in other words, to have a say in the economic strategy of the company. The union accepted that labor's input was restricted to issues that affected its members directly. The management of General Motors, for its part, accepted that prudent concessions to the unions could avert costly strikes.

By the end of the 1950s "escalator clauses," sometimes called COLA (cost of living adjustment) clauses, were written into about half of all union agreements. They were not entirely a matter for union celebration since wages went up if the cost of living increased but could also be reduced when the cost of living went down. However, a range of "fringe benefits" such as sick pay, paid vacations, life insurance, and favorable pension plans increasingly came to be included in labor agreements with large corporations. (Smaller businesses could not so easily afford them but tended in any case to have nonunionized employees.) Many unions also secured contracts that enshrined the principle of employee seniority (which meant first in, last out when workers were laid off) and included clearly defined procedures to deal with grievances and

Teamsters leader Jimmy Hoffa talks before a crowd of 10,000 union members at Madison Square Garden, New York City, in 1960. He was speaking out against the 1959 Landrum–Griffin Act.

TROUBLE AT THE STEEL MILLS

Although strikes declined sharply in the 1950s, the steelworkers downed tools twice in the space of three years at the end of the decade. The first strike, called in the summer of 1956, made 650,000 workers idle and shut down about 90 percent of the nation's steel mills. The major issues in the dispute were the length of contracts and wage increases (with more pay for weekend work). The strike was conducted in a peaceful manner and was settled after just a month.

Three years later the industry was once more hit by strike action. As the economy slid into recession, bad trading conditions led to weak steel figures for 1958, with production at its lowest level since 1946. Despite the downturn, steelworkers went on strike again in July 1959, when the contract agreed in 1956 came up for renewal, and the owners and union leaders were unable to reach a new agreement. About 500,000 workers joined the strike in pursuit of higher wages, shorter hours, and better working conditions, closing down 85 percent of steel capacity. Another 200,000 men were laid off.

The government used the Taft-Hartley Act to get a court injunction against the strike. The union appealed against the decision to the Supreme Court, which early in November ruled that the injunction was constitutional, bringing an end to the walkout after 116 days, the longest strike in the steel industry in American history.

It was a black day for labor because the Supreme Court decision implied a severe restriction on the legal right to strike. The workers trudged back to the mills with no settlement in sight (it was reached, with few gains to the workers, in January 1960) and with relations between management and the workers worse than they had been when the strike began. Throughout the strike the owners had protested over and over again that the cause of the steel industry's malaise was high prices forced on the industry by unreasonably high wages. And it was a sign of the pressures on domestic American workers to come that the owners highlighted the increasing inability of American industry to compete with foreign, especially Japanese, producers, and that wage levels were costing American firms out of the market.

A tavern owner in Chicago places a sign offering "strikers special" in a window near the plant of the U.S. Steel Corporation in July 1959.

dismissals. Occasionally rules of arbitration were laid down. Those fruits of labor–management cooperation increased job security and helped prevent strikes.

Strikes

The number of strikes and worker hours lost during labor disputes dropped sharply in the later part of the decade compared to the peaks of industrial unrest during the second half of the 1940s and during the Korean War (1950–1953). Stoppages reached a record high of 5,117 in 1952, then declined dramatically to fewer than 4,000 a year for the rest of the decade. The average number of workers involved in a strike also dropped. However, the exception to this was the great steel strike of 1959 (*see box*), when half a million steelworkers went on strike. The strike shook the nation because people had become used to a period of industrial calm.

One further sign of labor discontent in the 1950s was a series of "wildcat strikes" (walkouts staged without the authority of the union or a ballot of its members). One-third of all walkouts in the decade were wildcat strikes. Many were provoked by management efforts to speed up production processes. Others were sparked off by interference in established shopfloor rights and practices. Most union contracts outlawed wildcat strikes, and strikers who broke contracts were subject to union discipline. Wise managers, however, learned that strong unions could be an advantage to them in enforcing collective-bargaining agreements and in relieving them of some of the burden of disciplining their workers. Union leaders, backed by the AFL–CIO, sought to prevent wildcatters from inciting workers to take part in illegal strikes.

WHITE-COLLAR WORKERS

The economist John Kenneth Galbraith (1908–) looked with wry bewilderment on the reluctance of white-collar workers to organize themselves into unions and so increase their economic power. "School teachers, clerical workers, municipal employees and civil servants," he wrote in *American Capitalism* (1952), "have generally avoided organization as something not quite genteel or because it was believed that employers and community at large would recognize their importance and pay accordingly." He argued that the stance taken by such workers "has invariably been viewed with approval, even as a manifestation of patriotism and sound Americanism, by public authorities and private employers."

In his book *White Collar* (1951) the sociologist C. Wright Mills was more scathing about such workers: "They may be politically irritable, but they have no political passion. They are a chorus, too afraid to grumble, too hysterical in their applause." In the short run, he argued, the "new middle classes" would continue to "follow the panicky ways of prestige." But both Mills and Galbraith predicted that the "new middle classes" would would eventually seek power for themselves by organizing.

Two women teachers discuss their work in Maine, in 1954. Increasing numbers of women found both part-time and permanent employment.

In this way unions became part of the control system of management. They became what the American sociologist C. Wright Mills (1916–1962) called "managers of discontent." While they would have preferred to exercise undiluted authority, intelligent managers recognized that unions could perform vital functions for them. Labor unions could, for example, take care of the difficult job of ranking workers' grievances in order of priority. The management of a company was thus relieved of certain tasks, and the union acted as the buffer between the managers and the aggrieved workers. So there came into being an uneasy alliance between unions and the owners of industry.

This seal was selected to be the official insignia of the AFL–CIO in 1955. When the AFL and the CIO merged, they became the most powerful labor organization in America.

Casualties of the steel strike flock to the Ohio State Employment Service in Cleveland in June 1952. Most were laid off from the Chevrolet plant and Midland Steel Products Company.

The fact that unions made gains on behalf of their members without recourse to militant opposition to management helped keep conservative leaders in control of the labor movement. Although the UAW failed to win its demand for a guaranteed annual wage (as opposed to hourly rates) in 1955, in the same year the first genuine annual-wage guarantee was won by steelworkers employed by the American Can Company and the Continental Can Company. In 1956 steelworkers got a substantial pay rise after a five-week strike, and the United Mine Workers also won improved pay packages without going on strike. Prosperity bred relatively harmonious labor relations with management.

Landrum–Griffin Act

Some union activists, however, considered the compromise with management an abdication by their leaders of union power, and the more radical among them were incensed by further restrictions placed on union activity by the Labor-Management Reporting and Disclosure Act, better known as the Landrum–Griffin Act of 1959. The act banned secondary boycotts (boycotting of a company dealing with another company that was already being boycotted). It also outlawed what were called "hot cargo" agreements, by which unions out on strike attempted to persuade distributors not to handle "struck goods" produced by the companies against which they were striking.

In addition, in response to publicity about corruption in certain unions (in 1957 the AFL–CIO had expelled the Teamsters union on grounds that it was dominated by corrupt influences) the Landrum–Griffin Act introduced penalties for union officials who misued union funds or who prevented members from exercising their rights. It set out codes of practice for the conduct of union business and authorized the federal government to oversee the internal running of union affairs. Union leaders complained that federal interference in labor's affairs went far beyond what owners and managers would have tolerated.

The end of collective bargaining

Although organized labor in general opposed the Landrum–Griffin Act for strengthening what it considered the antilabor provisions of the Taft–Hartley Act, commentators suggest that most unionists in the 1950s were broadly contented with the postwar compromise stance adopted between management and labor. They argue

"HUMAN RELATIONS"

In the 1950s the management and control of workforces came to be called "human relations." Part of ensuring good "human relations" was personnel counseling, which had been introduced by the Bell Telephone Company before World War II. In the 1950s counseling spread throughout American industry and business as part of the medical service offered by companies to their employees.

In *The End of Ideology* (1960) the American sociologist and journalist Daniel Bell (1919–) poured scorn on human relations departments, denouncing them as a pretense. He argued that all that managers were doing was substituting "manipulation" and "psychological persuasion" for the open exercise of authority as a way of exerting control and replacing conflict with accommodation. The raucous foreman laying down the law gave way to the sweet-talking "human-relations oriented" supervisor. An academic at the Harvard Business School suggested that labor disputes, although ostensibly about wages and hours and conditions of work, were actually about deeper human needs such as personal recognition. Bell called this approach "the tyranny of psychology" and pointed out that its motive was the eagerness of business owners to discount the existence of "economic man." A sociologist who made a study of men on the shopfloor reached a contrary conclusion, however. He found that the workers "made noises like economic men," and that "[t]heir talk indicated that they were canny calculators and that the dollar sign fluttered at the masthead of every machine."

that a majority of labor unionists were in favor of "bread-and-butter" unionism—that is, unionism that emphasized the need for workers' rights rather than pushed for economic and political changes on a national scale. "We must stop treating labor and management like fighting cocks, taking sides and egging them on," the two-time Democratic Party presidential candidate Adlai Stevenson (1900–1965) told a rally of autoworkers at Flint, Michigan, the home of General Motors, in a well-received campaign speech in 1952. "This kind of fomented disagreement isn't good," he maintained. "We are talking ourselves into a kind of class hatred. And there can't be class hatreds or group antagonisms in a healthy democracy."

However, commentators also claim that in showing reluctance during the 1950s to mold labor into an instrument of national political force (other than maintaining its loose links to the Democratic Party), the labor movement was unable to be an effective voice for the general redistribution of wealth from the rich to the poor. By the 1960s there was a general acceptance that collective bargaining was near the limits of its achievements, and that wage increases had to be tied to productivity. That was not necessarily a bad thing for labor, however: By accepting wage deals tied to productivity, workers could, in years of low inflation, earn more money than they would have if pay increases were determined principally by rises in the cost of living.

In the background to the compromise, or partnership, between labor and capital was the United States' industrial supremacy and the relative weakness of foreign competitors compared to American producers. As long as booming sales continued to fatten corporate profits, and as long as foreign producers offered little challenge to domestic manufacturers, especially in the American market, the partnership worked well. When American corporations invested abroad, they did so chiefly to gain access to foreign markets, not—as was frequently the case at the end of the century—to undercut wages at home and reduce labor costs in order to compete successfully against overseas companies in the home market.

The nature of the relationship between labor and management was in many ways understandable given the strength of the American economy at the time. Wage rates and the standard of living were much higher in the United States than anywhere else in the world. Unemployment rates were lower than they had been even in the good times of the 1920s. In those circumstances it is not surprising that labor made peace with the leaders of industry so easily. American capitalists were more in tune, ideologically, with national opinion than their Japanese or European counterparts.

In addition, the government's role in protecting workers and providing for their financial security by means of such things as workers' compensation and retirement pensions made American labor unions less militant and more concerned to cooperate with management in areas such as profit-sharing and new patterns of work to accommodate automation. However, in agriculture and among the mass of African American and women workers the unions had almost no influence. At the end of the 1950s that was not an issue that unduly disturbed union leaders. The labor movement had entered a new era as a less powerful and progressive force in American society.

See Also:

American Federation of Labor–Congress of Industrial Organizations • Automobile Industry • Black Americans • Democratic Party • Economy • Fair Deal • Hoffa, Jimmy • Industry • Politics and Government • Poverty • Retail Industry • Supreme Court

LAW AND ORDER

Two major events particularly affected law and order in the 1950s: Senator Joseph McCarthy led a nationwide campaign against communist supporters, while black leaders pushed on with the civil rights campaign to change the discriminatory laws against black Americans.

In popular culture the 1950s have an image as something of a golden age of law and order. They form the background of the movie genre known as film noir, with malevolent criminals and hard-boiled cops, or such classic fiction as the late novels of Raymond Chandler (1888–1959), with somewhat sleazy detectives fighting crime in the "mean streets" of American cities. More recently the decade has provided the setting for crime novels by writers such as James Ellroy, whose book *L.A. Confidential* was made into an Oscar-winning movie in 1997.

The process of fictionalization began during the 1950s themselves. One of its chief instruments was the TV series *Dragnet*, which ran from 1952 to 1959 (it was syndicated under the title *Badge 714* and revived in the late 1960s under its original title). Some 38 million viewers a week tuned in to watch *Dragnet*'s hero, Joe Friday, an earnest Los Angeles cop with little interest in anything except fighting crime. A catchphrase the laconic Friday used when interviewing witnesses summed up the show's image of the forthright, trustworthy police force: "All we want are the facts, Ma'am." The show's great appeal was its claim to represent the truth about police work. Each episode was said to be based on files from the Los Angeles Police Department; announcer George Fenneman began each program by assuring the audience, "The story you are about to see is true. Only the names have been changed to protect the innocent." The show ended with the pronouncement of the court's verdict on the accused criminals. In 1954 *Time* magazine remarked that *Dragnet* had given Americans "a new appreciation of the underpaid, long-suffering, ordinary policeman."

In reality the 1950s had little to do with their fictional portrayal. The decade had lower serious crime levels than the 1980s and 1990s, although they were commensurate with today's levels. In many communities Americans were still happy to leave their homes unlocked when they went out. FBI records show that in 1950, five

Police officers escort a demonstrator to a patrol wagon during a student protest against a meeting of the House Committee on Un-American Activities in San Francisco in 1960.

TRAFFIC PATROLS AND HIGHWAY SAFETY

Sightings of state troopers patroling on horseback became less and less frequent as the 1940s drew to a close and the chief mode of transportation for the police became the automobile. Indeed, as the car became the nation's favorite means of travel, this in itself became one of the primary focuses of police activity and initiatives during the 1950s.

Traffic volumes greatly increased, and safety on the highways became a major concern for state police patrols. As Superintendent John A. Gaffney of the New York State Police observed in 1951: "[T]raffic congestion on summer weekends has reached the saturation point, particularly on parkways and highways leading to the State's metropolitan areas." Within a few years congestion was reaching similar levels during the working week; the era of commuter traffic had arrived in urban America.

With the rise in traffic volumes across the United States drunk driving also began to be a major problem for the police. In 1953 a law was passed in New York that allowed police patrols to obtain blood, breath, or urine from a driver for analysis to determine his or her blood alcohol content. The following year the police made a record number of arrests for drunk driving. By the end of the decade the use of breathalyzers was widespread, while the use of radar in traffic enforcement and helicopters to observe heavy traffic was also popular.

New York State police chiefs share a coffee at Niagara Falls while putting up a sign directing tired motorists to free coffee bars in 1959.

incidences of serious crime—murder, manslaughter, rape, robbery, and aggravated assault and burglary—were reported per 1,000 of the population. By 1960 the figure had risen to 5.9; it reached 22.8 in 1980, but by 2000 had fallen back to 5.06.

Such figures, however, should not suggest that there was little crime for the police to fight. In particular, law enforcement targeted organized crime perpetrated by gangs such as the Mafia, the extent of whose activities first came to light during the decade; juvenile delinquency and other problems caused by the new phenomenon in U.S. society, the teenager; and crime associated with a growing drug culture. On the roads, meanwhile, the police enforced legislation designed to prevent the number of road accidents (*see box*). Legislation to permit blood tests to check the alcohol level in drivers' blood was introduced in New York in 1953; the breathalyzer, which analyzes the alcoholic content of a driver's breath, was also introduced during the decade.

Unlike in fiction, however, much police work in the 1950s was not directed at established forms of criminal activity such as burglary or murder. Instead, law-enforcement agencies were heavily involved in two broader aspects of American life: public order issues related to the emerging campaign for civil rights and white reactions against it, and issues relating to the widespread Cold War suspicion of communist and other subversive activity in American life.

Trends in law enforcement

Across the United States police departments shared common approaches to the fight against crime. They completed the shift begun in the 1930s from foot patrols, which had aimed to deter crime through high visibility, to the motorization of officers in automobiles or on motorcycles. That not only cut response times—departments across the country set a common target of three minutes to respond to an emergency call; it also acted as a greater deterrent by increasing the possibility that officers might arrive on the scene while an incident or crime was still in progress. The theory at the time argued that the use of motor vehicles helped create the impression that the police were everywhere.

Meanwhile, technological development also changed policing. Patrol cars were linked to their base by radio, but in the early 1950s the introduction of "walkie-talkie" telephones allowed for two-way car-to-car communication. Late in the 1950s, meanwhile, the development of telephoto communications made it possible for the country's major police departments, such as Chicago after 1959, to transmit copies of photographs, fingerprints, and documents to other departments with the same technology.

Considerable reform in the first half of the 20th century, particularly under the auspices of August Vollmer and his protegee O.W. Wilson, had aimed to create a more professional police service. In particular reformers set out to decrease corruption within the police, in part by separating the police from political influence by creating a civil service to hire and promote officers and focusing police activity more narrowly on serious street crimes. Reforms also prevented officers from serving in the areas where they lived and varied their patrols so that they did not become too closely associated with particular neighborhoods. Police departments became more centralized and bureaucratic, with specialized squads tackling specific areas such as criminal investigation, traffic, vice and prostitution, and narcotics.

Despite reform initiatives, however, corruption remained a problem in some forces. So too did the use of violence against suspects and the routine harassment of black Americans. Although police departments had been hiring African Americans since the late 1800s, black officers were still largely recruited to patrol black areas. It was only in the mid-1960s that police departments began routinely to use black officers to patrol white as well as black areas.

Beyond local or state jurisdiction law enforcement was the responsibility of the Federal Bureau of Investigation (FBI), originally set up in 1908 to investigate criminal activities across the nation. Under its director, J. Edgar Hoover (1895–1972), the FBI had established a reputation for honesty during Prohibition in the 1920s. The bureau's jurisdictional responsibility for fighting crime was expanded in the late 1940s and 1950s. The agency also took on a much wider role in providing assistance to state and local police, using its resources to assist particularly with developments in technology and in forensic science. In 1950 the FBI also introduced its "10 Most Wanted Fugitives" program, which publicized criminals who were judged a serious threat to the country.

Civil rights and law enforcement

One of the growing areas of law enforcement concerned relations between black and white Americans, which became increasingly strained. The causes were partly social and economic, but also owed much to the introduction of new civil rights legislation, in particular the desegregation of transportation and education.

Changing social forces after the end of World War II (1939–1945) set the scene for the escalation in racial tension. There were huge demographic changes as many black Americans left the South to find jobs in northern industrial cities. Many of these new arrivals tried to move into all-white neighborhoods and job markets, creating economic competition. Many urban whites responded with the so-called "flight to the suburbs." Cities experienced suburban expansion and the subsequent relocation of urban manufacturing jobs to rural and suburban areas, while some downtown areas became virtual ghettos inhabited by African Americans or other disadvantaged groups such as Chinese or Japanese Americans.

Even with the postwar economic boom in the United States more than 50 percent of blacks lived in some degree of poverty, and unemployment levels were high. Racial discrimination remained common, particularly in the southern states. Institutionalized segregation governed areas such as housing, schools, restaurants, restrooms, and public transportation. Meanwhile, the raised social ambitions of, for example, black GIs returning after the war clashed with a white determination to keep black Americans in their place (*see box on p. 173*). African Americans could often expect little in the way of protection or even sympathy from law officers. Police officers were themselves commonly implicated in acts of violence and racial hatred.

A police officer records the names of African American students attempting a peaceful sit-down protest at a segregated lunch counter in Atlanta, Georgia, in 1960.

Where segregation was enshrined in law, the police played a major part in enforcing it. In December 1955 they arrested Rosa Parks in Montgomery, Alabama, for refusing to give up her seat to a white man on a bus. Parks's gesture led to a black boycott of Montgomery's buses that lasted a year before the Supreme Court ruled segregation on public buses unconstitutional. As civil rights pressure led to changes in legislation during the 1950s, however, the police were sometimes called on to ensure desegregation. As with other members of the white population, not all law-enforcement officials or their local commanders were happy at the prospect. The situation was particularly pronounced in the South, where local state policies and federal positions frequently clashed.

In 1957, for example, the governor of Arkansas, Orval Faubus (1910–1994), used his police powers to order the Arkansas National Guard to keep nine black students from attending classes at what had previously been an all-white high school in Little Rock. President Dwight D. Eisenhower (1953–1961) "federalized" the National Guard—bringing it under federal rather than state authority—and also sent in regular U.S. Army troops to ensure integration of the school.

Escalation in violence

Despite landmark decisions by the Supreme Court and the passage of the Civil Rights Act in 1957—the first piece of civil rights legislation in the 20th century—segregation remained a fact of life for many African Americans (particularly in the South) until 1968, by which time all forms of de jure, or legal, segregation had finally been declared unconstitutional.

The 1957 act provided for the establishment of a civil rights office as part of the Justice Department. The Civil Rights Division came into being on December 9, 1957, to enforce federal statutes related to civil rights and to coordinate the enforcement of civil rights more generally. The division was only small, however; it had fewer than 10 lawyers, whose initial priority was the investigation of voting rights violations in the South. In the early 1960s the U.S. Marshals were tasked with providing security to enforce desegregation laws. When James Meredith became the first black student to enroll at the University of Mississippi in 1962, for example, a team of 127 marshals provided a 24-hour guard for him for over a year.

As the civil rights movement gained momentum, so did the violent reaction against it. Baptist churches were bombed, as was the home of the prominent civil rights leader and Baptist minister Martin Luther King, Jr. Field agents for the National Association for the Advancement of Colored People (NAACP) were attacked and murdered. Racial violence increased as higher numbers of African Americans moved to industrial cities such as Cleveland, Chicago, Detroit, Boston, and Philadelphia. Crimes committed exclusively by white people against the first blacks to integrate into neighborhoods in-

Members of the Washington Freedom Riders Committee hang signs from bus windows to protest segregation en route to Washington, D.C., from New York in 1961.

ROUGH JUSTICE FOR BLACK AMERICANS

A number of brutal crimes against blacks helped mobilize the civil rights movement. During a bus journey in South Carolina in 1946 black former GI Isaac Woodard was insulted by the bus driver for taking too long in the "colored" bathroom. When Woodard protested against the insult, a heated argument broke out. The driver soon called for help from the police department, and Woodard was beaten by the police officers who arrived on the scene. He was then taken to the police station, where he had his eyes gouged out by a police nightstick. Woodard was left permanently blind.

Incidents such as this increased as the 1940s drew to a close and spilled over into the 1950s. The 1950s saw 11 lynchings of blacks in the South, when mobs hanged or otherwise executed blacks who committed a crime or in some way broke the code of southern race relations. Eight of those lynchings took place in 1955.

However, it took a particularly vicious murder in 1955—when a 14-year old black boy, Emmett Till, was beaten and shot for whistling at a white woman in Mississippi—before ordinary Americans began to question some of the shortcomings of their legal and law-enforcement institutions in their treatment of blacks and other minorities. Although the perpetrators of Till's murder (the woman's husband and his half-brother) were arrested and charged, the all-white jury found the men not guilty. Shortly after the trial they admitted to the killing.

Isaac Woodard (seated left), an African American veteran who was beaten and blinded by police, applies for maximum disability benefits.

cluded the stoning of houses, arson, and other vandalism of property. Such incidents went largely unreported by the mainstream media and were seldom investigated seriously or acted on by police.

In the early 1960s, too, local police were accused of not acting to prevent white violence against civil rights protesters such as the Freedom Riders. Black and white protesters rode buses through the South to test the desegregation of public transportation. They were often met with violence. In Montgomery, Alabama, a crowd attacked a white Freedom Rider and crippled him for life. In Jackson, Mississippi, the police arrested the Freedom Riders and put them in jail for between 40 and 60 days.

Some contemporary commentators believe that the inadequate response of law enforcement and civil authorities to the civil rights movement of the 1950s contributed in the following decade to the emergence of more militant forms of civil rights protest, which would present new challenges to the forces of law and order.

The "Red Scare"

Another important aspect of law and order during the 1950s concerned responses to anxiety about the threat of communism. The general suspicion of the Soviet Union during the Cold War was heightened by events such as the Korean War (1950–1953) and the trials of high-profile spies, such as Julius and Ethel Rosenberg, who were executed in 1953. Pro-Soviet individuals were widely feared to have infiltrated the U.S. government, while the Communist Party of the United States of America was thought to be working through front organizations to promote leftist causes.

Although the FBI had previously been authorized to investigate threats to national security, its role was greatly expanded under Presidents Harry S. Truman (1945–1953) and Eisenhower. Police departments began to display posters urging people to report "subversive activities" to the FBI. Executive Order 9835, issued in 1947, laid down a loyalty program for federal employees; in 1953 Executive Order 10450 set a procedure for vetting their political sympathies.

The main bodies for investigating communist activity were two government committees: the House Un-American Affairs Committee (HUAC) and from 1953 the Permanent Subcommittee on Investigations, part of the Senate Committee on Government Operations, chaired by Senator Joseph McCarthy (1908–1957) of Wisconsin. The senator gave his name to the extreme anticommunism of the period: McCarthyism. He was joined in his anticommunist enthusiasm by FBI boss Hoover, whose bureau used secret surveillance and paid informers to gather evidence.

Between 1947 and 1954 thousands of people in public life or federal

ENFORCING FEAR

During the late forties and early fifties Americans became increasingly concerned about the potential domestic threat from communists. Anxiety about the spread of communism led many people to suspect innocent civilians of being left-wing subversives. Police officers even arrested people on suspicion of being involved in left-wing activities.

For example, one evening in 1950 a Houston woman, a writer for radio, entered a Chinese restaurant with her husband. The woman was researching a program on recent Chinese history and engaged the proprietor in conversation. On overhearing the conversation, a man sitting nearby rushed out of the restaurant and called the police to inform them that people were "talking communism." The police arrested the couple immediately, jailing them for 14 hours before concluding there was no case to answer.

Another incident that took place in the early part of the decade involved a policeman in Wheeling, West Virginia. The officer discovered some machines dispensing candies containing tiny geography lessons within the wrappers. One of them, under the hammer-and-sickle Soviet flag, read "USSR population: 211,000,000. Capital: Moscow. Largest country in the world." The police officer reported the "subversive" candies immediately to the city manager, who quickly removed them from sale.

employment were investigated. Although no one was prosecuted for any crime, hundreds of people were fired from their jobs for "questionable loyalty." HUAC, meanwhile, concentrated on investigating subversion in the Hollywood movie industry.

Investigators largely "uncovered" liberals, labor leaders, civil rights activists, pacifists, atheists, and other individuals who did not conform to majority values. In a national survey in 1954 more than 50 percent of those interviewed agreed that known communists should be jailed; 78 percent thought it acceptable to report neighbors and acquaintances whom they suspected to be communists to the FBI. Yet only 3 percent of those polled had ever met anyone who admitted to being a communist (*see box*).

In 1950 the Internal Security Act (also known as the McCarran Act) created the Subversive Activities Control Board (SACB), which was empowered to order that communist and "communist-front" organizations register with the government. The SACB undertook many investigations into communist activity, summoning witnesses and subpoenaing documents. It explored the full history and workings of political organizations such as the Communist Party of the United States of America (CPUSA) along with labor unions and civil rights groups. Unlike HUAC and the Subcommittee on Investigations, the operations of SACB were open to judicial review.

The head of the FBI, J. Edgar Hoover (left), and Attorney General J. Howard McGrath (right) talk with President Truman at the Justice Department in 1950.

Organized crime

The popular image of organized crime in the United States in the 1950s—promoted by official statements during the decade—linked it almost exclusively with Italian mobsters connected to the Sicilian Mafia. In fact, as organized crime had developed, partly by bootlegging liquor during Prohibition from 1920 until 1933, it had outgrown ethnic groups to include many Jewish and Protestant gangsters. By the 1950s the national crime syndicate was run by a commission of six members.

After the end of Prohibition organized crime expanded from liquor to racketeering—getting money by extortion—gambling, and prostitution. In the postwar period the mobsters used their wealth to diversify into legitimate activities such as real estate and

Harry P. Cain, member of the Subversive Activities Control Board, sits beside a stack of testimony collected during his hearings into an alleged communist organization in 1955.

entertainment. They became involved in hotel chains, jukebox concerns, restaurants, and taverns.

Meyer Lansky, for example, a Belorussian-born Jewish gangster who had been instrumental in the creation of the crime syndicate in the 1930s, saw that legal gambling in places such as Las Vegas (*see p. 177*) would be more cost effective than illegal activities. When Fulgencio Batista became president of Cuba for the second time in 1952, he hired Lansky as a consultant. In 1954 Lansky opened the Montmartre Club in Havana and in 1955 the Gran Casino Nacional. Cuba became a popular American vacation and gambling destination. Lansky's 21-story Riviera Hotel opened in 1958. The following year, however, Batista was overthrown in a revolution led by Fidel Castro, and Lansky's businesses lost around $10 million.

Organized crime also gained influence in the country's labor unions, which were a potential source of funds and political power. The Mob already dominated labor organization among the longshoremen—who loaded and unloaded ships in the nation's docks—and fish markets. In the 1950s it expanded into the construction and building trades, hotels, and transportation. In 1952, for example, Teamsters Union official Jimmy Hoffa made a deal with the Outfit, the Chicago branch of the syndicate. In return for low-interest loans from the union's pension fund the Outfit had Hoffa made vice president of the Teamsters; he was elected union president in 1957.

Kefauver and McClellan hearings

The extent of organized crime's influence came to the attention of many Americans during the 1950s thanks to the Kefauver and McClellan committees, Senate bodies tasked with investigating crime's role in gambling and labor unions during the 1950s. Estes Kefauver (1903–1963), a Tennessee Democrat who served in the Senate from 1949 until his death, was chairman of the Special Committee to Investigate Organized Crime in Interstate Commerce, usually known as the Kefauver Committee. The hearings commenced in May 1950, lasted for 15 months, and questioned 800 witnesses in 14 cities around the United States. The committee's televised proceedings attracted a large audience in bars, restaurants, and businesses—few homes had televisions at the time.

The hearings mesmerized the nation, even though many witnesses "took the Fifth"—cited the Fifth Amendment to the Constitution, which provides protection from incriminating oneself—to avoid answering questions. Writing about the hearings in New York City, where witness after

Frank Costello testifies before the Kefauver Committee investigating organized crime in 1951. Costello was one of America's most notorious gangsters.

Meyer Lansky is brought in for booking on a vagrancy charge at a New York police station in 1958. Lansky was the financial mastermind behind "Lucky" Luciano's organization.

witness described the workings of the crime syndicate, *Life* magazine reported, "The week of March 12, 1951, will occupy a special place in history ... people had suddenly gone indoors into living rooms, taverns, and clubrooms, auditoriums and back-offices. There, in eerie half-light, looking at millions of small frosty screens, people sat as if charmed. Never before had the attention of the nation been riveted so completely on a single matter."

The Kefauver hearings found widespread evidence of skimming, which reduced casino profits to avoid taxation, and brought a crackdown on criminal influence in the casino industry. At the same time, more than 70 local crime commissions were set up across the United States. Of the committee's 19 legislative recommendations, however, none was enacted. Kefauver's conclusions, meanwhile, stressed that organized crime was "alien" to America, continuing the misleading stereotype that it remained dominated by the Italian Mafia. In fact, of the 134 people prosecuted for labor racketeering by the Justice Department from 1953 to 1959, only 15 percent were of Italian descent.

Meanwhile, what had been Joseph McCarthy's Senate Permanent Subcommittee on Investigations had a new chairman, Senator John McClellan (1896–1977). Helped by chief counsel Robert Kennedy, brother of John F. Kennedy, McClellan began hearings in 1957 into the influence of organized crime in labor unions. The hearings uncovered systematic racketeering in Jimmy Hoffa's International Brotherhood of Teamsters and in the Hotel Employees and Restaurant Employees International Union. It also found evidence of squandered and stolen union funds, collusion, coercion, and violence. The efforts of McClellan and Kennedy contributed to Hoffa's imprisonment for pension fund fraud in 1967.

Juvenile delinquency

The word "teenager" was first used in 1941; as time went on, it increasingly came to categorize individuals not only by their age but also by specific behavior, such as listening to certain types of music. Between 1946 and 1960 the number of teenagers in the United States rose from 5.6 million to 11.8 million. For many Americans the new phenomenon represented another source of fear. Teenagers rejected the values of their parents; they adopted uniforms such as leather jackets and jeans or baggy zoot suits; they formed gangs and fought turf wars. They intimidated families around fast-food cafes and drive-ins. They cruised Main Street or raced hot-rods. They drank and took drugs. They were delinquents.

Such fears were fueled by the movie industry, which portrayed teenagers as dangerous rebels in films such as *The Wild One* (1953) and *Rebel without a Cause* (1955). In the former movie, when a waitress asks the biker played by Marlon Brando, "What are you rebelling against?" he famously replies "Whaddya got?"

The media and politicians also emphasized the dangers posed by delinquency. When *New York Times* reporter Benjamin Fine wrote about the subject in 1955, he titled his book after the number of juveniles he predicted would get into trouble with the police each year: *1,000,000 Delinquents*. Within a couple of years the Senate Subcommittee to Investigate Juvenile Delinquency reported that the figure had been surpassed. Although the number of teenagers involved in serious crime was relatively small—car theft

BUGSY SIEGEL AND THE PINK FLAMINGO

Although many casinos in Nevada were financed by mobsters, the most notable was probably the Pink Flamingo Hotel and Casino in Las Vegas. The casino was built in 1946 and opened in 1947 by Meyer Lansky (1902–1983) and his partner, Benjamin "Bugsy" Siegel (1906–1947), a notorious and violent criminal famed for his role in arranging the murder of New York mobster "Dutch" Schultz. He nevertheless had influential political connections—partly the result of black market activities during the war—and was issued a gaming license.

The hotel housed 77 rooms, including the "Bugsy Suite," with its bullet-proof windows, single entrance, yet five possible exits (including a hidden ladder leading to a basement tunnel). The venture was initially unprofitable, and Siegel reportedly used too much Mafia money in building and keeping it afloat. Possibly as a consequence, he was gunned down at the Beverly Hills mansion of his girlfriend less than six months after the casino opened.

The Pink Flamingo went on to feature stars such as Jimmy Durante and George Raft, and undoubtedly played a part in putting Las Vegas on the map as the country's chief gaming destination during the 1950s and for decades to come.

Garish neon signs advertise gambling establishments in downtown Las Vegas in 1953.

LAW ENFORCEMENT AND THE MOB

Policing organized crime was notoriously difficult for several reasons: the established and central role played by crime families in local communities; the tactics employed to maintain that influence and control, including blackmail, extortion, and violence; and the Mafia's own strong political connections. Investigations throughout the 1950s were further hampered by a lack of federal laws covering mob activities. After Prohibition most crimes perpetrated by racketeers were carried out locally, and this prevented investigation on a larger scale by the FBI during much of the decade. Alternative tactics include the use of community policing, informants, surveillance, and undercover operations.

However, law enforcement's big break came in 1957, when Sergeant Croswell and a colleague, both of the New York State troopers, stumbled across a convention of mobsters from all over the United States at a motel in Apalachin, New York. The meeting disbanded when the criminals became aware of the troopers' presence, and they tried to escape through the surrounding woods. The FBI was able to collect information on the individuals identified at the meeting, which confirmed the existence of a national organized crime network. The incident marked the beginning of a concerted, nationwide war on the Mafia. It also provided impetus for federal legislation to tackle organized crime.

was the most common offense—many Americans identified with Boston judge John C. Connelly, quoted in *Newsweek* in 1953: "We have the spectacle of an entire city terrorized by one-half of one percent of its residents. And the terrorists are children." The period from 1948 to 1953 saw the number of juveniles charged with a crime increase by 45 percent in comparison to previous years.

Ordinary Americans were ready to try to combat the spread of delinquency. In 1954 *Newsweek* reported that the parents of an Ohio town had held a secret meeting to draft a code of behavior for their teenage children, including a time for curfew, the permissible number of nights out a week, and the age at which girls should start attending dances. Because all parents would apply the same rules, the theory went, children would not be able to argue, "But everyone else is doing it."

Explanations of the phenomenon of juvenile delinquency varied widely. Some people blamed parents for the failures of their children. FBI Director J. Edgar Hoover argued that lack of parental discipline and irreligion were both to blame: "In practically all homes where juvenile delinquency is bred there is an absence of religious training for children.... Most of them have never seen the inside of a church."

For other observers, however, teenage gang members from poor slums had been brutalized by their environment. In his book *Must You Conform?* (1956) psychiatrist Dr. Robert Lindner argued that teenagers were suffering a type of collective mental illness, but that above all they wanted to conform to one another. For other liberal commentators the delinquents' desire for power could even be taken as a positive quality. In 1957 educator Max Lerner wrote in *America as a Civilization*, "The violence with which intense slum youngsters imitate the values of culture, even while distorting them, may be seen as their own form of flattery. What they do is legally and morally wrong, but instead of being a sign of the decay of American life it may be taken almost as a sign of its vitality."

Other people looked for other scapegoats. Some blamed horror and

This police station in San Francisco was photographed in 1956. The centralization of police forces during the decade was in part aimed at fighting corruption in local stations.

crime comics for inspiring "copycat" behavior in young people. For example, in *Seduction of the Innocent* (1954) senior psychiatrist for the New York Department of Hospitals, Dr. Fredric Wertham, compared comic books to drugs that corrupted children and led to juvenile delinquency. In the wake of hearings by the Senate Subcommittee to Investigate Juvenile Delinquency in the United States, held in April 1954, self-regulation by publishers saw the virtual disappearance of crime and horror comics from the shelves.

Politicization of black youth

During the 1950s black American youth, in particular, found a new voice. Some of the earliest and most active supporters of desegregation were black students. Following World War II, many of the younger generation carried with them the expectation of their elders that they would be agents of democratic and social change. The school strikes and riots of the late 1940s and the 1950s frequently involved young people.

At the same time, gangs of black youths began to spring up in more and more of the poor urban neighborhoods of America's northern cities, where an entire generation was becoming increasingly isolated in substandard, overcrowded living conditions. The continuing segregation and discrimination, this time in a northern urban environment, were to boil over into race riots in the following decade. Many young blacks later found cultural identity by turning to the militant nationalistic groups that were to become prominent during the 1960s, such as the Black Panthers.

Narcotics and the law

During the 1950s many police departments witnessed the first signs that narcotics could become a major crime problem, although compared to the levels of drug use in later decades there were still relatively few drug users. The primary drug of concern for most

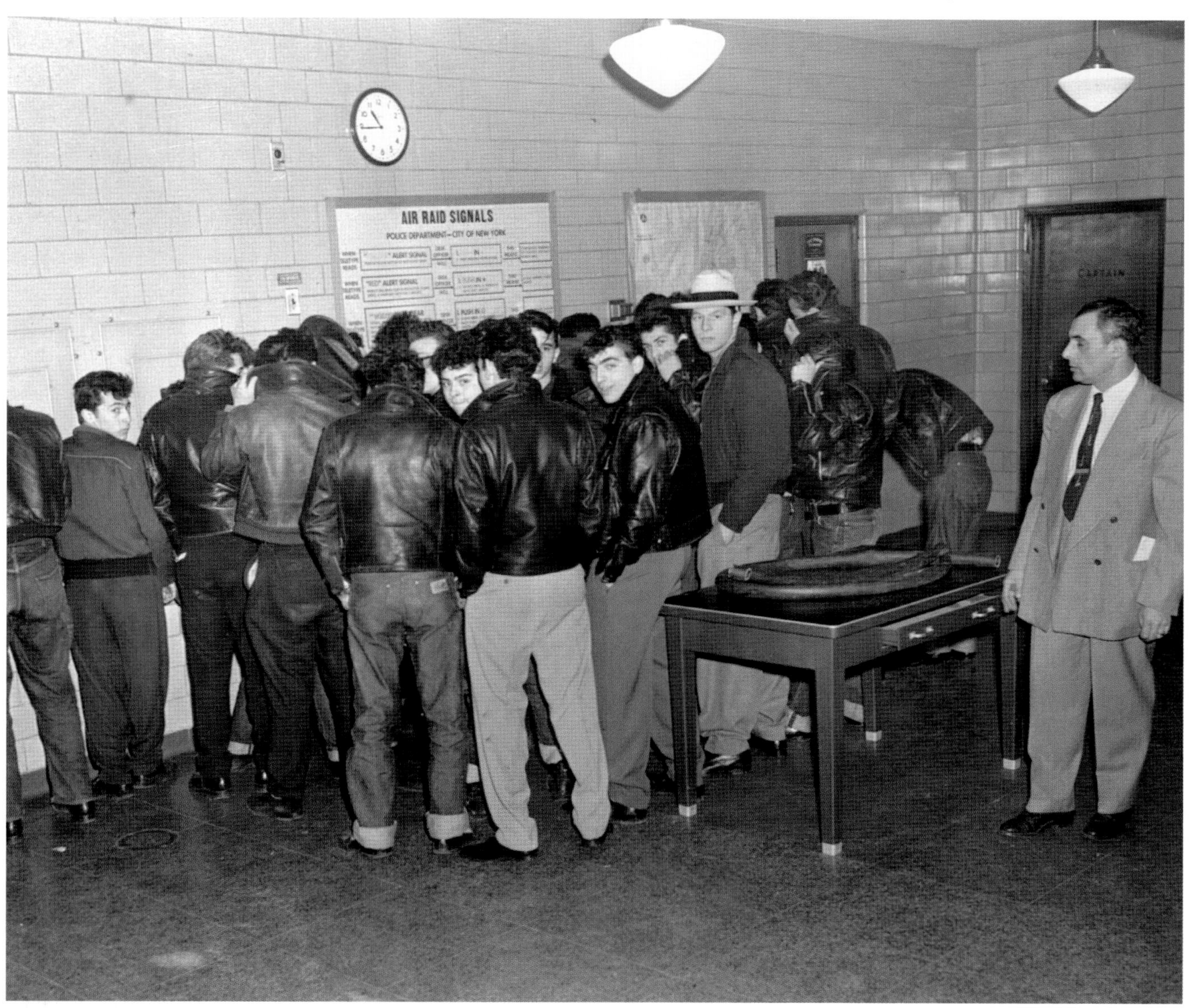

A group of youths stand together in a Brooklyn police station in 1954. Some of them were released into the custody of their parents on juvenile delinquency charges.

Police detectives in Harrisburg, Pennsylvania, pour 15,000 amphetamine sulfate pills into the city incinerator in 1960. The pills were confiscated from service station attendants.

police departments in terms of its use, abuse, and trafficking was heroin. Originally produced for medical use by the German company Bayer until 1913, heroin addiction was to become a major problem during the 1930s and 1940s, when its use came to be a part of the Harlem jazz scene and of the cultural identity of black "hipsters."

The Korean War (1950–1953) then introduced a generation of American servicemen to opium and its derivatives such as heroin. Levels of addiction grew among war veterans. Heroin was further integrated into America's subculture when it became fashionable among the Beatniks of the 1950s.

During the 1950s the major supply of heroin entering the United States came via the "French Connection"—a collaboration between Corsican gangsters in Marseilles, France, and the Sicilian Mafia. Attempts at targeting this supply and at busting heroin distributors and "pushers" on the streets increasingly involved cooperative investigations between local police departments and federal law-enforcement agents.

Marijuana

Between 1850 and 1937 marijuana could be purchased from pharmacies and general stores throughout the United States and was popular as a medicinal drug. An influx of Mexican immigrants and the years of Prohibition led to increased use of the drug for recreational purposes; "tea pads," places in which people could buy marijuana, began appearing in cities across the nation. However, during the Great Depression of the 1930s the drug became linked to a more negative attitude toward Mexican immigrants. Since research studies also linked the drug with crime and violence, Congress passed the Marijuana Tax Act in 1937, which criminalized use of the drug.

Marijuana remained popular in black jazz culture, however, and the 1950s saw its increased popularity with the Beatnik subculture (bebop jazz and Beat literature). Although the period 1951 to 1956 saw stricter sentencing laws set mandatory minimum sentences for drug-related offenses, the decade was to witness a slow rise in the number of arrests for marijuana possession and sale.

See Also:

Civil Rights • Drugs and Drug Abuse • Federal Bureau of Investigation • Hoffa, Jimmy • Hoover, J. Edgar • House Un-American Activities Committee • King, Martin Luther, Jr. • Labor Relations • Little Rock School Crisis • McCarthy Hearings • Teenage Culture

BOOKS

Altschuler, Glenn C. *All Shook Up: How Rock 'n' Roll Changed America.* New York: Oxford University Press, 2003

Ambrose, Stephen E. *Eisenhower: Soldier and President.* New York: Simon and Schuster, 1990

Bell, Daniel *The End of Ideology: On the Exhaustion of Political Ideas in the Fifties.* Cambridge, MA: Harvard University Press, 2000 (originally published 1960)

Boddy, William *Fifties Television: The Industry and Its Critics.* Urbana, IL: University of Illinois Press, 1990

Cross, Gary S. (ed.) *Encyclopedia of Recreation and Leisure in America.* Farmington Hills, MI: Charles Scribner's Sons, 2004

Doherty, Thomas *Teenagers and Teenpics: The Juvenilization of American Movies in the 1950s.* Philadelphia, PA: Temple University Press, 2002 (rev. edn)

Fried, Albert (ed.) *McCarthyism, the Great American Red Scare: A Documentary History.* New York: Oxford University Press, 1997

Galbraith, John Kenneth *The Affluent Society.* Boston, MA: Houghton Mifflin, 1998 (originally published 1958)

Hendershot, Cyndy *Anti-communism and Popular Culture in Mid-century America.* Jefferson, NC: McFarland, 2003

Johns, Michael *Moment of Grace: The American City in the 1950s.* Berkeley, CA: University of California Press, 2003

Judge, Edward H. and John W. Langdon (eds.) *The Cold War: A History Through Documents.* Upper Saddle River, NJ: Prentice Hall, 1999

Kaledin, Eugenia *Daily Life in the United States, 1940–1959: Shifting Worlds.* Westport, CT: Greenwood Press, 2000

Klingaman, William K. *Encyclopedia of the McCarthy Era.* New York: Facts on File, 1996

LaFeber, Walter *America, Russia, and the Cold War, 1945–2002.* Boston, MA: McGraw-Hill, 2004

Layman, Richard (ed.) *American Decades: 1950–1959.* Detroit, MI: Gale Research, 1994

Levy, Peter B. *The Civil Rights Movement.* Westport, CT: Greenwood Press, 1998

McCullough, David *Truman.* New York: Simon and Schuster, 1992

Oakley, J. Ronald *Baseball's Last Golden Age, 1946–1960: The National Pastime in a Time of Glory and Change.* Jefferson, NC: McFarland, 1994

Olson, James S. *Historical Dictionary of the 1950s.* Westport, CT: Greenwood Press, 2000

Palladino, Grace *Teenagers: An American History.* New York: Basic Books, 1996

Pierpaoli, Paul G., Jr. *Truman and Korea: The Political Culture of the Early Cold War.* Columbia, MO: University of Missouri Press, 1999

Salamone, Frank A. *Popular Culture in the Fifties.* Lanham, MD: University Press of America, 2001

Thumin, Janet (ed.) *Small Screens, Big Ideas: Television in the 1950s.* New York: I.B. Tauris, 2002

Young, William H. with Nancy K. Young *The 1950s* (American Popular Culture through History series). Westport, CT: Greenwood Press, 2004

USEFUL WEBSITES

Cold War
http://edition.cnn.com/SPECIALS/cold.war

Cold War International History Project
http://wwics.si.edu/index.cfm?fuseaction=topics.home&topic_id=1409

The Dwight D. Eisenhower Library
www.eisenhower.archives.gov

The Fifties Index
www.fiftiesweb.com

Greatest Space Events of the 20th Century: The 50s
http://www.space.com/news/spacehistory/greatest_space_events_1950s-1.html

The History of Rock 'n' Roll
www.history-of-rock.com

Kingwood College Library: American Cultural History 1950–1959
http://kclibrary.nhmccd.edu/decade50.html

The Korean War
www.korean-war.com

Literature and Culture of the American 1950s
http://www.writing.upenn.edu/~afilreis/50s/home.html

National Baseball Hall of Fame 1950–1959
http://www.baseballhalloffame.org/hof_weekend/hof_game/history/1950s.htm

Pro Football Hall of Fame: The Fifties
http://www.profootballhof.com/history/decades/index.jsp#50s

Voices of Civil Rights
www.voicesofcivilrights.org

PICTURE CREDITS

Front cover images supplied by Library of Congress, National Archives of America, and the Robert Hunt Library

Corbis: 13, 23, 25, 31, 36, 37, 58, 66, 100, 119, Bettmann 5, 15, 17, 19, 33, 34, 42, 43t, 43b, 51, 60, 70, 72, 78, 81, 82, 83, 99, 101, 103t, 103b, 104, 113, 117b, 126, 137, 140, 159, 161, 164, 165, 166b, 167, 169, 170, 171, 175t, 177, 178, 179, 180, William Gottlieb 11, Jack Moebes 32, Genevieve Naylor 18, Charles E. Rotkin 111, Mark L. Stephen 141; **Getty Images:** 4, 6, 7, 16, 20t, 20b, 21, 39, 40, 49, 57, 59, 65, 68, 71, 73, 76, 80, 91, 92, 98, 105, 106, 110, 116, 123, 127, 134, 138, 16, 163; **Lebrecht Collection:** 131, 132; **Library of Congress:** 22, 24, 26, 28, 29, 30, 38, 44, 45, 47t, 47b, 54, 55, 56, 61, 64, 67, 69, 74, 77, 79, 84, 85, 87, 88, 89, 90, 95b, 96, 97, 108, 114, 115, 117t, 118, 120, 121, 122, 124, 125, 129, 136, 160, 162, 166t, 172, 173, 174, 175b, 176; **National Archives:** 148, 149, 150, 152, 153, 154, 155, 156, 157t, 157b, 158; **Photos12.com:** 86; **Robert Hunt Library:** 10, 46, 53, 62, 63, 107, 130, 139, 143; **Topham Picturepoint:** 8, 9, 14, 50, 52, 75, 95t, 128, 133, 135. 142, 144, 145, 146.

PRE-1950

1945
April 12 President Franklin D. Roosevelt dies. His vice president, Harry S. Truman, replaces him.

May 12 British Prime Minister Winston Churchill first uses the phrase "Iron Curtain" to describe the invisible barrier that divides Eastern and Western Europe.

August 6 United States drops an atomic bomb on Hiroshima, Japan. A second bomb is dropped on Nagasaki on August 9.

September 2 Ho Chi Minh declares the founding of the Democratic Republic of Vietnam.

October 24 The United Nations Charter is ratified.

1947
March 12 President Truman commits the United States to defending Greece and Turkey against communism.

April 15 Jackie Robinson makes debut his for the Brooklyn Dodgers, becoming the first African American to play baseball for a major-league team.

June 5 Secretary of State George C. Marshall outlines a program of financial aid to help accelerate European economic recovery. The program becomes known as the Marshall Plan.

September 18 The Central Intelligence Agency (CIA) is established to coordinate U.S. intelligence efforts.

October 20 The House Un-American Activities Committee (HUAC) holds its first round of hearings into communist activity in the movie industry.

December 3 Tennessee Williams's play *A Streetcar Named Desire* opens on Broadway to widespread acclaim.

1948
April 30 The Organization of American States is formed.

June 24 The Soviet Union blocks road and rail access to West Berlin.

1949
April 4 The North Atlantic Treaty Organization is formed at a meeting in Washington, D.C.

October 1 The People's Republic of China is formed after the victory of Mao Zedong's Communists over Nationalist forces.

1950

January 21 Alger Hiss, a U.S. government official accused of spying for the Soviet Union, is convicted of perjury. He is later sentenced to five years' imprisonment.

February 9 In a speech delivered to a Republican women's group Senator Joseph McCarthy claims that the U.S. State Department is home to 205 communists.

March 1 Klaus Fuchs is convicted of spying for the Soviet Union and supplying it with top-secret information about British and American nuclear bomb research.

April 14 National Security Report NSC-68 is published. The document warns that the Soviet Union is aiming to bring Europe and Asia under its control.

May 11 The Kefauver Committee hearings into organized crime begin.

June 25 North Korean troops cross the border dividing North and South Korea; the Korean War begins.

July 17 Julius Rosenberg is arrested and charged with spying for the Soviet Union. His wife Ethel is arrested on August 11.

July 20 In a report to the Senate the Tydings Committee finds no substance to the allegations about communist activity made by McCarthy in February.

September 15 UN troops launch an amphibious assault on the port of Inchon to turn the tide of the Korean War.

October 2 "Peanuts," the comic strip by Charles M. Schulz, is published for the first time.

November 1 Puerto Rican nationalists Griselio Torresola and Oscar Collazo attempt to assassinate President Harry S. Truman. The attempt fails.

November 11 The first gay liberation organization, the Mattachine Society, is founded in Los Angeles.

November 26 Chinese troops take part in their first major battle of the Korean War when they surround UN forces at the Chosin Reservoir.

November 30 U.S. troops begin to retreat from the Chosin Reservoir.

December 10 Ralph Bunche wins the Nobel Peace Prize for his efforts to bring peace to the Middle East.

1951

February 1 The United Nations General Assembly denounces China's entry into the Korean War as an act of aggression.

February 27 The Twenty-Second Amendment to the United States Constitution is ratified. The amendment limits presidents to two terms in office.

March 30 The first UNIVAC I computer is delivered to the United States Census Bureau by Remington Rand.

April 11 President Truman relieves General Douglas MacArthur of his command in Korea after the latter openly criticizes the president's foreign policy.

April 18 Six Western European nations sign the Treaty of Paris, establishing the European Coal and Steel Community.

June 25 Arthur Godfrey, Ed Sullivan, and Faye Emerson appear in CBS's first commercial color telecast.

July 16 J.D. Salinger's novel *The Catcher in the Rye* is published.

August 14 U.S. newspaper publisher William Randolph Hearst dies.

September 1 The ANZUS Treaty, a mutual defense pact, is signed by the United States, Australia, and New Zealand.

September 4 The first live coast-to-coast TV broadcast in the United States features President Truman at the opening of the Japanese Peace Conference in San Francisco.

September 8 The end of the Pacific War is officially recognized when 48 countries sign the San Francisco Peace Treaty with Japan.

October 15 The first episode of *I Love Lucy* is broadcast.

November 1 In the Nevada Desert U.S. troops hold the first military exercises aimed at preparing for nuclear war.

November 24 The play *Gigi*, starring Audrey Hepburn, opens on Broadway.

December 20 The nuclear reactor Experimental Breeder Reactor I produces enough power to illuminate four 150-watt light bulbs.

December 25 The black civil rights activist Harry T. Moore is murdered. No one is arrested for the crime.

1952

March 21 The Moondog Coronation Ball takes place at the Cleveland Arena. The show, which was to feature a number of rock-'n'-roll artists, is stopped after just one song because of overcrowding.

March 29 President Truman announces that he will not be running for reelection.

July 2 Scientist Jonas Salk tests an early version of the polio vaccine on children.

July 24 *High Noon* opens. The movie would go on to win four Oscars; star Gary Cooper would win the best actor award.

July 25 Former colony Puerto Rico becomes a self-governing commonwealth of the United States.

August 1 The first Holiday Inn hotel opens in Memphis, Tennessee.

August 29 *4' 33"* by John Cage is performed for the first time.

September 1 *Life* magazine publishes Ernest Hemingway's *The Old Man and the Sea*.

September 19 U.S. Attorney General Thomas McGranery issues an order that actor Charlie Chaplin should be held by immigration services if he tries to return to the United States. Chaplin is suspected of holding left-wing political views.

September 23 Rocky Marciano defeats Jersey Joe Walcott to claim the boxing world heavyweight title.

Vice-presidential candidate Richard M. Nixon appears on television to counter corruption charges.

November 1 The United States successfully detonates its first hydrogen bomb, "Mike," on Enewetak Atoll in the Pacific Ocean.

November 4 Republican candidate Dwight D. Eisenhower defeats Democrat Adlai Stevenson in the presidential election. The Republicans regain control of both houses of Congress.

November 29 Eisenhower fulfills an election campaign promise and travels to Korea in an attempt to bring the Korean War to a close.

December 14 Conjoined twins are successfully separated by surgery at Mount Sinai Hospital in Ohio, the first time that such an operation has been performed.

1953

January 1 Country singer Hank Williams dies of a heart attack at age 29.

January 7 President Truman announces that the United States has developed a hydrogen bomb.

January 20 Eisenhower takes over the presidency from Truman.

January 22 Arthur Miller's play *The Crucible*, an attack on the anticommunist fervor of the decade, opens on Broadway.

February 18 Lucille Ball and Desi Arnaz sign an $8 million contract to continue the *I Love Lucy* TV series until the end of 1955.

February 28 James D. Watson and Francis Crick announce that they have determined the chemical structure of DNA.

March 5 Soviet leader Joseph Stalin dies after ruling the country for 29 years.

April 7 Dag Hammarskjöld is elected secretary-general of the United Nations.

June 19 Julius and Ethel Rosenberg are executed following their conviction for conspiracy to commit espionage in 1951.

July 26 A small band of revolutionaries led by Fidel Castro attacks Moncada Army Barracks in Cuba.

July 27 The Korean War ends. The United Nations Command, People's Republic of China, and North Korea sign an armistice agreement at Panmunjom.

August 12 The Soviet Union explodes its first hydrogen bomb.

September 7 Nikita Khrushchev becomes first secretary of the Soviet Union's Central Committee.

Tennis player Maureen Connolly wins the U.S. National Singles Championship to become the first woman to win all four grand slam titles in a single year.

October 5 Earl Warren is sworn in as chief justice of the U.S. Supreme Court.

December 8 President Eisenhower delivers what becomes known as the "Atoms for Peace" speech to the United Nations; he proposes the formation of an international atomic energy agency.

December 30 The first commercially available color TV set goes on sale.

1954

January 14 Actress Marilyn Monroe marries baseball star Joe DiMaggio.

January 25 The foreign ministers of the "big four"—the United States, Britain, France, and the Soviet Union—meet at the Berlin Conference.

February 23 The first mass vaccination of children against polio begins in Pittsburgh, Pennsylvania.

March 1 The United States conducts a hydrogen bomb test on Bikini Atoll in the Pacific Ocean.

April 7 In a speech at a news conference President Eisenhower outlines the "domino theory," which states that if one nation falls to communism, its neighbors will soon follow.

April 22 Television coverage of the Army–McCarthy hearings in the U.S. Senate begins.

May 7 The siege of Dien Bien Phu ends in victory for the Vietminh over French colonial forces.

May 17 The Supreme Court rules that racial segregation in public schools is unconstitutional in the case of *Brown v. Board of Education*.

June 18 Rebel troops trained by the CIA cross the border from Honduras to topple President Jacobo Arbenz of Guatemala.

July 17 The first Newport Jazz Festival opens. Billie Holiday, Dizzy Gillespie, Stan Getz, and Louis Armstrong are among the musicians to appear.

July 21 An agreement at the Geneva Conference results in the division of Vietnam at the 17th parallel.

September 8 The Southeast Asia Collective Defense Treaty is signed in Manila in the Philippines. It provides the basis for the formation of the Southeast Asia Treaty Organization the following year.

December 2 The U.S. Senate censures McCarthy for conduct that tends "to bring the Senate into dishonor and disrepute."

December 10 Ernest Hemingway wins the Nobel Prize for literature.

December 15 The first episode of *Davy Crockett* appears on television as part of the *Disneyland* show.

1955

January 28 Congress approves a presidential request to allow U.S. forces to defend Formosa (Taiwan) against Communist aggression.

March 12 Jazz saxophonist and bebop pioneer Charlie Parker dies.

March 30 *On the Waterfront* wins the Oscar for best picture. Its star, Marlon Brando, receives the award for best actor, while Elia Kazan is named best director.

May 5 West Germany becomes a sovereign state, with Bonn as its capital. Allied troops remain in occupation to protect the country from Soviet threat.

May 9 West Germany joins the North Atlantic Treaty Organization.

May 14 After a three-day conference in Poland the Soviet Union, Poland, East Germany, Czechoslovakia, Hungary, Romania, Bulgaria, and Albania sign the Warsaw Pact.

May 31 The Supreme Court orders that public schools be desegregated with "all deliberate speed."

June 12 The radio show *Monitor* is broadcast for the first time.

July 9 "Rock around the Clock" by Bill Haley and His Comets reaches number one on the pop charts.

July 17 The Disneyland theme park opens in Anaheim, California.

August 19 Hurricane Diane causes severe flooding in the northeastern United States and claims 200 lives.

September 30 Film star James Dean dies in a car crash.

October 13 Beat writer Allen Ginsberg gives a reading of his poem "Howl" at San Francisco's Six Gallery.

December 1 On a bus in Montgomery, Alabama, Rosa Parks refuses to give her seat to a white man and is arrested for violating the city's racial segregation laws.

December 5 The Montgomery Bus Boycott begins under the leadership of Baptist minister Martin Luther King, Jr.

The American Federation of Labor and the Congress of Industrial Organizations merge to form the AFL–CIO.

1956

February 22 Elvis Presley makes his chart debut with "Heartbreak Hotel." The single reaches number one.

February 25 Khrushchev denounces Stalin at the 20th Soviet Party Congress.

March 12 More than 100 southern representatives and senators sign a manifesto pledging to use "all lawful means" to reverse the Supreme Court ruling on segregation.

March 15 The musical *My Fair Lady* opens on Broadway.

May 21 Bikini Atoll in the Pacific Ocean is almost obliterated during a nuclear test following the first airborne explosion of a hydrogen bomb.

June 29 Actress Marilyn Monroe marries playwright Arthur Miller.

President Eisenhower signs the Federal-Aid Highway Act, authorizing the construction of a 41,000-mile (65,970-km) highway network linking the major urban centers.

July 30 The phrase "In God We Trust" is adopted as the national motto of the United States.

August 11 Abstract expressionist painter Jackson Pollock dies.

August 25 Dr. Alfred Kinsey, author of two groundbreaking reports on sexual behavior, dies.

September 9 Elvis Presley makes his first TV appearance on *The Ed Sullivan Show.*

October 23 Thousands of people take to the streets of Budapest, Hungary, in antigovernment protests.

October 29 The Suez Crisis begins; Israeli troops invade the Sinai Peninsula and push Egyptian forces back toward the Suez Canal.

November 4 Soviet tanks roll into Budapest and crush the Hungarian Uprising.

November 6 In a rerun of the 1952 presidential election Republican incumbent Dwight D. Eisenhower again defeats his Democrat opponent Adlai Stevenson.

November 13 The Montgomery Bus Boycott ends in a victory for civil rights activists when the Supreme Court declares that segregation on public buses is unconstitutional.

1957

January 2 The San Francisco and Los Angeles stock exchanges merge.

January 5 In a speech to a joint session of Congress Eisenhower pledges U.S. military support to any Middle Eastern country threatened by communism. The policy becomes known as the Eisenhower Doctrine.

January 13 The Wham-O Company produces its first frisbee, called the Pluto Platter.

March 13 The FBI arrests Jimmy Hoffa, general president of the Teamsters labor union, and charges him with bribery.

March 25 The European Economic Community is created by the signing of the Treaties of Rome.

April 10 The Suez Canal reopens.

May 2 Joseph McCarthy dies.

July 6 Althea Gibson wins the Wimbledon women's singles title, becoming the first African American to do so.

July 16 United States Marine Major John Glenn flies an F8U supersonic jet from California to New York in 3 hours, 23 minutes, and 8 seconds, setting a new transcontinental speed record.

August 5 The first program of *American Bandstand* is broadcast across the nation.

September 4 The Little Rock crisis begins; Orval Faubus, governor of Arkansas, calls out the National Guard to prevent black students from enrolling at Central High School in Little Rock.

September 9 President Eisenhower signs the 1957 Civil Rights Act, which seeks to protect voting rights.

October 4 The Soviet Union launches the first artificial satellite, *Sputnik 1*, into orbit around Earth. The ball-shaped satellite weighs 184 pounds (83kg).

November 3 The Soviet satellite *Sputnik 2* is sent into orbit around Earth with a dog, Laika, on board.

November 25 President Eisenhower suffers a stroke and is partially incapacitated.

December 6 The first attempt by the United States to launch a satellite, *Vanguard TV3*, fails when the rocket explodes on the launchpad.

1958

January 20 Elvis Presley is drafted into the U.S. Army. He serves until March 1960, largely in West Germany.

January 31 A team led by Wernher Von Braun successfully launches the first U.S. artificial satellite, *Explorer I*. The 31-pound (14-kg) cylindrical spacecraft detects the Van Allen radiation belt that surrounds Earth.

March 17 The U.S. satellite *Vanguard 1* finally makes it into orbit. The 3-pound (1.4-kg) satellite proves that Earth is not a perfect sphere but is slightly flattened at the poles.

March 27 Khrushchev becomes premier of the Soviet Union.

May 13 A group of anti-American demonstrators attack Vice President Richard M. Nixon's car during an official visit to Caracas, Venezuela.

July 14 A military coup in Iraq brings Brigadier Abdul Karim Kassem to power. Under Kassem's leadership Iraq withdraws from the pro-Western Baghdad Pact and forges closer ties with the Soviet Union.

July 24 At the opening of the American National Exhibition in Moscow Khrushchev and Nixon discuss the respective merits of the capitalist and communist economic systems.

July 29 President Eisenhower signs the National Aeronautics and Space Act; the the National Aeronautics and Space Administration (NASA) comes into being on October 1.

August 7 A federal court quashes Arthur Miller's conviction for contempt of Congress. Miller had refused to "name names" of possible communists when called before HUAC.

September 22 Sherman Adams, the White House chief of staff, is forced to resign over allegations that he accepted a gift from a friend who had business dealings with the government.

October 26 Pan American World Airways makes its first scheduled jet fight from New York to Paris.

December 28 The Baltimore Colts beat the New York Giants in sudden-death overtime in the NFL Championship Game, which *Sports Illustrated* calls "the best football game ever played."

1959

January 1 President Fulgencio Batista of Cuba flees the country as rebel troops march on the capital Havana.

January 2 The Soviet space probe *Luna 1* becomes the first artificial object to fly past the moon and escape Earth's gravitational field.

January 3 Alaska is admitted as the 49th state of the Union.

February 3 Rock-'n'-roll stars Buddy Holly, Ritchie Valens, and The Big Bopper are killed in a plane crash.

February 16 Fidel Castro becomes the prime minister of Cuba.

March 9 The first Barbie doll goes on sale.

May 24 Former Secretary of State John Foster Dulles dies.

June 26 The St. Lawrence Seaway, which links the North American Great Lakes to the Atlantic Ocean, officially opens to shipping.

July 15 Steelworkers go on strike in pursuit of higher wages, shorter hours, and better working conditions.

July 17 Jazz and blues singer Billie Holiday dies.

August 17 *Kind of Blue* by trumpeter Miles Davis is released. It is eventually recognized as one of the greatest jazz albums ever recorded.

August 21 Hawaii is admitted as the 50th state of the Union.

September 15 Khrushchev begins a visit to the United States.

October 4 The first photographs of the far side of the moon are taken from the Soviet space satellite *Luna 3*.

October 21 The Solomon R. Guggenheim Museum opens to the public in New York City. It was designed by Frank Lloyd Wright, who died in April.

December 1 The Antarctic Treaty is signed by 12 countries, including the United States and the Soviet Union. It bans military activity on the continent and is the first arms control agreement established during the Cold War.

December 14 Berry Gordy, Jr., founds Motown Records.

POST-1959

1960

May 1 An American U-2 spy plane is shot down while flying over the Soviet Union. The incident places a considerable strain on U.S.–Soviet relations.

November 8 John F. Kennedy is elected president of the United States in the closest election in the country's history.

1961

January 3 President Eisenhower cuts diplomatic ties to Cuba.

April 12 Yuri Gagarin makes the first manned space flight for the Soviet Union.

April 17 Cuban rebels, trained and funded by the CIA, land at the Bay of Pigs in an attempt to topple the Castro regime. In a humiliating setback for the United States they are quickly defeated.

August 13 The Berlin Wall is erected, separating East from West Berlin.

1962

August 5 Actress Marilyn Monroe is found dead after a drug overdose.

October 14 U.S. reconnaissance planes spot a Soviet ballistic missile on a military base in Cuba. The discovery prompts the Cuban Missile Crisis, a period of tension that ends only when the Soviet Union agrees to withdraw the missiles.

1963

August 28 250,000 people take part in a civil rights march in Washington, D.C.

November 22 President Kennedy is assassinated by Lee Harvey Oswald in Dallas, Texas. Vice President Lyndon Baines Johnson takes over as president.

1964

February 9 British pop group the Beatles appears on *The Ed Sullivan Show*. An estimated 73 million viewers watch the performance.

February 25 Cassius Clay defeats Sonny Liston to win the world heavyweight boxing title. Shortly afterward Clay adopts the Muslim name Muhammad Ali.

1965

February 21 African American political activist Malcolm X is shot dead in New York City.

1968

April 4 Martin Luther King, Jr., is assassinated in Memphis, Tennessee.

SET INDEX

Volume numbers are in **bold**. Page numbers in **bold** refer to main articles; those in *italics* refer to picture captions.

A

B

H

L

M